# Fundamentals of Lighting

*fb*

# Fundamentals of Lighting

## SECOND EDITION

SUSAN M. WINCHIP, PhD, LEED AP, MIES
ILLINOIS STATE UNIVERSITY
PROFESSOR EMERITA

FAIRCHILD BOOKS | NEW YORK

Executive Editor: **Olga T. Kontzias**
Assistant Acquisitions Editor:
**Amanda Breccia**
Development Editor: **Rob Phelps**
Assistant Art Director: **Sarah Silberg**
Production Director: **Ginger Hillman**
Production Editor: **Andrew Fargnoli**
Copyeditor: **Susan Hobbs**
Ancillaries Editor: **Noah Schwartzberg**
Text and Cover Design:
**Carolyn Eckert**
Compositor: **Dedicated Book**
**Services (DBS)**
Cover Art: **Courtesy of 7Gods**
Illustrations: **Precision Graphics**

10 06630812

Library of Congress Catalog Card
Number: 2010937545
ISBN: 978-1-60901-086-7
GST R 133004424
Printed in Canada

# CONTENTS

# EXTENDED CONTENTS

# PREFACE

*Fundamentals of Lighting*, Second Edition, builds upon the first edition's answer to the need for a textbook on quality lighting from a design perspective with pedagogical strategies that particularly appeal to the millennial generation. This second edition retains the essence of the content presented in the first edition with major improvements to the art program and emphasis on the sustainability characteristics of daylighting and electrical lighting. Conceptualizing and designing a quality lighting environment requires an understanding of how daylight, luminaires, electrical sources, and control systems will affect people and the built environment. To help students understand these effects, this second edition has almost an entirely new art program with more than 300 photographs of global interiors and new lighting systems. Photographs and text include innovative approaches to lighting from nontraditional sources, such as the visual arts, nanotechnologies, and textiles.

Additional case studies further enhance comprehension, and instructional features supplement many of the illustrations. For example, to help clarify lighting concepts photographs now include explanatory text accompanied with arrows that point to specific details. To explain lighting systems, multiple images are grouped together. For example, a single photograph of a metal halide lamp does not demonstrate how the lamp will illuminate a space; therefore, the figure that illustrates a metal halide lamp also has a photograph of an interior that is illuminated with a metal halide lamp. Grouping these two illustrations together

provides the image that the student needs to identify a metal halide lamp as well showing them what the space looks like when using a metal halide lamp. This approach has been applied to understanding many aspects related to lighting systems, including LEDs, common lamps, recessed fixtures, the light distribution patterns of luminaires, photometric charts, and controls.

The second edition also has updated lamp technologies, luminaires, controls, human factor research, and energy codes and standards. New information regarding solid-state lighting technologies, including LEDs and OLEDs, is emphasized, and reader-friendly tables have been created to present updated characteristics of common lamps. A reader-friendly approach also applies to daylighting strategies and the new energy codes and standards associated with EPAct 2005 and the Energy Independence and Security Act 2007. Lighting calculations have been simplified and color-coded to assist visual learners. Color-coding also has been applied to demonstrate the relationship between manufacturers' photometric charts and calculations.

## A New Emphasis on Sustainable Design

A substantial amount of text and images have been added to demonstrate lighting's important role in creating sustainable designs. Considerable new content relates to sustainability concepts, daylighting design, controls, and efficient lamps and luminaires. Sustainability-related characteristics of lamps are presented in Table 3.1 as well as suggested appropriate applications, whereas Table 4.2 summarizes daylighting strategies by providing numerous suggestions for maximizing daylight and controlling for sunlight.

## LEED CERTIFICATION AND LIGHTING DESIGN

The new sustainability-related content in this second edition includes valuable suggestions on how to achieve top environmental and other sustainable design standards in lighting design. Ten chapters feature boxes and tables that summarize how the content in each chapter relates to the LEED (Leadership in Energy and Environmental Design) certification requirements. These boxes and tables also lay out the LEED credit categories that can help take one's lighting design to the highest standards of sustainability. Case studies in the concluding chapters of the text further illustrate daylighting and electrical sources used in top-rated LEED-certified buildings, providing examples of successful sustainable lighting design.

# An Integrated Approach to Quality Lighting

*Fundamentals of Lighting*, Second Edition, is written for college students who are studying lighting in their quest to become interior designers. The textbook is an approach to quality lighting with a focus on the design process and sustainability. Specifically, the textbook uses an integrative approach to lighting that not only includes the basics of lighting systems, but also demonstrates how

lighting is interrelated with the design process, human factors, sustainability, global issues, design fundamentals, regulations, business practices, and the LEED building certification program.

Many of the topics and suggestions provided in the text reflect the results of research studies. The exercises and pedagogical suggestions in the accompanying Instructor's Guide are written to reinforce the content of the textbook and help to develop critical skills for practicing professionals, such as programming, schematic design, concept development, design development, drafting, sketching, and teamwork.

The text can be used in a variety of courses and formats. It can serve as the primary textbook in introductory lighting courses, or as a supplementary resource in other courses, such as sustainable design, and commercial and residential studio courses. As with all discipline-specific books, students should be encouraged to keep their books after an initial lighting course and then use the text as a reference when they develop lighting plans in other courses and in their future professional practices. The interdisciplinary nature of the content makes the book an excellent choice for reinforcing concepts throughout the curriculum. For example, in non-lighting courses, this textbook could be used as a reference when discussing topics, such as sustainable design, energy standards, codes, human factors, or the phases of the design process.

## ORGANIZATION OF THE TEXTBOOK

This textbook is organized sequentially to develop fundamental understanding of how to design quality lighting environments with an emphasis on sustainability. It is divided into two parts.

Part One, "Principles of Lighting," explores basic concepts and elements of a quality lighting environment, including components of lighting systems, daylighting, energy considerations, sustainability, human factors, and color and directional effects of illumination. Each chapter in Part One ends with a boxed feature that includes steps to apply the chapter content toward sustainability and LEED certification requirements.

In Chapter 1, "Introduction to Quality Lighting," we explore and assess the importance of quality lighting. Chapter 2, "Color and Directional Effects of Lighting," covers the basic concepts associated with color and lamps. In Chapter 3, "Natural and Artificial Light Sources," we examine the advantages and disadvantages of using daylight as a lighting source.

Chapter 4, "Energy, the Environment, and Sustainable Design," defines sustainable design, applies the concept and practice to lighting systems, and analyzes the energy required for lighting systems. In Chapter 5, "Illumination and Human Health and Behavior," we explore the physical, psychological, and behavioral effects of light on people as well as the principles of universal design as it applies to lighting.

Chapter 6, "Lighting Systems: Luminaires," examines the specification and placement of fixtures in an environment, whereas Chapter 7: "Lighting Systems: Controls," covers the basic equipment of controls in a lighting system and identifies the primary ways in which

controls can conserve energy. In Chapter 8: "Quantity of Light," we master the basic units of measurement used in lighting, including luminous intensity, luminous flux, illuminance, luminance, and luminance exitance, and comprehend the relationships among them.

Part One serves as the foundation for exploring specific applications in Part Two, "Lighting Design Applications and the Design Process." These applications include the phases of the design process: (1) project planning; (2) comprehensive programming; (3) schematic design; (4) design development; (5) contract documentation; (6) contract administration; and (7) evaluation—outlined as they apply to lighting design in Chapters 9 and 10, "Lighting Design Process: Project Planning through Design Development," and "Lighting Design Process: Contract Documents through Postoccupancy Evaluation." Both Chapters 9 and 10 also feature tables that highlight connections between the design process and suggestions for proceeding through the LEED certification process.

Chapters 11, "Residential Applications," and 12, "Commercial Applications," conclude with lighting case studies that reflect the principles of sustainability as illustrated by top-rated LEED buildings.

For more information, go to www .fairchildbooks.com and search for *Fundamentals of Lighting*, Second Edition.

## PEDAGOGICAL FEATURES

Every chapter in the textbook has pedagogical features that are designed to assist teaching and enhance learning. To help explain concepts and techniques, every chapter has numerous full-color illustrations, many of which have been further enhanced with pedagogical features. In addition, each chapter begins with a list of objectives, which can be used as an assessment tool at the beginning and end of a lesson. The summary, list of key terms, and exercises in every chapter are designed to reinforce the content and develop important professional skills.

The appendices are very important to learning the content of the book and can be an excellent reference for practicing professionals. They include lists of contact information for lighting manufacturers, distributors, suppliers, professional organizations, government agencies, and trade associations.

The Instructor's Guide that accompanies this text offers additional activities and assignments designed to enhance teaching and learning. This guide explains in full detail the pedagogical approach of the text and elaborates on the content embodied in *Fundamentals of Lighting*, Second Edition.

## Acknowledgments

An author is only one individual in the process of publishing a second edition of a textbook. I am not only grateful to all of the talented professionals working at Fairchild Books who were involved with both editions; I am very appreciative to the faculty who selected the first edition as well as the students who read the pages. Without their support this book would not be possible. In addition, I am grateful to the reviewers for both editions for their thoughtful reading, and excellent recommendations: Roxane Berger, Cal State University Northridge; Michelle Brown, Baylor University; Eugenia Ellis, Drexel University; Ellen Goode, Meredith College; Jessica Mahne, Madison Area Technical College; Kathleen Lugosch, University of Massachusetts; Nam-Kyu Park, University of Florida; Pam Shofner, International Academy of Design & Technology, Tampa; and Beth Stokes, Art Institute of Portland. Their insights always help to improve the text.

As always, I extend my deep gratitude to Olga Kontzias, executive editor, for her continuing support and enthusiasm for my work as well as the interior design profession. Our profession is fortunate that she is dedicated to quality and progressive educational experiences. I am also appreciative of my dear husband, Galen, and my children, Kristi, Kyle, and Amy. They always have supported my work and provide the encouragement that an author needs to successfully complete the countless hours of writing.

# Fundamentals of Lighting

PART ONE  PRINCIPLES OF LIGHTING

Conceptualizing and designing a quality lighting environment requires an understanding of how daylight, luminaires, electrical sources, and control systems affect people and the built environment. In twenty-first-century design, quality lighting must also carefully encompass attention to environmental and other sustainable standards.

In these first chapters, we explore basic concepts and elements of a quality lighting environment, including components of lighting systems, daylighting, energy considerations, sustainability, human factors, and color and directional effects of illumination. Each chapter ends with a checklist of steps you can use to apply quality lighting to LEED-certified building design.

# 1 Introduction to Quality Lighting

Light is one of the essential elements of life; without it we could not exist. Designers must consider both natural and electrical sources of light when they plan a quality lighting environment. A working knowledge of natural and electrical lighting systems has never been as important as it is today. The global emphasis on **sustainable designs** has prompted significant attention to maximizing daylight and specifying energy-efficient lighting systems (Box 1.1). Natural and electrical sources are key components in green interior design rating systems, such as **LEED (Leadership in Energy and Environmental Design)** (Box 1.1). In reviewing LEED's categories (refer to Table Box 1.1c), it may appear that lighting would be examined only in the credits that specifically address lighting, such as EA 1.1, 1.2, and IEQ 6.1, 8.1, and 8.2. However, as illustrated in future boxes in this textbook, lighting does impact several other LEED categories and credits. Designing interiors that are LEED certified as well as reflecting the principles of sustainability includes a thorough understanding of the concepts, policies, codes, materials, and technologies that are presented in this book.

To understand natural and electrical light, it is important to review historical developments of light sources and how civilizations invented technologies to produce light. Electric light, the form to which we

**OBJECTIVES**

o Comprehend and assess the importance of quality lighting

o Identify the key characteristics of light and some of the effects light has on the human response

o Analyze the basic parts of the eye and the vision process

o Describe general, task, accent, and decorative lighting techniques

o Identify fixtures that are used for general, task, accent, and decorative lighting

o Develop a fundamental understanding of the factors that affect quality in general as well as task and accent lighting

are accustomed, has been in existence for approximately 100 years. This is an extremely short period of time compared to the thousands of years of civilization. (See Timeline.) Advancements in lighting will continue to transform our lives and society.

As a form of energy, light travels through space and affects every living organism. Light sources and the physiological process of vision affect what we see. Poor lighting has a negative effect on vision, our ability to perform tasks, and our psychological responses. Designing functional, sustainable, and aesthetic interiors requires a focus on planning principles that include the fundamentals of illumination, elements of lighting systems, and specific interior applications.

Lighting requirements in a space can be divided into three main categories: general, task, and accent. The first is **general lighting**, or **ambient lighting**, which provides overall illumination in a space, including lighting that allows people to navigate an area safely (Figure 1.1). The second is **task lighting**, which is the lighting specified for each task (such as reading, for example) that is performed in a space (Figure 1.2). The third is **accent lighting**, which is used to create interest and to highlight special features such as architectural details, artwork, plant foliage, or decorative accessories (Figure 1.3).

For a well-planned lighting environment, it is critical to include daylight as well as electrical light, and to specify general, task, and accent lighting in every space in an interior. Using a variety of types of lighting allows the designer to create a lighting plan that is adapted to the purpose of the space, the needs of its users, and energy conservation. **Decorative lighting** is ornamental and should not be included in the three categories; it includes light sources that provide illumination and are also artistic pieces themselves (Figure 1.4).

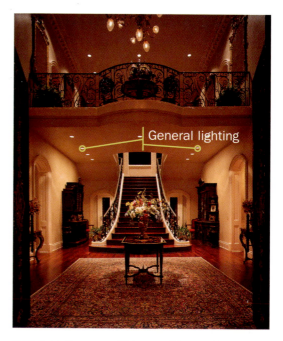

General lighting

FIGURE 1.1 The recessed fixtures provide general illumination in this space. (© 2000–2010 Cooper Industries, Inc.)

**BOX 1.1 Sustainable Design and LEED**

## SUSTAINABLE DESIGN

Sustainable design holistically concentrates on reducing negative impacts on the environment by optimizing the interactions between the earth, people, the built environment, and the economy for current and future generations. Sustainable designs emphasize healthy indoor environments, environmentally friendly products, minimal waste, and reduced consumption of energy and non-renewable resources.

**TABLE BOX 1.1A LEED Green Building Rating System***

| CATEGORIES | POSSIBLE POINTS |
|---|---|
| *Environmental* | |
| Sustainable Sites (SS) | 21 |
| Water Efficiency (WE) | 11 |
| Energy and Atmosphere (EA) | 37 |
| Materials and Resources (MR) | 14 |
| Indoor Environmental Quality (IEQ) | 17 |
| *Additional* | |
| Innovation in Design (ID) | 6 |
| Regional Priority (RP) | 4 |

**TABLE BOX 1.1B LEED Certification Levels***

| CERTIFICATION LEVELS | 100 POSSIBLE POINTS PLUS 10 BONUS POINTS |
|---|---|
| Platinum | 80+ |
| Gold | 60–79 |
| Silver | 50–59 |
| Certified | 40–49 |

*For projects that may exceed prescribed performance levels LEED has exemplary performance points for selected environmental categories.

## LEED

The U.S. Green Building Council (USGBC) developed the Leadership in Energy and Environmental Design (LEED) system, which is an internationally recognized green building certification system. LEED is a voluntary standard that provides "third-party verification that a building or community was designed and built using strategies aimed at improving performance across all the metrics that matter most: energy savings, water efficiency, $CO_2$ emissions reduction, improved indoor environmental quality, and stewardship of resources and sensitivity to their impacts" (www.usgbc.org, p. 1).

For the purpose of this textbook, examples are derived from the USGBC's *LEED Reference Guide for Green Interior Design and Construction 2009*. LEED's other rating systems are Core & Shell, New Construction, Schools, Neighborhood Development, Retail, Healthcare, and Homes—all of these can be found at www.usgbc.org.

### *Overall Certification Process*

1. Adherence to LEED's minimum program requirements.
2. Register.
3. Manage the documentation process using LEED-Online (https://leedonline.usgbc.org/). LEED for commercial interiors allows a two-step certification application process

(continued)

(design phase review and construction phase review).

**4.** Request Credit Interpretations and Rulings when necessary.

**5.** Review and Certification.

**6.** Appeals (as necessary).

**TABLE BOX 1.1C** **LEED Environmental Categories Related to Quality Lighting**

| LEED CREDIT CATEGORY | LEED INTENT |
|---|---|
| SS (Sustainable Sites) Credit 1 Option 2 Path 6: Light Pollution Reduction | To encourage tenants to select buildings that employ best practices systems and green strategies. |
| EA (Energy and Atmosphere) Prerequisite 1 Fundamental Commissioning of Building Energy Systems | To verify that the project's energy-related systems are installed and calibrated to performing according to the owner's project requirements, basis of design and construction documents. Benefits of commissioning include reduced energy use, lower operating costs, fewer contractor callbacks, better building documentation, improved occupant productivity, and verification that the systems perform is in accordance with the owner's project requirements. |
| EA Prerequisite 2 Minimum Energy Performance | To establish the minimum level of energy efficiency for the tenant space systems to reduce environmental and economic impacts associated with excessive energy use. |
| EA Credit 1.1 Optimize Energy Performance—Lighting Power | To achieve increasing levels of energy conservation beyond the referenced standard to reduce environmental and economic impacts associated with excessive energy use. |
| EA Credit 1.2 Optimize Energy Performance—Lighting Controls | To achieve increasing levels of energy conservation beyond the prerequisite standard to reduce environmental and economic impacts associated with excessive energy use. |
| EA Credit 2 Enhanced Commissioning | To verify and ensure that the tenant space is designed, constructed, and calibrated to operate as intended. |
| EA Credit 3 Measurement and Verification | To provide for the ongoing accountability and optimization of tenant energy and water consumption performance over time. |
| MR (Material and Resources) Credit 1.2 Building Reuse—Maintain Interior Nonstructural Components | To extend the life cycle of existing building stock, conserve resources, retain cultural resources, reduce waste, and reduce environmental impacts of new buildings as they relate to materials, manufacturing and transport. |
| MR Credit 2 Construction Waste Management | To divert construction and demolition debris from disposal in landfills and incineration facilities. Redirect recyclable recovered resources back to the manufacturing process and reusable materials to appropriate sites. |
| MR Credit 3.2 Materials—Reuse—Furniture and Furnishings | To reuse building materials and products to reduce demand for virgin materials and reduce waste, thereby reducing impacts associated with the extraction and processing of virgin resources. |

**TABLE BOX 1.1C** LEED Environmental Categories Related to Quality Lighting (continued)

| LEED CREDIT CATEGORY | LEED INTENT |
|---|---|
| MR Credit 4<br>Recycled Content | To increase demand for building products that incorporate recycled content materials, thereby reducing impacts resulting from extraction and processing of virgin materials. |
| MR Credit 5<br>Regional Materials | To increase demand for building materials and products that are extracted and manufactured within the region, thereby supporting the regional economy and reducing the environment impacts resulting from transportation. |
| MR Credit 6<br>Rapidly Renewable Materials | To reduce the use and depletion of finite raw materials and long-cycle renewable materials by replacing them with rapidly renewable materials. |
| MR Credit 7<br>Certified Wood | To encourage environmentally responsible forest management. |
| IEQ (Indoor Environmental Quality) Credit 4.2 Low-Emitting Materials—Paints and Coatings | To reduce the quantity of indoor air contaminants that are odorous, irritating, and/or harmful to the comfort and well-being of installers and occupants. |
| IEQ Credit 6.1<br>Controllability of Systems—Lighting | To provide a high level of lighting system control for individual occupants or groups in multi-occupant spaces (e.g., classrooms and conference areas) and promote their productivity, comfort and well-being. |
| IEQ Credit 6.2<br>Controllability of Systems—Thermal Comfort | To provide a high level of thermal comfort system control for individual occupants or groups in multi-occupant spaces (e.g., classrooms and conference areas) and promote their productivity, comfort, and well-being. |
| IEQ Credit 7.1<br>Thermal Comfort—Design | To provide a comfortable thermal environment that promotes occupant productivity and well-being. |
| IEQ Credit 7.2<br>Thermal Comfort—Verification | To provide for the assessment of occupant thermal comfort over time. |
| IEQ Credit 8.1<br>Daylight and Views—Daylight | To provide occupants with a connection between indoor spaces and the outdoors through the introduction of daylight and views into the regularly occupied areas of the tenant space. |
| IEQ Credit 8.2<br>Daylight and Views—Views for Seated Spaces | To provide the building occupants a connection to the outdoors through the introduction of daylight and views into the regularly occupied areas of the tenant space. |
| ID (Innovation in Design) Credit 1<br>Innovation in Design | To provide design teams and projects the opportunity to achieve exceptional performance above the requirements set by the LEED Green Building Rating System and/or innovative performance in Green Building categories not specifically addressed by the LEED Green Building Rating System. |

Source: USGBC (2009). *LEED reference guide for green interior design and construction*. Washington, D.C.: U.S. Green Building Council.

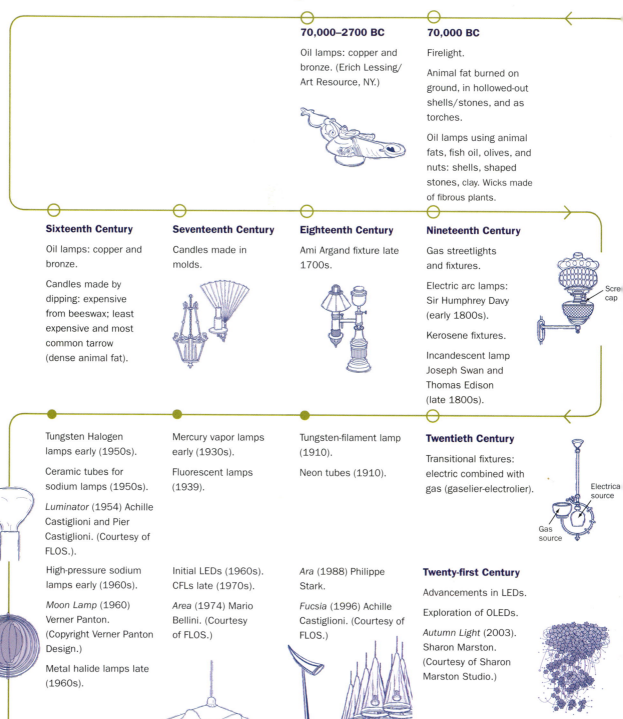

# Major Historical Developments of Light Sources and Selected Luminaires

**70,000–2700 BC**

Oil lamps: copper and bronze. (Erich Lessing/Art Resource, NY.)

**70,000 BC**

Firelight.

Animal fat burned on ground, in hollowed-out shells/stones, and as torches.

Oil lamps using animal fats, fish oil, olives, and nuts: shells, shaped stones, clay. Wicks made of fibrous plants.

**Sixteenth Century**

Oil lamps: copper and bronze.

Candles made by dipping: expensive from beeswax; least expensive and most common tarrow (dense animal fat).

**Seventeenth Century**

Candles made in molds.

**Eighteenth Century**

Ami Argand fixture late 1700s.

**Nineteenth Century**

Gas streetlights and fixtures.

Electric arc lamps: Sir Humphrey Davy (early 1800s).

Kerosene fixtures.

Incandescent lamp Joseph Swan and Thomas Edison (late 1800s).

Screw cap

Tungsten Halogen lamps early (1950s).

Ceramic tubes for sodium lamps (1950s).

*Luminator* (1954) Achille Castiglioni and Pier Castiglioni. (Courtesy of FLOS.).

High-pressure sodium lamps early (1960s).

*Moon Lamp* (1960) Verner Panton. (Copyright Verner Panton Design.)

Metal halide lamps late (1960s).

Mercury vapor lamps early (1930s).

Fluorescent lamps (1939).

Initial LEDs (1960s). CFLs late (1970s).

*Area* (1974) Mario Bellini. (Courtesy of FLOS.)

Tungsten-filament lamp (1910).

Neon tubes (1910).

*Ara* (1988) Philippe Stark.

*Fucsia* (1996) Achille Castiglioni. (Courtesy of FLOS.)

**Twentieth Century**

Transitional fixtures: electric combined with gas (gaselier-electrolier).

Electrical source

Gas source

**Twenty-first Century**

Advancements in LEDs.

Exploration of OLEDs.

*Autumn Light* (2003). Sharon Marston. (Courtesy of Sharon Marston Studio.)

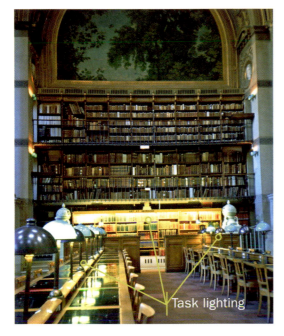

**FIGURE 1.2** Task lighting is installed in the center of the tables and above the books in the main Reading Room, National Public Library, Paris. (© Directphoto.org/Alamy.)

**FIGURE 1.4** Resin was used to fabricate the decorative chandelier. (3-Form Inc.)

**FIGURE 1.3** LEDs (light emitting diodes) are used to accent several elements in an Asian-inspired restaurant in Los Angeles. (Robert Berger Photography.)

## What Is Light?

Technically, **light** is a form of energy that is part of the electromagnetic spectrum visible to the human eye. The spectrum also includes cosmic rays, microwaves, gamma rays, radar, radio waves, ultraviolet, and X-rays (Figure 1.5). The human eye is able to see light in only a relatively small spectrum, from violet (about 400 nanometers) to red (about 750 nanometers) wavelengths. (A nanometer is extremely small, about one billionth of a meter.)

Light travels at a speed of 186,000 miles per second (or about 300,000 kilometers per

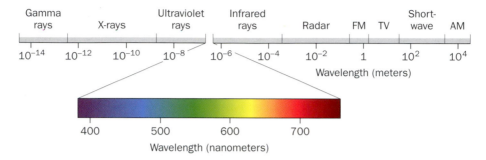

**FIGURE 1.5** Light is a form of energy that is part of the electromagnetic spectrum which also includes cosmic rays, microwaves, gamma rays, radar, radio waves, ultraviolet, and X-rays.

second), theoretically the fastest speed in the universe. **Natural light** includes direct light from the sun and the stars. **Indirect natural light** is the result of reflection from clouds, structures, and the landscape. The unit for measuring the quantity of light emitted by a light source is the **lumen (lm)**.

## QUALITY LIGHTING

**Quality lighting** is a relatively new concept. The discovery of electricity and the invention of the incandescent light bulb in the 1800s prompted engineers to develop new and better **lamps** and lighting systems. Since then, the focus has been primarily on the quantity of light needed in a space. Because we can measure light, it is fairly easy to have an adequate amount of lighting in a space.

Now that scientists and engineers have developed systems that produce a large quantity of light, it is necessary for designers to focus on the quality of lighting. There is a subjective aspect to quality lighting that extends beyond scientific measurement into psychology and mood, making it complicated

and difficult to accomplish. The *IESNA Lighting Handbook*, 10th Edition, focuses on the importance of quality lighting and the quantity of lighting.

### What Is Quality Lighting?

Quality lighting allows users to function comfortably in an interior, feel safe in it, and appreciate its aesthetic components. Achieving a quality lighting environment requires complete control over the lighting system. Environments with quality lighting are specifically designed for particular uses in special locations. These environments reflect a skillful application of the principles of design by integrating and layering light into the entire composition.

**Layered lighting** includes natural light and multiple electrical light sources (Figure 1.6). With the focus on quality, lighting is no longer an afterthought that is simply added on to a design plan. Quality lighting includes the art of balancing and integrating daylight and general, task, and accent lighting. Designing quality lighting environments also results in reduced energy costs and conservation of

FIGURE 1.6  Using natural light and reducing electrical light saved energy at the Bronx library center in Bronx, New York, a LEED silver-certified building. (© Jeff Goldberg/Esto.)

natural resources. Throughout this text, the principles of quality lighting are applied to the fundamentals of lighting, elements of lighting systems, case studies, and presentations of lighting solutions. The goal of every chapter is to build the knowledge and skills designers need to create quality lighting environments.

## VISION AND LIGHTING

The vision process starts when light enters the pupil, the aperture of the iris of the eye (Figure 1.7). The lens adjusts the perception of light for near and far vision, and the cornea focuses light on the retina of the eye by refraction. This function is known as **accommodation**. The

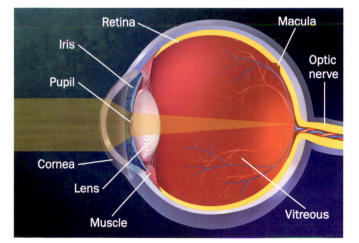

FIGURE 1.7 Cross section of the eye.

retina is the inner, light-sensitive lining of the eye, and the fovea of the retina is where light is focused.

Rods and cones are detector cells located at the back of the retina. Rods are activated primarily at lower illuminance levels and are important in night vision; cones are activated by bright light, color, and detail. The fovea does not contain any rods. The cones and rods convert light energy into nerve impulses, which are sent by the optic nerve from the retina to the brain for interpretation. Through this entire process, brightness and color are adjusted, and images are compared to experiences in memory.

**Adaptation** is what happens when the eye adjusts itself to the amount of brightness entering the pupil. Similar to a camera lens, the pupil constricts in bright light and expands in the dark. The adaptation process can take some time. When you enter a dark movie theater on a bright sunny day, your eyes require more time to adjust from bright to dark than from dark to light.

To assist the adaptation that occurs in the vision process, designers should consider a lighting system that provides a transition in light levels. For low-level illuminated interiors used during daylight times, a transitional system should begin with higher light levels as one enters the space, lowering gradually as one travels through the interior. If possible, the amount of time required for a person to reach the darkest space should be equal to the amount of time it takes for adaptation to occur in the vision process. Seating should be provided for those individuals, such as the elderly, who need more time for their eyes to adapt. During evening hours, to reduce the contrast in lighting from outdoors to indoors, the lighting levels should be decreased in the entry area and gradually increased as one progresses through the interior.

## Conditions Affecting Vision

The **eye's field of vision** is also an important consideration in designing quality lighting environments. It is most natural to see objects within a horizontal field. The field of vision includes a central and a peripheral area. The central field of vision for the eye is approximately 2 degrees above and 2 degrees below the direct line of sight (Figure 1.8). **Visual acuity**, the ability of the eye to see detail and color, is best in this small range. The peripheral area is the area to the sides of the central field of vision and above and below the central field of vision. Brightness and motion, such as flashing lights, are best seen in peripheral vision.

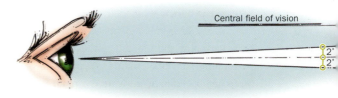

Central field of vision

2°
2°

**FIGURE 1.8** The central field of vision for the eye is approximately 2 degrees above and 2 degrees below the direct line of sight.

Designers should consider the eye's field of vision when they plan the lighting for detailed visual tasks or when specifying bright or flashing lighting systems. For example, when planning the lighting for a work surface, a designer should position the light source to illuminate the work area in the central field of vision. Flashing emergency light fixtures are best located in areas within the peripheral field of vision. Because the location of the eye's field of vision changes when a person moves from a sitting to a standing position, a designer might have to specify several light sources to accommodate all the lighting needs.

The aging process of the eye affects visual acuity, color identification, adaptation, peripheral vision, depth perception, and tolerance for glare. As one ages, the lens of the eye yellows and **presbyopia** occurs. That is the decline in the eye's ability to adjust the shape of the lens. As a result, when designing spaces for the elderly, designers must specify higher illumination levels, especially in areas where detailed tasks are performed and where there are potential hazards such as stairs.

## LIGHT AND EMOTIVE RESPONSES

Light is a remarkable element that can be exciting, mysterious, magical, or terrifying. Paris, known as the City of Light, evokes excitement. Fireworks, used in Chinese New Year's celebrations as early as the ninth century, are an excellent example of how lights can create a festive atmosphere. Lights are often used to inspire people during prayer as well as in sorrowful times. The Metropolitan Cathedral of Brasilia (1970) in Brasilia, Brazil by architect Oscar Niemeyer is an excellent example of the inspirational effects that can occur when daylight and stained glass are blended together (Figure 1.9). In differing from a traditional location of stained-glass windows along the exterior walls of a church, Niemeyer's placement of illuminated colors and shapes prompts worshippers to look to the heavens.

To memorialize the victims of the 1995 Oklahoma City bombing, the Butzer Design Partnership firm designed clear chairs, one for each of the 168 victims, which are illuminated during the evening (Figure 1.10). There are 19 small chairs that represent each child who was killed while they were in the building's childcare center. In another example, the life of President John F. Kennedy is honored in a memorial with a cenotaph, a monument, designed by the architect Philip Johnson. The words "John Fitzgerald Kennedy" are engraved in gold on black granite in the center of the sculpture. These are the only words on the sculpture, and they are illuminated only by the reflections of the surrounding white walls. The words are dark during the evening hours, thus representing the loss of a leader.

Although these lighting examples demonstrate inspirational uses, light also can be very frightening, as with lightning or a severe fire. For example, lightning is often used in movies and on the stage to create a fearful setting. A raging fire can create panic in people and animals. Flashing red lights on fire trucks or ambulances cause apprehensive feelings of being in a crisis or a life-threatening situation.

**FIGURE 1.9** The Metropolitan Cathedral of Brasilia (1970) in Brasilia, Brazil by architect Oscar Niemeyer illustrates the beauty of natural light passing through stained glass. (© Ludovic Maisant/Hemis/Corbis.)

## Layered Lighting

The integration and control of daylight can be applied to each category of lighting, including general, task, and accent. This requires layered lighting utilizing multiple light sources, each with its own purpose. This gives the users of the space the flexibility of selecting and adjusting the lighting for each specific activity. An important element in achieving a flexible light plan is to have multiple switching and dimming controls. The overall theme of an interior should be reflected in the selection of the light fixtures and the illumination levels for each of the three categories of lighting—general, task, and accent.

### GENERAL LIGHTING

As mentioned earlier in this chapter, general lighting is sometimes referred to as ambient lighting, and is designed to provide uniform lighting to a space. Often, light fixtures for general lighting are designed for indirect or reflected illumination and are hidden from view. General lighting allows people to walk safely through a space by reducing sharp contrasts between light sources. This enables people to perceive the overall shape and size of a space.

FIGURE 1.10 To memorialize the victims of the 1995 Oklahoma City bombing, the Butzer Design Partnership firm designed clear chairs, one for each of the 168 victims, which are illuminated during the evening. (© Danita Delimont / Alamy.)

General lighting also establishes the mood or character of an interior (Figure 1.11).

The design of a general lighting plan should be based upon the purpose of the space and the needs of its users. General lighting is the source that establishes the overall impression of a space and is determined by the light level, light source, and fixtures. For example, as shown in Figure 1.11, the general lighting in a high-end restaurant or retail store will usually be dimmer than in a fast-food restaurant or discount store. High-end spaces usually have a flexible lighting system, including electrical fixtures that promote a certain mood and image. Designers of low-end or discount settings plan systems that are functional but economize on electrical usage, maintenance, and fixtures.

Daylight can be the source of general lighting on sunny days in spaces with many windows or skylights (Figure 1.12). But those spaces should be designed to provide general lighting from electrical sources during the evenings or on dark, cloudy days. A variety of light fixtures and structural lighting systems are available to provide the lighting required for general illumination. (Lighting systems and styles of fixtures are discussed in Chapter 6.) To have an adequate level of illumination, the space must have several indirect fixtures in various locations. Any light fixture that provides indirect light could be used for general lighting, or it may be supplemented with light that is integrated into walls, ceilings, or furniture.

## TASK LIGHTING

Task lighting is another category of lighting that is used in both commercial and residential

FIGURE 1.11 The general lighting in this restaurant set the tone for a relaxed and upscale experience. (© MARKA/Alamy.)

FIGURE 1.12 Patterned surfaces can reduce glare and enhance the effects of daylight. (Fotodesign Andreas Braun, Hameln,Germany © FotodesignAndreasBraun.de.)

lighting be excellent for activities that require precision, such as surgery. The more time is spent engaged in an activity, the more important it is to specify appropriate task lighting. Any quality task lighting design must take into account individuals with less than perfect eyesight, such as the elderly.

In planning a task lighting system, it is important to build in flexibility and control for the users of the space. For example, adjustable **luminaires** and dimmers can customize the lighting for the specific needs of a user at a particular time and save energy by localizing the high-illumination levels where they are required (Figure 1.13). Conserving energy is one of the reasons why LEED

environments to provide quality lighting for specific activities and tasks. Task lighting is a direct form of lighting that enables users to see the critical details of an activity (Figure 1.2). A quality lighting environment includes the appropriate balance of general lighting and task lighting. The illumination level of task lighting should be approximately three times the level of general lighting. This ratio ensures a level of lighting that allows the eye to shift from the task to the surrounding area and vice versa with a minimum amount of adjustment in the eye's lens.

Some task lighting requires special consideration. For example, it is critical that

Fixtures controlled by individuals

FIGURE 1.13 By including such features as these canopies to workstations, individuals can control their task lighting; a credit category for LEED certified buildings. (HermanMiller.)

provides credit (IEQ 6.1) for interiors that have lighting system controls for individuals or groups of people. Other important considerations related to individual controls are enhanced productivity, comfort, and well-being (USGBC, 2009).

Lighting plans that specify an illumination level for an entire area regardless of the specific needs of the users result in a waste of electricity because some individuals do not need a high level of illumination or are not always present in the space (Figure 1.14). Customized task lighting in a large, open, office space allows individual users to have flexibility and control, providing the appropriate illumination level at the brightness required for the duration of an activity.

Potential problems should be considered in planning quality task lighting. Task lighting can become a problem because the illumination levels needed for many activities can be very high, which can lead to difficulty for the eye in adapting to the varying light levels and contrasts. The light source may create glare, **veiling reflections**, or shadows. Glare and veiling reflections occur when the light source is reflected on the work space. For example, computer monitors can reflect fixtures mounted on a ceiling, or light can cause glare on shiny surfaces such as glossy magazines.

The eye can have problems adjusting between light and dark areas because of severe contrast in illumination levels between the task and its surrounding area. It is especially difficult to ensure the proper lighting levels for tasks that require high levels of illumination, such as sewing black fabric with black thread or reading very small type.

Sources that should be dimmed when daylight levels are sufficient

FIGURE 1.14 Power is wasted when lights are on when people are not in the space and when electrical sources are not dimmed when there is adequate daylight levels. (© GLOBETROTTER/Alamy.)

Close work fatigues the eye by creating strain. Generally, the more light on the task, the less strain there will be on the eye.

To reduce strain on eyes, a designer can do other things besides increasing the brightness of the lighting. One possibility would be to increase the contrast or size of the objects used in a task. For example, most books are printed with black type on white paper because the extreme contrast between black and white results in the greatest amount of visibility. To improve visibility, a designer might also change the color of a work surface or the position of a piece of furniture. Designers can use computerized analytical tools to predict visibility patterns and illumination levels in an environment.

## Task Lighting: Planning and Placement

In planning task lighting, a designer must first identify the activities that occur in a space and then determine which characteristics of those tasks need to receive special lighting treatment. National codes and standards have been established for task illumination levels for commercial and residential spaces. Excellent sources for this information include the *National Handbook of the Illuminating Engineering Society of North America (IESNA)* and the *Chartered Institute of Building Services Engineers (CIBSE) Code for Lighting* in the United Kingdom. The recommended illumination levels are averages, not minimum requirements, which is why it is important to avoid overlighting an area while also providing adequate illumination for special needs groups, such as seniors with aging eyes. For example, higher illumination levels should be specified for long-term care facilities for the elderly.

In addition to illumination levels for a task, a designer must consider the design and placement of each luminaire. Luminaires for task lighting include portable fixtures, pendants, and recessed, track, and structural lighting (Figure 1.15). As illustrated in Figure 1.13, some office furniture has task lighting built into it. This lighting includes sources for both task lighting and ambient lighting, whereby direct light is positioned for tasks and indirect light for the general or ambient light surrounding the workstation. Task-ambient

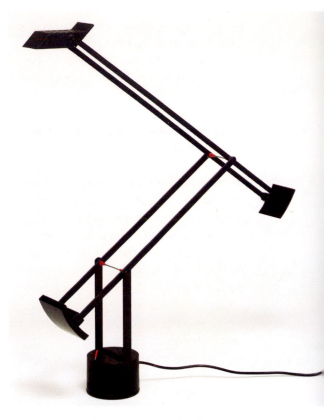

**FIGURE 1.15** One of the most well-known task luminaires, Tizio was designed by Richard Sapper in 1971. Tizio is an adjustable table luminaire that was originally made with a halogen bulb, but is currently manufactured with LED lighting. (Digital Image © The Museum of Modern Art/Licensed by SCALA/Art Resource, NY.)

furniture systems can be an effective way to illuminate a large, open office space that accommodates users with a variety of needs.

Daylight can also be a part of task lighting. Daylight is excellent for helping people to discern critical details, for example, in reading and writing, and to make color distinctions. That is why daylight can be very effective in interiors such as schools, offices, and libraries. Supplemental electrical sources have to be planned, however, to meet the needs of the users on dark days and in the evenings.

## ACCENT LIGHTING

Accent or **focal lighting** is another layer of illumination in a quality lighting environment (Figure 1.3). It can be as simple as a single spotlight trained on a piece of art on a wall. Some of the illumination from accent lighting can also contribute to the interior's general lighting, but the purpose of accent or focal lighting is to bring attention to an object or element in a space. Accent lighting creates drama, variety, interest, and excitement in an interior. The form and style of accent lighting should be designed to contribute to the room's atmosphere and theme.

In planning accent lighting, it is important for the designer to identify the things needing to be highlighted and the characteristics of the surrounding areas. Designers use accent lighting to emphasize artwork, sculptures, water, fabrics, architectural details, textures, forms, and plants. The location and aiming angle must be chosen so as to avoid direct glare to the eyes of users. To avoid problems with viewing, the preferred angle to a wall is 30 degrees (Figure 1.16). Exterior views, especially in the evening, can also be excellent focal points of an interior (Figure 1.17).

Creating contrast and determining the best angle at which to position a light are key to successful accent lighting. To attract the eye to an object or area requires contrast, so the characteristics of the surrounding area of the accented object are important. For example, a

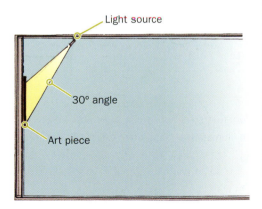

FIGURE 1.16 To accent artwork on a wall, the preferred angle to the wall is 30 degrees.

FIGURE 1.17 The proposed extension to the Tate Modern in London illustrates how interior lighting can provide dramatic impressions of the architecture. (Courtesy of Hayes Davidson.)

white object will blend into white walls around it, whereas a dark object will stand out by contrast. An illumination level that is the same for both the accented item and the surrounding area will not emphasize the item effectively (Figure 1.18). Contrasts in illumination levels enhance the accent item and distinguish it from the surrounding area (Figure 1.19).

The drama and emphasis of extreme light and shadow is often illustrated in paintings. As demonstrated in Figure 1.20, the artist skillfully used light, shade, and shadows to emphasize architectural lines, forms, and space. One approach to achieving contrast is to illuminate the object to be accented with a greater amount of light than its surrounding area. Because the eye is attracted to light, the users of the space will focus their attention on the areas of the room with the highest illumination levels. Generally, to create enough contrast to accent an object requires a minimum ratio of 5 to 1 between the accent and general lighting. Ratios lower than this will generally not provide enough contrast to be considered accent lighting. Extreme drama can be accomplished with a 10 to 1 ratio, but the ratio should not exceed 20 to 1. Differentials higher than this create a setting that does not allow the eye to adjust to the contrasts between light and dark.

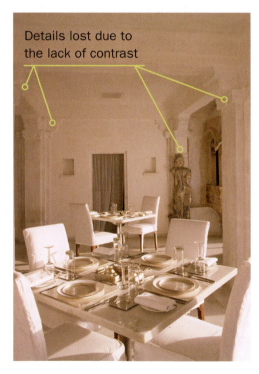

FIGURE 1.18 Using lighting to create contrast between the characteristics of the surrounding area and the accented object is especially important in an all-white interior. (© Robert Harding Picture Library Ltd/Alamy.)

FIGURE 1.19 Contrasts in illumination levels enhance the merchandise and distinguish it from the surroundings areas. (Courtesy of Philips Lightolier.)

FIGURE 1.20 This painting of a Gothic church in 1636 by Pieter Neeffs, the elder, illustrates how light, shade, and shadows emphasize architectural lines, forms, and space. (Image copyright © The Metropolitan Museum of Art/Art Resource, NY.)

Specifying effective contrast ratios is difficult in spaces that have many accented areas or objects. For example, a retailer might want to emphasize several displays that are close to one another in the store. But this may result in the objects blending together, eliminating the contrast required to bring attention to the individual items. In addition to varying the illumination levels, a designer might have to contrast other elements in the space by employing complementary colors and varying textures, forms, shapes, and lines. Motion is also an excellent technique for attracting the eye, especially peripheral vision.

Direction and angle of a source are also key considerations in accent lighting. The perceived shapes of three-dimensional objects or people can be affected if the direction and angle of light are not well planned. In contrast, a specific direction and angle of light can create dramatic shadows that the designer wants to emphasize. For example, plant foliage can provide interesting patterns and shadows on walls and ceilings if a light source is placed close to a plant. In fact, revealing the textures and form of an object often requires that the light source be close to the object (Figure 1.21). This technique is referred to as **grazing**. Shapes and other details also can be enhanced by placing a light source behind an object or architectural element (Figure 2.22). This **backlighting** technique results in a decorative pattern of silhouettes.

Accent lighting allows a designer to be very creative in highlighting areas or objects. It can often be more interesting and effective if the designer selects a specific point of emphasis on an accent piece. For example, instead of providing a uniform distribution of light to a sculpture or architectural detail, it might be far more dramatic to illuminate only portions of a sculpture or only one interesting detail of a column, a fireplace, or other architectural details (Figure 1.23). Highlighting flower petals that have fallen from a bouquet sitting on a table, rather than the entire arrangement, is another creative example of accent lighting. Spotlighting the specific element and having the appropriate contrast in illumination levels can focus the emphasis on the focal point. The best approach to accenting a sculpture or objet d'art is to have two light sources aimed at the piece from two different angles.

**FIGURE 1.21** Grazing created by placing LEDs close to the wall emphasizes the textures of the bricks. (Courtesy of Pure Lighting.)

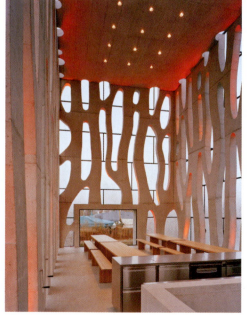

**FIGURE 1.22** A transparent pavilion, Nordwesthaus in Austria (2008) illustrates how architectural elements can be enhanced by backlighting. (Eduard Hueber/archphoto.com.)

FIGURE 1.23 A dramatic effect is created by highlighting only selected points beneath the arches and upon the stone walls within Ajloun Castle near Jerash, Jordan. (© Dynamic Light Arabia/Alamy.)

Shadows play an important role in accent lighting. A strong spotlight can create some undesirable shadows on a surface. For example, the frame of a painting could create a shadow from the spotlight on the artwork. It is, therefore, critical to position the spotlight at the proper mounting location and aiming angle. Of course, shadows can be planned as unique focal points of a surface or object, such as shadows of architectural elements on walls (Figure 1.24). The shadow of a unique form, such as an abstract sculpture, could also be the accented element. Shadows of architectural details of an interior enhance the sculptural elements and the three-dimensional aspect of a façade; the location and aiming angle are critical to ensure that a façade is viewed as having three dimensions rather than two. Depending on the intensity of a

FIGURE 1.24 Interior view of the Sweeney Chapel (1987) at Christian Theological Seminary in Indianapolis designed by Edward Larrabee Barnes illustrates dramatic effects that can be created with light and shadows. (Balthazar Korab.)

light source, its distance from the object, and the aiming angle, shadow lines can be hard or soft. From a design perspective, a hard shadow line will project an image that is dramatic and harsh. A soft shadow line does not attract the eye easily and promotes a subdued theme.

Light fixtures used for accent lighting include **uplights**, **recessed spots**, **spotlight projectors** with optical control, and wall brackets. Depending on their location in a space, luminaires for accent lighting can form a decorative element of an interior or they can be hidden from view. Some furniture is designed with accent lighting hidden from direct view. Curio cabinets, breakfronts, and other cabinets often have accent lighting to enhance crystal, china, and objects d'art. As with general lighting, it is often intriguing to hide the light source when specifying accent lighting. Viewing an object or area enhanced by illumination without seeing the source of the light adds mystery and drama to a setting (Figure 1.25).

Daylight could be a bright source that accents an object or area in a space through narrow slits or small openings. The variability of daylight, depending on the weather, the time of day, and so on, will affect the quality of the accent. As a note of caution, because

accent lighting is often a small, bright light source, unexpected glare can create a safety concern.

## DECORATIVE LIGHTING

Decorative lighting is designed to be a focal point in a space. It can be a fixture that is designed to be an ornamental element of the interior, or it can be a specialty architectural lighting solution. Chandeliers, Tiffany glass shades, neon tubes, lasers, holograms, holiday lights, wall sconces, and some fiber optics are examples of decorative lighting (Figure 1.26). Daylight can be a source of decorative lighting when it illuminates a stained glass window. To appreciate the stained glass window in the evening, exterior lighting should be included in the lighting plan.

Decorative lighting can also be an art form. Candles and flames in a fireplace are decorative sources that add warmth and

FIGURE 1.25 Dramatic lighting effects using light sources that are hidden from view. (Julian Taylor Design Associates.)

FIGURE 1.26 *Wo bist du, Edison,...?* (1997) by Ingo Maurer is a decorative luminaire that is a hologram. (Ingo Maurer GmbH, Munich, Germany, info@ingo-maurer .com, www.ingo-maurer.com/photographer: Tom Vack, Munich.)

enhance the appearance of people and objects in an environment. Whenever possible, candles should be considered an important element of the layered lighting in a space.

The purpose of a decorative fixture should remain ornamental. For example, whereas most chandeliers are designed to be only decorative, quite frequently a chandelier in a dining room is used as the source for general, task, and accent lighting (Figure 1.27). As a result, the high illumination level required to meet all three needs could discourage people from viewing the chandelier, negating the purpose of having it as a decorative fixture. This is especially problematic if the chandelier has exposed **flame-shaped lamps**, which are quite common. Decorative lighting serves an important role in reinforcing the theme and style of the space. These sources should supplement the lighting specified for general, task, and accent purposes.

To design quality lighting environments, an interior designer must understand the power and effect of light on people within the context of the setting. This requires an understanding of the purpose of the space and characteristics of the users. For example, low levels of illumination are appropriate for a romantic restaurant, but they would be very wrong for a workplace. Flashing lights can promote excitement in a nightclub, but they would be very annoying in a museum. An important element in addressing the needs of the users of the space focuses on the variability of the vision process. Quality lighting must support the basic functions of vision. This requires an understanding of what happens when light enters the eye and the conditions that alter the vision process.

**FIGURE 1.27** One light fixture cannot be the general, task, and accent lighting in a space. (© mauritius images GmbH/Alamy.)

# Fundamental Projects

**1. Human Factors Research Project**

Identify several experiences you have had with changes in lighting, such as entering a movie theater on a bright, sunny day. Describe what occurs in the vision process as you experience these changes.

**2. Research Design Project**

Select photographs of five residential interiors and five nonresidential interiors. Identify the electrical fixtures in the space and determine the category (general, task, accent) of each fixture. If a fixture does not exist for a category of lighting, suggest an effective fixture. The identification and analysis should be submitted in written form. Photographs must be included.

## Application Projects

**1. Human Factors Research Project**

Developing observational and problem-solving skills is critical to success as a designer. Identify five public spaces you can observe during various times of the day and on different days of the week. Write a report that could include sketches and photographs responding to the items listed below:

a. Determine whether the space meets all the criteria for a quality lighting environment.

b. Given the users and elements of the space, identify special needs for vision.

c. Determine the human response elicited from the space and identify the lighting techniques that contribute to the response.

d. Compare and contrast how the space would work with non-electrical light fixtures.

**2. Research Design Project**

The purpose of this project is to develop an understanding of how to integrate daylight with general, task, and accent lighting. As a designer you have been commissioned to create layered lighting plans for an elementary school in a warm climate and for a discount retail store in a cold climate. You are to submit to each client a written document, optionally accompanied by sketches and photographs, that includes the following information:

a. Critical spaces for integrating daylight.

b. For each space in the interior, an identification of the needs for general, task, and accent lighting.

# Summary

o The global emphasis on sustainable designs, including LEED certification, has prompted significant attention to maximizing daylight and specifying energy-efficient lighting systems.

o Light is a form of energy that is part of the electromagnetic spectrum visible to the human eye. Light has the ability to elicit significant emotional responses from people.

o Quality lighting environments allow users to function in a space, feel safe in it, and appreciate its aesthetic components. These environments reflect a skillful application of the principles of design by integrating and layering lighting into the entire composition.

o The vision process starts when light enters the pupil. The lens adjusts the light for near and far vision, and the cornea focuses light on the retina by refraction. Rods and cones are detector cells located at the back of the retina. Rods are activated primarily in lower illumination levels, and cones are activated by bright light, color, and detail. The optic nerve sends impulses from the retina to the brain for interpretation.

o Because light/dark adaptation occurs in the vision process, designers should consider a lighting system that provides a transition in light levels.

o The eye's field of vision includes a central and peripheral area.

o The aging of the eye affects visual acuity, color identification, the adaptation process, peripheral vision, depth perception, and tolerance for glare.

o General or ambient lighting is a category of lighting designed to provide uniform lighting to a space.

o Task lighting is a direct form of lighting that enables users to see the critical details of an activity.

o The purpose of accent or highlight lighting is to bring attention to an object or element in a space. Creating contrast and determining the direction and angle of a source are key considerations in accent lighting.

o Decorative lighting is designed to be an ornamental element of an interior.

## KEY TERMS

accent lighting (focal lighting)
accommodation
adaptation
backlighting
decorative lighting
eye's field of vision
flame-shaped lamp
focal lighting (accent lighting)
general lighting/ ambient lighting
grazing

indirect natural light
lamp
layered lighting
Leadership in Energy and
    Environmental Design (LEED)
light
lumen (lm)
luminaire
natural light
presbyopia

quality lighting
recessed spot
spotlight projector
sustainable design
task lighting
uplight
veiling reflection
visual acuity

## References

USGBC (2009). *Green Interior Design and Construction*. Washington, D.C.: U.S. Green Building Council.

## Resources

Gordon, G. (2003). *Interior lighting for designers* (4th ed.). New York: John Wiley & Sons.

Illuminating Engineering Society of North America (IESNA) (2011). *IESNA lighting handbook* (10th ed.). New York: Illuminating Engineering Society of North America.

Phillips, D. (2000). *Lighting modern buildings*. Oxford: Architectural Press.

Veitch, J. (July 9–11, 2000). *Lighting guidelines from lighting quality research*. CIBSE/ILE Lighting 2000 Conference. New York, United Kingdom.

# 2 Color and Directional Effects of Lighting

In Chapter 1 you learned the fundamentals of the vision process and how color activates cone cells that are located at the back of the retina. Generally, people perceive daylight to reveal an object's "true" color. However, weather conditions, reflections, and the time of day can affect perceived color. The type of light source will affect perceived color, which influences the work of an interior designer. This is especially challenging with electrical light sources because each lamp has unique color-rendering properties.

As introduced in Chapter 1, designing a quality lighting environment requires an understanding of the impact of the intensity and direction of a light source on an object's appearance, the effect of architectural features, the ability to perform a task, and the quantity of illumination. In layered lighting plans, an interior designer must coordinate the intensity and directional effects from all the light sources. A lighting plan must be developed that is in harmony with the physical attributes of furniture, objects, walls, floors, window treatments, and interior architecture. Colors, textures, shapes, forms, and size are affected by the intensity and directional qualities of light sources. Concurrently, the elements of design can affect the quantity and direction of light.

## OBJECTIVES

o Summarize the basic concepts associated with color and lamps

o Explain how chromaticity and the color-rendering index can be used to specify lamps and color

o Identify the elements of an environment that contribute to brightness and glare

o Provide design solutions that maximize the positive attributes of brightness and control glare

o Describe the reflectance properties of colors and materials

o Apply the principles of reflectance and optical control to an environment

## Lamps and Color

The eye can detect more than five million colors. The perception of all these colors is affected by numerous factors, but most importantly by the source of light. For example, the wavelengths of daylight vary according to the time of day, sky conditions, time of year, and geographic location. Daylight at sunset appears to be redder than it does at noon, because the light will have more red and yellow wavelengths than blue or green ones. Northern daylight has more blue and green wavelengths than does southern daylight, resulting in a cooler appearance. Impressionist artists studied extensively how the appearance of colors and objects changed with the conditions of light and atmosphere. For example, Claude Monet painted the western façade of Rouen

FIGURE 2.1A Effect of noon sunlight on the façade of Rouen Cathedral as painted by Claude Monet. (Scala/Art Resource, NY.)

FIGURE 2.1B Effect of a cloudy day on the façade of Rouen Cathedral as painted by Claude Monet. (Scala/Art Resource, NY.)

Cathedral at many different times of the day and under a variety of weather conditions (Figures 2.1a and b). From 1892 to 1894, he created 20 paintings of Rouen Cathedral.

Color cannot be seen without light. To prove this to yourself, walk through a room at dusk and attempt to identify and distinguish colors. You will notice that you can see objects but that it is nearly impossible to discern the colors of these objects and surfaces. Once the lights are turned on, the colors become visible. These facts are important when a lighting designer selects a light source. If a light source does not have a balanced spectrum of colors, the color of the object being illuminated will be altered. In specifying a quality lighting system, a designer selects lamps that will enhance the colors in the environment. To assist designers with the lamp selection process, lamp manufacturers provide data about lamp color specifications, such as **chromaticity** ratings and the **color-rendering index (CRI)**.

## CHROMATICITY

The chromaticity, or **color temperature**, of a light source helps to create the atmosphere of a space and often reflects the quality of the interior. The color temperature indicates the degree of red or blue in the light supplied by a light source. It is measured in kelvins (K) and is part of the information provided by lamp manufacturers about their lamps. On a kelvin scale, the warmer the apparent color of a light source, the lower the number of kelvins will be (Figure 2.2). A higher number on the scale represents a cooler or bluer color. For example, the warm color of light emitted from a candle is approximately 2000K, whereas the color of

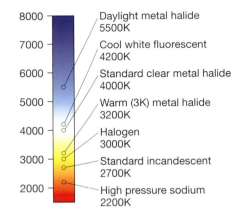

FIGURE 2.2 A kelvin scale illustrates that the warmer the apparent color of a light source, the lower the number of kelvins and a higher number on the scale represents a cooler or bluer color. Labeling includes typical color temperatures associated with daylight and selected lamps.

cool daylight is 5000K. A neutral color falls at about 3500K. Lamps that provide a warm and cool appearance have chromaticity ratings of 3000K and 4100K, respectively.

One way to understand the scale is to imagine the heating of a hard material such as steel. As the steel is heated, it will first turn red, followed by yellow, then white, and finally blue-white, so that the temperature of the steel is reflected in the relative coolness of its color. Similarly, an interior that has a warm glow will have a relatively low chromaticity rating (3000K) (Figure 2.3). In contrast, an interior that appears to be cool and bright will have a relatively high chromaticity rating (4100K). To comply with state energy codes, the most common chromaticity ratings for fluorescent sources are 3000K, 3500K, and 4100K. These lamps are available with CRIs in the 70s and

Warm below 3500K    Midrange 3500K–4500 K    Cool above 4000K

**FIGURE 2.3** Lamps with three different color temperatures illuminate these floral bouquets. Examine the differences in colors and textures of the three arrangements and their backgrounds. (Photographs courtesy Con-Tech Lighting.)

80s; some manufacturers produce lamps with CRIs in the 90s.

In an attempt to measure color, an international organization for color, the International Commission on Illumination or Commission Internationale de l'Eclairage (CIE), developed a diagram consisting of a graph on which colors ranging from red to violet are plotted on x and y axes (Figure 2.4). The diagram represents **correlated color temperature (CCT)**. The mathematics of the colors form the triangular-shaped diagram: the wavelengths of the colors, in nanometers, are identified around the perimeter of the color triangle, and all colors in the spectrum blend in the center to become white.

The x and y coordinates on the diagram help designers locate a color. In the center of the triangle is the black body locus. This black curved line demonstrates the progression in

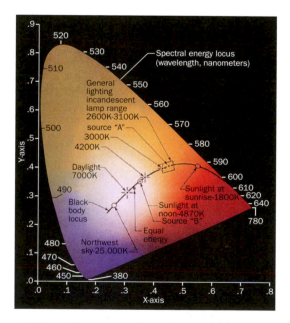

**FIGURE 2.4** CIE chromaticity diagram for natural and artificial light sources.

color temperature in kelvins (K). As illustrated in Figure 2.4, one of the circles on the black body locus represents sunlight at noon, with a color temperature of 4870K. The light from a lamp with warm color appearance is shown to have a color temperature of 3000K.

In practice, designers can use the CIE chromaticity diagram to determine quickly how a specific lamp compares to sunlight or the cool northwest sky. For example, 3000K lamps are located on the black curved line midway between sunlight at sunrise and sunlight at noon, indicating that these lamps tend to enhance warm colors. Another lamp is located in the blue-green colored area, indicating that it tends to enhance cool colors. The diagram also makes it easy for a designer to compare the chromaticity ratings of various lamps.

## COLOR RENDERING INDEX

A designer must know the color temperature and rendering ratings of lamps in order to specify those that are appropriate. The color rendering index (CRI) measures how faithfully a light source reveals the true colors of objects, and is another piece of information provided by manufacturers of lamps. The index ranges from 0 to 100. The higher the CRI number, the better the color-rendering ability of a lamp. The number is based upon an average of how eight colors appear in the light of different lamps in comparison to a standard test lamp. Thus, a source may be very good on most of the hues but not as good on others. Incandescent lamps have a CRI of 95 to 100 because they produce nearly perfect renditions of colors.

When color is important, select a lamp with a CRI in the 80s or higher. A CRI in the 90s

should be specified in settings where color appearance is very important. Compared to lamps with a CRI in the 70s, the cost of lamps with a CRI in the 80s or higher is greater because of additional rare earth phosphors used and a slightly lower efficacy rating. To determine the colors of objects and surfaces, an interior designer should always examine samples under the lamps and/or any daylight in the space.

To integrate a lamp's color temperature and rendering ability, General Electric developed a chart that demonstrates the relationship between chromaticity in kelvins and the CRI (Figure 2.5). As shown in Figure 2.5, a warm (3000K) fluorescent lamp has approximately the same chromaticity as a different fluorescent lamp. However, the

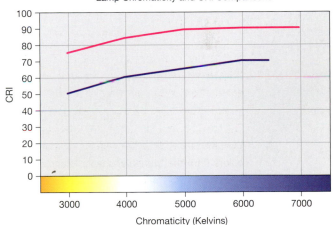

FIGURE 2.5 The CRI and chromaticity of artificial light sources. Notice how two lamps can have the same chromaticity (3000K) but two very different CRIs. Also notice how the CRI changes as the chromaticity becomes cooler (7000K).

## TABLE 2.1 Lamp Color Specifications and Suggested Applications

| LAMPS | | | CCT (K) (approx.) | CRI (approx.) | SUGGESTED APPLICATIONS |
|---|---|---|---|---|---|
| **Incandescent** | | | 2500–2800K | 97–100 | Residential, special applications such as niches, historic fixtures, sconces, nightlights, pendants |
| **Halogen** | | | 2800–3000K | 97–100 | Residential, hospitality, gallery, retail (high end) |
| **Fluorescent F32T8's** | | | | | |
| **General Electric Initial/Mean Lumen** | **Osram Sylvania** | **Philips** | | | |
| SPX50/ECO 2715/2580 | 850/ECO | TL850/ALTO | 5000K | 80s | Color-critical areas in galleries, printing, jewelry displays, medical examinations |
| SP50/ECO 2665/2530 | 750/ECO | TL750/ALTO | 5000K | 70s | Galleries, printing, jewelry displays, medical examinations |
| SPX41/ECO 2860/2710 | 841/ECO | TL841/ALTO | 4100K | 80s | Color-critical areas in offices, retail (discount), and hospitality, florists, classrooms, conference rooms |
| SP41/ECO 2715/2580 | 741/ECO | TL741/ALTO | 4100K | 70s | Offices, retail (discount), and hospitality, florists, classrooms, conference rooms |
| SPX35/ECO 2860/2710 | 835/ECO | TL835/ALTO | 3500K | 80s | Color-critical areas in offices, reception areas, retail, hospitality, hospital, residential |
| SP35/ECO 2715/2580 | 735/ECO | TL735/ALTO | 3500K | 70s | Offices, reception areas, retail, hospitality, hospital |
| SPX30/ECO 2860/2710 | 830/ECO | TL830/ALTO | 3000K | 80s | Color-critical areas in offices, retail (high end), and hospitality, libraries, hospital, residential |
| SP30/ECO 2715/2580 | 730/ECO | TL730/ALTO | 3000K | 70s | Offices, retail (high end), and hospitality, libraries, hospital, residential |
| **Ceramic Metal Halide Initial/Mean Lumen** | | | | | |
| **General Electric Initial Lumens** | **Osram Sylvania** | **Philips** | 3000–4200K | 80–93 | |
| CMH70/PAR38 4800/NA | MCP70PAR38 | CDM70/ PAR38 | 3000K | 80s | Offices, retail, hospitality, hospital |
| CMH150/T6 13000/11000 | MC150T6 | CDM150/ T6 | 4000K-4200K | 90s | Offices, retail, hospitality, hospital |
| High-Pressure Sodium Initial/Mean Lumen | | | 1900–2100K | 22 | |
| LU250/D 28000/27000 | LU250/D | C250S50/D | 2100K | 22 | Efficiency critical: industrial, outdoors |
| LU250/DX 22500/20700 | N/A | C250S50/C | 2200K | 65< | Industrial, outdoors |

color rendering capability of the two lamps is approximately 80 and 50, respectively. Thus, because their chromaticity is similar, both lamps will appear to be a cool light source, but color rendering will be better with the lamp having a CRI of 80. A designer selecting lamps for a high-end retail store could first select lamps with a lower chromaticity rating, and then select from within this grouping the lamp with the highest CRI.

Table 2.1 summarizes color properties of common lamps produced by three major manufacturers. (It also indicates initial and mean lumens; according to the chart, a 4100K fluorescent lamp with a CRI in the 80s has initial and mean lumens of 2860 and 2710, respectively. **Initial lumens** is the light output when the luminaire is first installed, and **mean lumens** is the average light output over the life of the lamp.) It should be noted that for each of the major CCT ratings (3000K, 3500K, 4100K), fluorescent lamps are available in two CRI ratings (70s and 80s). Table 2.1 also provides some lamp suggestions for specific applications. For example, according to the chart, a 5000K fluorescent lamp is excellent for checking the color of textiles during the printing process and other situations where the quality of color is evaluated.

## Directional Effects of Lighting

### BRIGHTNESS AND GLARE

To have a quality lighting environment, an interior designer must develop a plan that maximizes the positive attributes of **brightness** and that controls glare. Brightness is a subjective concept that has positive and negative connotations. The bright lights we see during the Christmas holidays are exciting and contribute to the gaiety of festivities. In contrast, the bright lights of an automobile's high beams directed toward a driver on a dark highway are distracting and dangerous. Ideally, an interior designer plans an environment that results in only positive reactions to brightness.

Technically, brightness is the result of the interaction between an illumination level and the amount of light reflected off various surfaces, known as **reflectance**. An interior designer can measure the quantity of light in a space that results from the reflectance of objects and surfaces. (Measuring illumination is reviewed in Chapter 8.) The light level or illuminance that falls on a surface can be measured in **foot-candles**, or **lux (lx)**. A foot-candle (fc) is a unit of illumance equal to the amount of light that falls on a surface within a one-foot radius of the source (Figure 2.6).

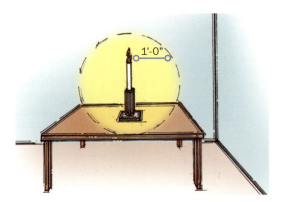

FIGURE 2.6 A foot-candle is the amount of light that falls on a surface within a one-foot radius of the source.

However, reflectance and **illuminance** are only two factors that affect brightness. Illumination levels can be significantly increased without appearing to be brighter. For example, even though foot-candle levels are very high on a cloudy day, people perceive the day as gloomy. Furthermore, an increase in illumination levels does not necessarily improve the quality of lighting; sometimes, changing the direction of a light source, rather than increasing the quantity of lighting, is the best way to improve a dark work area. To deal with brightness successfully, an interior designer must consider all the factors involved, including subjective responses, the context of the situation, the vision attributes of the individuals using the space, light sources, directional qualities, and characteristics of elements of the design.

Brightness is generally a subjective reaction to an environment and is dependent upon individuals' expectations and comparative contexts as well as the physical condition of their eyes. In analyzing the perceived brightness of an environment, an interior designer must anticipate expectations of a setting within the variability of different times of the day and year. Through their accumulated experiences, people develop expectations for illumination levels and perceived brightness. For example, people generally expect light levels to be lower in the evening than during the day, and higher during the summer months than in the winter. Expectations of brightness are also related to the specific activity to be undertaken in a space. For example, a lighting plan for an office may not appear to be too

bright, whereas the same illumination level in a romantic restaurant would most likely be perceived as too bright.

## Perceived Brightness

Perceived brightness is also affected by the physical condition of the eyes. Elderly people might not consider a light source as bright because age affects their vision. A younger individual, on the other hand, might perceive the same environment as very bright. The eye has the ability to adjust to an enormous range of illumination levels; however, this adaptation affects perceived brightness. For example, if an individual moves from a very dark space to a lighter area, the lighter area may appear very bright until the eye adjusts to the higher illumination level.

The perceived brightness of an environment is also affected by light sources and their directional qualities. The design of a luminaire and the type of lamp used affect the perceived brightness of electrical sources. A luminaire that provides direct illumination can be perceived as bright, whereas the light from indirect light sources generally appears softer (Figures 2.7a and b). Exposed lamps, especially those with clear glass, can appear to be bright. The perceived brightness of a light source also depends upon the location of the luminaire in relation to users: if a luminaire appears to be bright only when one looks directly at the exposed lamps, the perceived brightness can be altered by moving the location of the task or changing the direction of the light source.

The perceived brightness of a setting is affected by its surroundings: an object will

(a)                                    (b)

FIGURE 2.7A Light from a direct fixture can be perceived as too bright. (© Image Source/Alamy.)

FIGURE 2.7B Light from indirect fixtures generally appears to be soft illumination. (Jay Graham.)

appear to be brighter when the area surrounding the light source is dark, and dimmer when the surrounding area is lighter. For example, high-beam headlights on an automobile appear to be bright at night, but not during the day.

The color, texture, and finish of objects also affect the perceived brightness of an interior. White and light colors will appear to be brighter than black and dark colors. Smooth and shiny textures will be perceived as brighter than rough and matte finishes. For example, a room painted white in a high-gloss finish will appear to be brighter than a room paneled in a dark, rough wood.

## Glare

Excessive brightness is known as **glare**. As with perceived brightness, there are a variety of factors that affect glare. Glare can easily occur in illumination settings that require contrast for effective visibility and attention. For example, retail displays designed to attract attention to a product will often have a higher illumination level on the product than on the surrounding area. If the contrast between the two areas is too great, glare can occur. When the eye has to adjust to contrasting light levels, there is a loss in visual acuity and a potential for eye fatigue and strain, resulting in a negative subjective reaction. Glare due to contrast and high illumination levels can also occur with activities that require task lighting—for example, if concentrated light is shed on a task while the rest of the room is in darkness, or when bright, concentrated light sources are located above and in front of where the task is performed (Figure 2.8).

**Direct Glare**  Both direct and indirect glare occur as a result of the intensity and direction of a light source. **Direct glare** occurs when a light source is at a high-illumination level and is usually not covered or shielded. It also often occurs on a bright sunny day if there is no window treatment. Any lamp that is exposed and illuminated at a high level can cause direct glare. Generally, any unshielded lamp greater than 25 watts can cause glare. A flame-shaped lamp in a chandelier can cause glare at a high-illumination level, but the same lamp appears to glitter or sparkle at lower light levels. (For more information regarding types of luminaires, refer to Chapter 5.) Direct glare can also be the result of extreme contrast in illumination levels

between rooms. This can occur in a residential interior, for example, when the living room and dining room are located next to each other, and one of these rooms is in darkness while the other is highly illuminated. To help reduce glare, all spaces adjoining a room should have some illumination (Figure 2.9).

**Indirect Glare**  When light is reflected from surfaces or objects, indirect light occurs. It is important to examine how an individual can

**FIGURE 2.9** To help reduce glare adjoining rooms should have some illumination. (© Corbis RF/Alamy.)

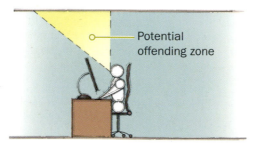

Potential offending zone

**FIGURE 2.8** Luminaire locations can cause glare to the user of the desk.

be affected by the reflections from indirect light sources. For example, on a sunny day, one can experience indirect glare from the sunlight reflected off light-colored surfaces or materials such as snow, concrete, or sand. Indoors, **indirect glare** can be the result of reflection of a light source from a light-colored or shiny surface. Glass, mirrors, and high-gloss surfaces, such as highly polished wood or the ink on a printed page, can cause indirect glare when the light source is directed toward these specular materials. Often an indirect light source can cause glare on visual display terminal (VDT) screens. As discussed

in Chapter 1, indirect light that is reflected from a surface in a task area is termed *veiling reflections*.

### Discomfort and Disability Glare

Discomfort glare and disability glare are terms that describe the degree of disturbance caused by a bright light source (Figure 2.10). **Discomfort glare** occurs when a natural or electrical light source causes glare that is uncomfortable, but still allows an individual to see objects and perform tasks. Discomfort glare can be especially annoying when an individual is exposed to the glare for a long time. **Disability**

**FIGURE 2.10** Electronically tintable architectural glass was used to reduce visible light on just one window that is across from the visible computer screen. Notice how difficult it is to see the screens on the other three monitors. (Courtesy Sage Electronics Inc.)

**FIGURE 2.11** Disability glare in this café is the result of the bright daylight that is behind the people. (© David Wells/ Alamy.)

**glare** arises when the glare from a light source is so severe that the individual is unable to see. This can happen, for example, when an individual is unable to see people in front of a window on a sunny day (Figure 2.11), or has difficulty seeing the faces of people approaching in a dark hallway with windows behind them. Disability glare can also occur when an individual is unable to read text on a glossy magazine page because of the reflection of the light on the surface. The high gloss of oil paints can cause disability glare on artwork. Some interior designers rely upon disability glare to discourage users from looking at undesirable elements in an interior, such as mechanical systems in an exposed ceiling.

### Controlling Glare

Glare must be controlled in a quality lighting environment, and there are many approaches for an interior designer to consider depending upon the specific elements of an interior and the users of the space (refer to Figures 2.7b and 2.10). Glare is easier to control when using more luminaires with lower wattages compared to fewer high-wattage luminaires. Locating luminaires out of the field of vision can also control glare. This requires an examination of the direction of a light source and all locations where people are sitting, standing, or walking.

Unshielded downlights can be problematic because they are permanent installations and because of the direct angle of the beam of light. For example, a restaurant lighting plan that utilizes downlights above the tables can result in glare. The original lighting plan might have the downlights located directly in the center of the tables, avoiding glare for the patrons; however, tables in restaurants are frequently moved to accommodate various groups of people, to clean the floor, or through carelessness. When the tables are moved, the downlights are no longer centered and might cause glare by being positioned directly over the faces of people. The glare is disturbing, and the mottling effect on faces can be very unflattering. Using elements in a luminaire, such as a **shade**, **baffle**, **louver**, or lens, can reduce glare (Figures 2.12a and b).

Reducing brightness ratios is a means of controlling glare and is achieved by examining a variety of factors in the environment, including the illumination levels between areas in a space and the size of the opening in the luminaire. Generally, smaller luminaire openings have a greater potential for glare than larger apertures. Therefore, a luminaire that disperses light from a large area can help to reduce glare. An interior designer must also reduce brightness ratios from daylight by specifying window treatments that either prevent direct sunlight from entering the room or soften the light penetration. Exterior devices, such as awnings or roof overhangs, can also

(a)

(a)

**FIGURE 2.12A** A luminaire with a baffle painted black and a white flange. (Courtesy Philips Lightolier.)

**FIGURE 2.12B** A luminaire with a parabolic aluminum louver with a semi-specular finish. (© Peerless Lighting.)

be used to reduce glare from sunlight (Devices to control sunlight are reviewed in Chapter 3.).

## REFLECTANCE, OPTICAL CONTROL, AND TRANSMISSION

An object's appearance, the architectural features of an interior, the quantity of illumination, and the ability to perform a task are all affected by reflectance, optical control, and transmission. Reflectance is another factor that is affected by the direction of a light source and demonstrates the interaction between lighting and surface qualities of objects and materials. Determining the reflectance of a surface or object involves examining the **angles of incidence** and reflection (Figure 2.13a). Changing the angle of the light source affects the angle of reflection (Figure 2.13b).

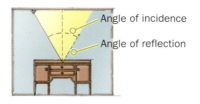

FIGURE 2.13A Angle of incidence of light coming from a light source, striking a surface, and reflecting to the interior.

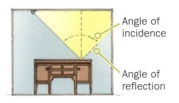

FIGURE 2.13B Changing the direction of the light source alters the angle of incident.

The type of lamp and shielding device on a luminaire also affects the angle of incidence. For example, a lamp with a clear glass covering allows light to travel in a straight direction. Frosted or milky materials alter the angle of direction; light emitted from a frosted incandescent lamp will be diffused. Luminaires may be designed with shielding devices that direct incident light in one or multiple directions. Some luminaires, such as a pendant globe with a white painted finish, will emit a multidirectional angle of incidence. **Interreflection** occurs when light is contained within a structure and is continuously reflected from its surfaces (Figure 2.14).

Reflectance is affected by the color and texture of an object or surface. Depending upon the characteristics of a material, when light strikes a surface, it is reflected or absorbed.

A specular object is one that reflects light. **Specular reflectance** results when all the falling light is reflected (Figure 2.15a). This occurs when light strikes a glossy surface. Reflection from a shiny material or bright color can cause discomfort or disability glare. When most of the light is reflected, **semi-specular reflectance** occurs (Figure 2.15b). This can occur when light strikes a surface that has some specular or reflecting qualities but is irregular, such as etched glass or a hammered finish. **Diffused reflectance** (Figure 2.15c) arises when the light is scattered at a variety of angles, such as when light strikes a matte finish.

Materials can also be rated according to their reflecting ability. Smooth and shiny materials will reflect more light than rough and heavily textured materials. Reflectance values of various materials are provided in Table 2.2. To

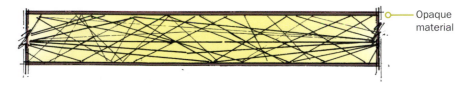

FIGURE 2.14 Interreflection occurs when light reflects back and forth within an enclosed area.

FIGURE 2.15A Light coming from a light source, striking a glossy surface, and reflecting to the interior.

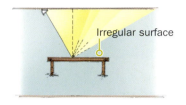

FIGURE 2.15B Light coming from a light source, striking an irregular surface, and reflecting to the interior.

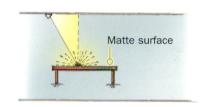

FIGURE 2.15C Light coming from a light source, striking a matte surface, and reflecting to the interior.

compensate for luminous reflectance values in an interior with light colors and smooth surfaces, the illumination level may need to be reduced. In contrast, in an environment that has dark colors and rough materials, the illumination level might have to be increased. However, before increasing or decreasing the illumination level, an interior designer must examine other environmental factors that affect reflectance values in a space, including the size of the room, the location of a surface, and light sources.

Because light reflects off surfaces and between surfaces—known as interreflection—reflectance levels are affected by the size of a room. The walls are close together in a small room, so the light reflected from the walls strikes other walls and increases the reflectance level of the color. In a large room with high ceilings, the surfaces may be too far apart to cause interreflection, thus resulting in a lower reflectance level. Remember, even light-colored walls absorb some light.

The location of a surface also affects reflectance levels. For instance, ceilings and walls cause interreflection because of their location, while floors reflect less light. Light sources that are close to a light-colored surface and have a high-illumination level will elicit the greatest amount of reflection.

Recommended reflectance levels for surfaces are summarized in Table 2.3. This table can serve as an important guideline when energy conservation is a design criterion.

Some lamps and luminaries are designed to control illumination. Reflector lamps, such as R, PAR, and MR lamps, have an optical system designed within the lamp to control light. As described in Chapter 6, shielding devices, reflection, refraction, and diffusion are all elements of luminaires that are designed to control illumination. Shielding devices for luminaires include baffles, louvers, and fascias. Because light cannot penetrate the shielding units within the luminaire, additional illumination is produced by reflection. Luminaires designed to control light through reflection have materials such as shiny aluminum on the inside surfaces. These materials are known as specular because

**TABLE 2.2 Reflecting Materials**

| MATERIAL | REFLECTANCE[a, b] (PERCENT) | CHARACTERISTICS |
|---|---|---|
| *Specular* | | |
| Mirrored and optical coated glass | 80–99 | Provide directional control of light and brightness at specific viewing angles. Effective as efficient reflectors and for special decorative lighting effects. |
| Metallized and optical coated plastic | 75–97 | |
| Processed anodized and optical coated aluminum | 75–95 | |
| Polished aluminum | 60–70 | |
| Chromium | 60–65 | |
| Stainless steel | 55–65 | |
| Black structural glass | 5 | |
| *Spread* | | |
| Processed aluminum (diffuse) | 70–80 | General diffuse reflection with a high specular surface reflection of from 5 to 10 percent of light. |
| Etched aluminum | 70–85 | |
| Satin chromium | 50–55 | |
| Brushed aluminum | 55–58 | |
| Aluminum paint | 60–70 | |
| *Diffuse* | | |
| White plaster | 90–92 | Diffuse reflection results in uniform surface brightness at all viewing angles. Materials of this type are good reflecting backgrounds for coves and luminous forms. |
| White paint | 75–90 | |
| Porcelain enamel | 65–90 | |
| White terra cotta | 65–80 | |
| White structural glass | 75–80 | |
| Limestone | 35–65 | |

**a |** Inasmuch as the amount of light transmitted depends upon the thickness of the material and the angle of incidence of light, the figures given are based on thickness generally used in lighting applications and on near-normal angles of incidence.

**b |** These provide compound diffuse-specular reflection unless matte finished.

Source: Reprinted from the *IESNA Lighting Handbook* (9th ed.), pp. 1–22, with permission from the Illuminating Engineering Society of North America.

**TABLE 2.3** Recommended Reflectance for Interior Surfaces of Residences

| SURFACE | REFLECTANCE (PERCENT) | APPROXIMATE MUNSELL VALUE |
|---|---|---|
| Ceiling | 60–99 | 8 and above |
| Curtain and drapery treatment on large wall areas | 35–60 | 6.5–8 |
| Walls | 35–60* | 6.5–8 |
| Floors | 15–35* | 4.0–6.5 |

*In areas where lighting for specific visual tasks takes precedence over lighting for the environment, the minimum reflectance should be 40 percent for walls, 25 percent for floors.

Source: Reprinted from the *IESNA Lighting Handbook* (9th ed.), pp. 18–22, with permission from the Illuminating Engineering Society of North America.

they reflect light. Light is emitted from the lamp and is reflected off the material to a surface or object (Figure 2.16).

A luminaire with an interior surface made from a specular material can reflect a high percentage of the lamp's illumination. However, these luminaires can also cause glare. Luminaires made from a specular material but having a brushed or etched finish, on the other hand, will diffuse some of the incident light rays, while matte finishes and dark colors will diffuse more. Some luminaires are designed with **reflector contours** to maximize the amount of illumination emitted from a lamp by increasing reflection into a space. Common shapes for these luminaires include ellipses, parabolas, and circles.

Some luminaires are made of materials designed to let light through rather than control it. **Transmission** is the term used to describe the passage of light through a material. The three types of transmission are direct, diffused, and mixed (Figures 2.17 a–c). Direct transmission occurs when the majority of the light passes through the material (Figure 2.17a). Clear glass is an example of a material that allows direct transmission. Material that creates diffused transmission, such as plastic, causes the light to be scattered in many directions (Figure 2.17b). Mixed transmission occurs with materials that allow most of the light to pass through in a semi-scattered manner (Figure 2.17c). Etched and sandblasted glass are examples of such materials. Keep in mind that white plastics can be a source of glare. (For more information on the design of luminaires, see Chapter 6.)

Color and the directional effects of lighting explored in this chapter are important elements in a lighting system. In specifying a lighting plan, an interior designer must consider how color and the intensity and direction of a light source affect an object's appearance, the architectural features of a

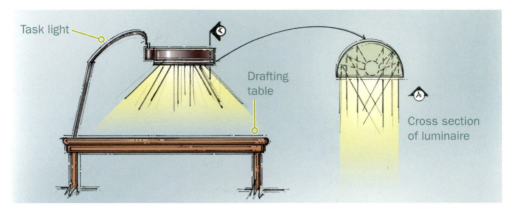

FIGURE 2.16 Light strikes the interior of a luminaire and then reflects into an interior space.

space, the ability of people in the space to perform a task, and quantity of illumination. The next chapter covers how to determine the quantity of illumination required in a quality lighting environment.

## Color, Directional Effects, and LEED Certification

For a checklist of how you can apply color and directional effects of lighting in creating a LEED-certified building, see Box 2.1.

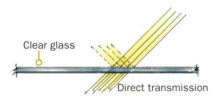

FIGURE 2.17A Direct transmission occurs when most of the light passes through clear glass in a straight direction.

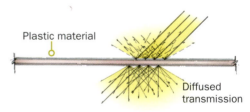

FIGURE 2.17B Diffused transmission occurs when some of the light passes through a plastic material in a scattered direction.

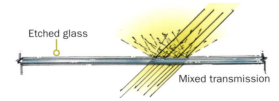

FIGURE 2.17C Mixed transmission occurs when most of the light passes through an etched glass in semi-scattered direction.

**BOX 2.1** Color, Directional Effects of Lighting, and LEED Certification

You can put the content of this chapter to work for you to create LEED-certified buildings by considering the following strategies:

○ Control and redirect interior light sources to reduce light pollution.

○ Compare the energy efficiency of lamps with different color temperatures and CRI ratings. Specify lamps that have the optimum combination of energy efficiency, and the appropriate color temperature and CRI rating for a specific application.

○ Minimize and optimize energy performance by selecting lamps and luminaires that direct the light where it is needed without spill to other areas or to the outdoors.

○ Minimize and optimize energy performance by controlling for daylight.

○ Minimize and optimize energy performance by selecting materials that optimize the transmission (direct, diffused, mixed transmission) of electrical light and daylight for an intended purpose.

○ Minimize and optimize energy performance by optimizing reflectance of materials and colors.

○ Minimize and optimize energy performance by maximizing the perceived brightness of a space by daylighting and the selection of interior colors, finishes, texture, and type of fixture.

○ Optimize energy performance of lighting controls by controlling for daylight and selecting lamps and luminaires that direct the light where it is needed without spill to other areas or to the outdoors.

○ Optimize users' ability to eliminate glare and direct light by specifying individual controls.

○ In the fundamental/enhanced commissioning of the building energy systems, monitor the directional effects of lighting, reflectance, and optical control.

○ Measure and verify the directional effects of lighting, reflectance, and optical control over time.

LEED CREDIT CATEGORIES RELATED TO CONTENT IN CHAPTER 2

SS (Sustainable Sites) Credit 1, Option 2, Path 6: Light Pollution Reduction

EA (Energy and Atmosphere) Prerequisite 1: Fundamental Commissioning of Building Energy Systems

EA Prerequisite 2: Minimum Energy Performance

EA Credit 1.1: Optimize Energy Performance—Lighting Power

EA Credit 1.2: Optimize Energy Performance—Lighting Controls

EA Credit 2: Enhanced Commissioning

EA Credit 3: Measurement and Verification

IEQ Credit 6.1: Controllability of Systems—Lighting

ID (Innovation in Design) Credit 1: Innovation in Design

Source: USGBC (2009). *LEED reference guide for green interior design and construction*. Washington, D.C.: U.S. Green Building Council.

# Fundamental Projects

**1. Research Design Project**

Draw a CRI and chromaticity graph similar to General Electric's chart illustrated in Figure 2.5. Using the data in Table 2.1, identify and locate on the graph three lamps, each with chromaticity ratings in the ranges of 3000K, 4000K, and 5000K.

**2. Research Design Project**

Select eight different materials having a variety of textures. Utilizing a clamp light, direct the light source at each material and record the resultant reflection properties. Position the light source at a variety of angles and distances from the material. Record all results and write a report that provides a summary and recommendations for future practice.

**3. Research Design Project**

Using the Internet, locate luminaires that are designed with each of the following control devices: (a) reflection, (b) diffusion, and (c) shielding unit. Print the pictures of the luminaires and then mount them in a notebook. Identify the advantages and disadvantages of each.

# Application Projects

**1. Human Factors Research Project**

In groups of three to four individuals, select four fabrics with warm and cool colors in a variety of textures, and four wall coverings with warm and cool colors. Take the material samples to a variety of commercial settings, including a grocery store, retail stores, a residence, and a library. Examine the fabrics and wall coverings under the various light sources. For each of the settings, record the type of light source and each group member's subjective reactions to the appearance of the colors.

**2. Human Factors Research Project**

Identify five different commercial spaces and ask at least ten people in each space whether they perceive any of the light sources as bright. Be sure to ask people of various ages. Record their responses, the type of luminaire, lamp, illumination level (high, medium, low), and the location of the light sources. Analyze the data and write a report that summarizes the results and provides recommendations for future illumination applications.

# Summary

o The wavelengths of daylight vary according to the time of day, sky conditions, time of year, and geographic location.

o Chromaticity ratings and the color-rendering index are two types of data about lamp color.

o Chromaticity, or the color temperature of a light source, helps to create the atmosphere of a space and often reflects the quality of the interior. The color temperature indicates the degree of red or blue in the light emitted by a light source. Chromaticity of a light source is measured in kelvins (K) and is part of the information provided by lamp manufacturers.

o The warmer the apparent color of a light source, the lower the number on the kelvin scale. For example, the warm color of light emitted from a candle is 2000K, whereas the color appearance of cool daylight is 5000K.

o The color rendering index (CRI) measures how faithfully a light source reveals the color of objects. The index ranges from 0 to 100. The higher the CRI number, the better the color rendering ability of the lamp.

o The ability to perform a task or view an object is affected by a variety of factors, including glare, contrast, colors, illumination levels, and the physical condition of the eyes.

o The direction of a light source can affect the quantity of light required in a space.

o To ensure a quality lighting environment, an interior designer must develop a plan that maximizes the positive attributes of brightness and controls glare.

o Brightness is generally a subjective reaction to an environment and is dependent upon individuals' expectations, their comparative contexts, and the physical condition of their eyes.

o A variety of factors affect glare, including individual perceptions, condition of the eyes, and extreme contrast in illumination levels.

o Reflectance is an example of the interaction between lighting and the surface qualities of objects and materials.

o Controlling the directional qualities of light sources is a key element in creating the desired atmosphere in an environment and in ensuring effective accent lighting.

## KEY TERMS

angle of incidence
baffle
brightness
chromaticity
color-rendering
   index (CRI)
color temperature

correlated color
   temperature (CCT)
diffused reflectance
direct glare
disability glare
discomfort glare
foot-candle (fc)

glare
illuminance
indirect glare
initial lumens
interreflection
louver
lux (lx)

mean lumens
reflectance
reflector contour
semi-specular reflectance
shade
specular reflectance
transmission

# Resources

Benya, J., Heschong, L., McGowan, T., Miller, N., & Rubinstein, F. (2001). *Advanced lighting guidelines*. White Salmon, WA: New Buildings Institute.

Bierman, A., and Conway, K. (2000). Characterizing daylight photosensor systems performance to help overcome market barriers. *Journal of the Illuminating Engineering Society, 29*(1), 101–115.

Boyce, P. N., Eklund, N., & Simpson, S. (2000). Individual lighting control: Task performance, mood and illuminance. *Journal of the Illuminating Engineering Society, 29*(1), 131–142.

Gordon, G. (2003). *Interior lighting for designers* (4th ed.). New York: John Wiley & Sons.

Illuminating Engineering Society of North America (IESNA) (2011). *IESNA lighting handbook* (10th ed.). New York: Illuminating Engineering Society of North America.

Jennings, J. F., Rubinstein, R., & DiBartolomeo, D. R. (2000). Comparisons of control options in private offices in an advanced lighting controls test bed. *Journal of the Illuminating Engineering Society, 29*(2), 39–60.

Maniccia, D., Von Neida, B., & Tweed, A. (2000). Analysis of the energy and cost savings potential of occupancy sensors for commercial lighting systems. Proceedings of the 2000 Annual Conference of the Illuminating Engineering Society of North America.

Mistrick, R., Chen, C., Bierman, B., & Felts, D. (2000). A comparison of photosensor-controlled electronic dimming systems. *Proceedings of the 2000 Annual Conference of the Illuminating Engineering Society, 29*(1), 66–80.

Narendran, A. N., Bullough, J .D., Maliyagoda, N., & Bierman, A. (July/August, 2000). What is useful life for white light LEDs? Proceedings of the 2000 Annual Conference of the Illuminating Engineering Society of North America. Washington, D.C.

Navvab, M. (2000). A comparison of visual performance under high and low color temperature fluorescent lamps. Proceedings of the 2000 Annual Conference of the Illuminating Engineering Society of North America. Washington, D.C.

Phillips, D. (2000). *Lighting modern buildings*. Oxford: Architectural Press.

Steffy, G. R. (2002). *Architectural lighting design* (2nd ed.). New York: Van Nostrand Reinhold.

Veitch, J., & Newsham, G. (2000). Exercised control, lighting choices, and energy use: An office simulation experiment. *Journal of Environmental Psychology, 20*(3), 219–237.

# 3 Natural and Artificial Light Sources

Creating a quality lighting environment requires a comprehensive plan based on both natural and artificial light. Integrating and controlling daylight involves an understanding of solar geometry, the distribution of daylight into spaces, glazing technologies, and energy considerations. **Solar geometry** is the movement of the earth around the sun.

This chapter covers characteristics of electrical sources that are utilized in interiors, including incandescent-filament, halogen (tungsten-halogen), fluorescent, high-intensity discharge (HID), fiber optics, and solid-state lighting (SSL). Electrical sources are used to complement daylight and to provide general, task, and accent lighting in an environment.

An electrical lighting system is composed of the electrical power, light source, luminaire, controls, maintenance, and service. All these elements affect the quantity and quality of illumination in an interior. In reviewing electrical sources, it is critical to study all the elements of quality lighting systems.

## OBJECTIVES

- Identify the advantages and disadvantages of using daylight as a lighting source

- Describe the factors and conditions that affect the quantity and quality of daylight in an interior

- Identify the primary functional components of incandescent-filament, halogen, fluorescent, and high-intensity discharge lamps

- Compare and contrast the advantages and disadvantages of incandescent-filament, halogen, fluorescent, and high-intensity discharge lamps

- Identify the primary functional components and operating principles of fiber optics and **solid-state lighting (SSL)**

- Determine applications for fiber optics and light-emitting diodes (LEDs)

# Daylighting Design

Daylight is not only essential to life but is critical to sustainable designs, and the psychological and biological well-being of people. To protect people's rights to access to the sun many countries and cities have enacted solar zoning legislation. In the United States, the Zoning Resolution of 1916 in New York City initiated laws that were created to provide access to the sun by establishing height and setback requirements for buildings. Many other cities with tall buildings followed New York City's zoning policies. Subsequently, in response to new building materials, technologies, urban plans, and population growths, cities have been amending solar zoning legislation.

From an architectural perspective, daylight enters an interior through **apertures** that include windows and skylights. Everyone appreciates windows in most interior spaces. Offices that have windows, especially on more than one side, are usually associated with status. Daylight is generally perceived as constant and is considered the standard for determining "true" colors. To determine an object's color accurately, people will often take the item outdoors or examine it near a window. Restaurants with a beautiful view of a city skyline, water, or golf course have prime seating close to these windows. Unfortunately, with the invention of electrical light sources and air conditioning, many contemporary buildings do not effectively integrate daylight into spaces. Many buildings have spaces with no windows or skylights.

The integration of daylight into interiors, or **daylighting**, is vital to creating quality and sustainable environments. This practice includes **daylight harvesting,** that is, capturing daylight for the purpose of illuminating interiors and saving energy. Daylight can be gathered by light coming through the roof (**toplighting**) or the walls (**sidelighting**) of a building. To maximize the harvesting of daylight, there are several elements to consider as well as the most appropriate strategies for controlling the negative effects of **sunlight** (Figures 3.1 and 3.2). Daylighting strategies for sustainable designs are discussed in Chapter 4.

Distinguishing between sunlight and daylight is important to a quality lighting environment. Sunlight is considered light that enters a space directly from the sun. This type of light is generally not good lighting for an interior. Direct sunlight can produce glare and excessive heat, and it can cause materials to fade. **Daylight,**

**FIGURE 3.1** One approach to controlling the negative effects of sunlight is shades in the shape of sails. Designed for the Peabody Essex Maritime Museum in response to sunlight, these shades automatically open and close. (Copyright 2007 Peabody Essex Museum. Photographer Walter Silver.)

**FIGURE 3.2** Automatically controlled light-blocking window shades help keep cool the LEED-certified headquarters of Novus International, located in St. Louis. (© James Leynse/Corbis.)

or skylight, is the term that describes the desirable natural light in a space. Daylight results in a perceived even distribution of light that avoids the glare and ill effects of direct sunlight (Figure 3.3). A designer should always focus on ways to integrate daylight into an interior while avoiding the glare of sunlight.

## ADVANTAGES AND DISADVANTAGES OF NATURAL LIGHT

There are advantages and disadvantages to using natural light as part of a quality lighting plan. Advantages of integrating daylight into interiors include energy savings resulting from a reduction in electrical lights and from passive solar energy penetration in the winter. Another advantage to daylight is the even distribution of light that appears to reveal the "true" colors of

**FIGURE 3.3** The arched ceilings painted white help to maximize daylight in Boston's Old North Church. (John Brandon Miller.)

objects and surfaces. Daylight also enhances visual acuity by providing better light for reading and writing. Advantages of integrating daylight into interiors also include benefits associated with windows, such as providing a view and ventilation.

In addition, daylight has positive psychological and physiological effects on people: It reduces stress, satisfies circadian rhythms, and encourages positive attitudes. A **circadian rhythm** is the biological function that coordinates sleeping and waking times through hormones and metabolic processes. Research done in hospitals, offices, schools, and retail stores indicates that daylight has positive effects on human performance (Heschong, 2003; Heschong, 2001; Heschong, 1999; Littlefair, 1996). Littlefair reported on the positive effects of using **light shelves** to maximize daylight in the patient rooms of hospitals. Light shelves are horizontal units placed high on an interior or exterior wall for the purpose of reflecting daylight into a space.

In 2003, research results indicated that compared to office workers without a view, individuals with a view performed better on tests involving mental functions and memory recall (Heschong). Moreover, individuals in an office with views reported good health conditions. The Heschong Group (1999) found that students in classrooms with significant daylight had 7 to 18 percent higher scores than students working in classrooms with little or no daylight. It also found that retail stores with skylights reported 40 percent higher sales. (Human factors related to lighting are examined in detail in Chapter 5.)

## Disadvantages of Natural Light

Disadvantages of natural light are often a result of direct sunlight penetrating a space. Research has demonstrated that glare from sunlight has a negative effect on the performance of individuals in classrooms and offices. In addition, the ultraviolet rays of the sun can fade fabrics and artwork. The fabric's fiber and weave determine how easily the material will be damaged. Natural fibers such as silk, cotton, or linen are more susceptible to damage than acrylics or polyesters, and tight weaves, shiny fabrics, and thick fibers are more resistant to damage from the sun. Infrared rays of the sun also cause some woods to crack and peel. If direct sunlight cannot be avoided, a designer can specify a fabric that deteriorates less readily than others. Other solutions to controlling direct

**FIGURE 3.4** Electronically tinted glass is used to help control glare and heat from the sun. (Courtesy Sage Electronics/Maritime & Co.)

sunlight are illustrated in Figure 3.4 and are discussed in Chapter 4.

Disadvantages associated with windows include glare, noise penetration, the problem of cleaning and maintenance, lack of privacy, and heat gain in the summer. In addition, the beautiful views enjoyed during the day can become "black holes" at night. Windows at night resemble mirrors by reflecting distracting images into the room. This problem can be resolved with appropriate window treatments and measures to reduce contrast, for example, by adding exterior lighting to the landscaping.

The key to resolving problems associated with sunlight is first awareness that these negative consequences exist, and then planning solutions that address the concerns. Many solutions include installing appropriate devices that help to control sunlight and layering light so that daylight penetration is integrated with electrical systems. (Detailed information on daylighting and controls is discussed in Chapter 7.)

## SOLAR GEOMETRY AND THE VARIABILITY OF SUNLIGHT

Designing buildings that maximize penetration of daylight requires a great deal of analysis and planning, beginning with an understanding of solar geometry and the variability of sunlight. Solar geometry examines the movement of the earth around the sun. Sunlight changes daily, hourly, by the season, with the weather, and with geographical location (Figure 3.5). Colors, shadows, forms, and shapes vary during the day according to the sun's position. The oblique shafts of light produced by midmorning and late afternoon sun create long and soft shadows. The

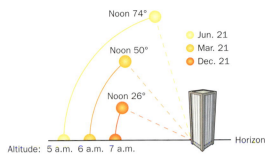

**FIGURE 3.5** Sunlight changes daily, hourly, by the season, with the weather, and with geographical location.

harsh shadows produced by sunlight at noon, on the other hand, emphasize the three dimensions of objects; this **modeling** is best achieved with sidelighting rather than toplighting.

As illustrated in Figure 3.5, the path of the sun is dramatically different in summer and winter. In the northern hemisphere during the summer, the sun rises in the northeast and sets in the northwest. In contrast, the path of the winter sun is lower; it rises in the southeast and sets in the southwest. On October 21 and March 21, the sun's path is identical. The directional qualities of the sun are determined by the earth's latitude; a more northerly sunrise and sunset will occur in higher latitudes. To determine the sun's path in a specific location, one can contact the American Society of Heating, Refrigerating, and Air-Conditioning Engineers (ASHRAE).

To maximize quality daylight, a designer utilizes this solar geometry to specify the size, shape, and location of windows. Ideally, window and shielding units should be positioned to allow the maximum amount of sunlight into a space during the winter and the minimum amount

(a)

(b)

(c)

**FIGURE 3.6A** Sun shield louvers help to reduce the glare and heat from daylight. (Bill Timmerman.)

**FIGURE 3.6B** External sun louvers help to reduce the glare and heat from daylight. (© Aardvark/Alamy.)

**FIGURE 3.6C** External sun louvers help to reduce the glare and heat from daylight in the Agbar Tower, Barcelona, Spain. (© Richard Bryant/Arcaid/Corbis.)

**FIGURE 3.6D** Louvers positioned in a horizontal plane help to reduce the glare and heat from daylight. (Hunter Douglas.)

(d)

during the hot summer. Shielding devices can include roof overhangs, shades, louvers, and deciduous trees (Figures 3.6 a–d). A very sophisticated shielding device was designed for the Arab World Institute in Paris. The south side of the building is a glass wall covered with photo-electrical control units (Figure 3.7). The metallic structure of the control units is aesthetically pleasing, and the photosensing mechanism allows the lenses to change according to the daylight levels. Functioning like a camera lens, on a cloudy day the aperture opens very wide to allow the maximum amount of daylight into the building. On a sunny day the lenses close to prevent a great deal of heat and sunlight penetration. This design helps to reduce energy costs, while the variability of daylight creates an ever-changing artistic composition on the south wall of the Institute.

In addition to the geometry of the solar system, there are several other factors that influence the level and quality of daylight entering a space. These include clouds, weather, atmospheric pollution, orientation, landscaping, and surrounding structures. The amount and type of cloud affects the characteristics of daylight. Atmospheric pollution tends to create a hazy lighting condition, especially at sunset. Overcast days generally provide a uniform level of intensity that lacks the dynamic qualities of bright sunlight. Cloudy days reduce contrast and shadows.

The U.S. Weather Bureau provides the number of overcast days per year by geographical location. A designer needs this information in planning the integration of daylight with electrical systems. For example, if a building is located in an area that experiences a high number of overcast days, it may be necessary to have extra large windows and an adequate number of electrical sources in order to have enough illumination.

**FIGURE 3.7** The south side of the Arab World Institute in Paris is a glass wall covered with photo-electrical control units. The photosensing mechanism allows the lenses to change according to the daylight levels. (© Oliver Knight / Alamy.)

## Characteristics of Electrical Light Sources

An understanding of electrical light sources begins with an examination of the general characteristics of lamps. Lamps are commonly referred to as lightbulbs; they are the term for any source that produces optical radiation (Figure 3.8). Having a working knowledge of electrical light sources requires a review of a lamp's light output, efficacy, **lamp life**, color, maintenance factors, and cost.

As introduced in Chapter 2, the light level or illuminance that falls on a surface can be measured in foot-candles or lux. Figure 3.9 illustrates foot-candle measurements on a wall

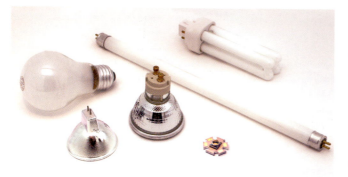

FIGURE 3.8 Examples of common lamps. (Courtesy Pure Lighting.)

that were created by a fixture recessed in the ceiling. It is appropriate for designers to review the guidelines established by the Illuminating Engineering Society of North America (IESNA) regarding the amount of light necessary to perform a specific task adequately.

The **candlepower** of a light source, measured in **candelas** (**cd**), is its intensity in a specific direction (Figure 3.10). The **watt** (**W**) is a unit measuring an electrical circuit's ability to do work, such as producing light and heat, in terms of the amount of electricity drawn.

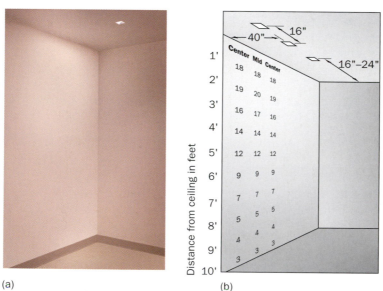

(a)                                                    (b)

FIGURE 3.9 The (a) photograph illustrates foot-candle measurements on a wall from fixtures recessed in the ceiling. The (b) graph depicts foot-candles on the wall and the location of the fixtures. While examining the photograph and the drawing to help visualize foot-candle measurements, compare the numbers on the drawing with their location on the wall. (Photograph courtesy Pure Lighting.)

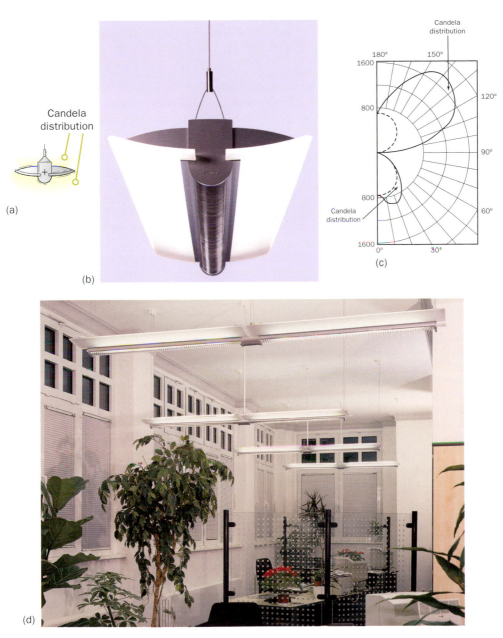

Candela
distribution

(a)

(b)

Candela
distribution

180°        150°
1600

800                        120°

800                        90°

800

Candela
distribution                60°

1600
0°        30°
(c)

(d)

**FIGURE 3.10** This (a) drawing shows how light is distributed from the (b) photographed fixture. The (c) chart graphically illustrates the candela distribution of the right side of the fixture. Examine the effects of the candela distribution in the (d) photograph of a room. (Courtesy of Selux.)

Therefore, a 20-watt lamp consumes 20 watts of electricity.

The **lumens per watt** (**lpW**) is a measure of the **light output** for each watt of electricity consumed and is used to determine energy efficiency. The resulting rating is known as the lamp's **efficacy**. The more lumens produced by a lamp per watt, the more efficient the lamp is and the more energy is saved. Typical lamp efficacies are provided in Table 3.1. Lamp life is a calculation derived from a record of how long it takes for approximately 50 percent of 100 lamps to burn out.

As discussed in Chapter 2, chromaticity and the color-rendering index are used to specify lamps and color. The chromaticity or the color temperature of a light source indicates the degree of red or blue in the light produced and is measured in kelvins (K). The color-rendering index (CRI) measures how faithfully a light source reveals the colors of objects. The index range is from 0 to 100. The higher the CRI number, the better the color-rendering ability of the lamp.

Maintenance factors include cleaning lamps, and replacement considerations based upon lamp life and reduced light output. Costs include the initial cost of the lamp, installation, energy requirements, cleaning, and replacement considerations. The location of a lamp and the high cost of labor are factors to be considered when planning the cleaning and replacement of lamps.

A lamp's size, wattage, shape, lpW, luminous intensity, life, color temperature, and CRI are provided in a lamp manufacturer's catalog. Figure 3.11 is a lamp manufacturer's chart for a halogen lamp. A designer should always refer to such charts when selecting and specifying lamps; the most current information will be found on the manufacturer's website. Figure 3.11 also explains how a designer uses the information in a specific application.

## INCANDESCENT AND HALOGEN LAMPS

The **incandescent carbon-filament lamp** is the oldest electrical light source and provides the greatest amount of flexibility for designers. However, recent legislation in countries throughout the world has mandated a phased elimination of many commonly used incandescent lamps as well as other lamps that do not meet specific energy efficient criteria. (Chapter 4 discusses energy policies and legislation.) Because of the simultaneous work conducted by Edison in the United States and Swan in England, 1879 is the year credited with the start of the lamp. Figure 3.12 illustrates a drawing of the basic components of an

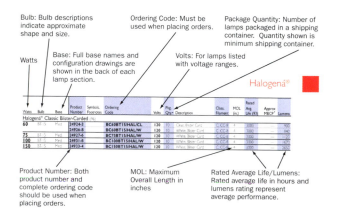

**FIGURE 3.11** A lamp manufacturer's chart for halogen lamps.

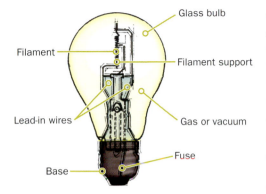

Glass bulb

Filament

Filament support

Lead-in wires

Gas or vacuum

Base

Fuse

FIGURE 3.12 The basic components of an incandescent lamp.

incandescent lamp. An electrical current heats the tungsten filament until incandescence is reached, at which point an incandescent lamp is said to be lit (Benya, Heschong, McGowan, Miller, and Rubinstein, 2001; Coaton and Marsden, 1997; IESNA, 2000). **Tungsten** is usually the conductive material used for this purpose because it has a high melting point and a low evaporation point.

Heating the tungsten filament oxidizes it, causing fragments of tungsten to be deposited on the glass of the bulb. Eventually the tungsten accumulation will cause the bulb to burn out. Inert gases have been added to bulbs to reduce the oxidization of the tungsten filament. A standard incandescent lamp has argon with some nitrogen to prevent arcing. Adding krypton is expensive, but it increases the lumens per watt rating and extends the life of an incandescent lamp.

Use of a halogen, either iodine or bromine gas, improves the performance of an incandescent lamp by redistributing the

oxidizing tungsten on the filament rather than allowing it to accumulate on the glass (Benya, Heschong, McGowan, Miller, and Rubinstein, 2001; Coaton and Marsden, 1997; IESNA, 2000). These **tungsten-halogen lamps** are available in line (120 volts, typical household current) and low (generally 12 volts) voltage. Low-voltage lamps can produce more light output per watt.

The efficacy of the incandescent lamp is affected by the amount of heat produced by the lamp. Generally only 10 percent of the energy consumed to illuminate an incandescent lamp produces light, whereas 90 percent of the energy consumed produces heat. This can be observed by someone feeling the heat produced by an incandescent lamp after it has been on for a period of time. Heat generated by the lamp not only affects the lamp's efficacy and life, but can damage artwork, fabrics, and other precious materials. In commercial environments the heat can seriously affect the load on air-conditioning systems. Dimming will reduce the amount of light and heat generated by the lamp.

Incandescent lamps are available in a variety of sizes, wattages, shapes, and colors (Tables 3.1 and 3.2). Sizes of incandescent lamps range from very small holiday lights to extremely large exterior search lamps. The variety in sizes corresponds to a wide range of wattages; a small night-light lamp can be just 3 watts, and large theater lamps can be as high as 10,000 watts. Incandescent lamps have been manufactured in a variety of shapes; however, there are standard shapes used throughout the industry. Codes developed by the American National Standards Institute (ANSI) include a letter that designates the shape of

**TABLE 3.1 Typical Characteristics of Electrical Light Sources and Selected Applications**

| | INCANDESCENT | HALOGEN | LINEAR FLUORESCENT (T12/T8/T5) | COMPACT FLUORESCENT CFL | METAL HALIDE (CERAMIC AND QUARTZ) | HIGH-PRESSURE SODIUM | LEDS |
|---|---|---|---|---|---|---|---|
| **Mean efficacy (lm/W)** | 5–22 | 12–36 | 75–100 | 27–80 | Ceramic: 80–95 Quartz: 80–115 | 90–140 | 45–107 |
| **Color temperature (°K)** | 2800 | 3000 | 2700 3000 3500 4100 5000 6500 | 2700 3000 3500 4100 5000 6500 | 2900 3100 4100 5000 | 1900 2100 2200 2700 | 2700 3000 warm white 4000 cool white 6500 daylight Up to 10,000 |
| **CRI** | 100 | 100 | T12: 58–62 T8: 75–98 T5: 80s | 80–85 | Ceramic: 85–95 Quartz: 65–70 | 22 standard 65 85 (rare) | 50–90 |
| **Average rated life (hours)** | 750–2,000 | 2,000–6,000 | 5,000–36,000 | 9,000–20,000 | 10,000–20,000 | 10,000–40,000 | 50,000 (time output degraded to 70% initial output) |
| **Life cycle cost** | High | Moderate—High | Low | Low | Moderate | Low | Moderate-Low |
| **Optics** | Point (good optical control) | Point (good optical control) | Diffuse | Diffuse | Point (good optical control) | Point (good optical control) | Point (good optical control) |
| **Start-to full brightness** | Immediate | Immediate | 0–5 seconds | 0–5 seconds | 3–5 minutes | 3–4 minutes | Immediate |
| **Restrike time** | Immediate | Immediate | Immediate | Immediate | 4–20 minutes | 1 minute | Immediate |
| **Lumen maintenance** | Very Good/ Excellent | Excellent | Excellent | Excellent | Ceramic: Very Good Quartz: Good | Excellent | Good |
| **Mercury content** | No | No | Yes | Yes | No | No | No |

| | INCANDESCENT | HALOGEN | LINEAR FLUORESCENT (T12/T8/T5) | COMPACT FLUORESCENT CFL | METAL HALIDE (CERAMIC AND QUARTZ) | HIGH-PRESSURE SODIUM | LEDS |
|---|---|---|---|---|---|---|---|
| **Suggested applications** | Minimal applications: Historical Accent Specialty Safety Rough service | General/task/ accent/ decorative Residential Hospitality Retail | General/task Offices Classrooms Hospitality Retail Residential Industrial Outdoors (limited) | General/task/ accent/decorative Office Classrooms Hospitality Retail Residential Industrial | General/task/ accent **Ceramic:** High-bay areas Downlights Offices Retail Healthcare **Quartz:** Outdoors High-bay areas Remote-source Retail Gymnasiums | Outdoors Warehouses Industrial Security | General/ task/ accent/decorative Bright color applications, exit signs, linear applications (cove/cornice, slot), mounted lights under cabinets and shelves, portable desk luminaires, recessed downlights, steps, outdoors, underwater, refrigerator cases |
| **Notes** | Phased-out elimination of lamps not meeting efficiency standards. | Advanced halogens possible substitutes for phased-out incandescents. | T5- only in metric High-performance T8 replace T12s. Dimming expensive. | Excellent incandescent replacement (3:1 ratio). Replace 75-W incandescent with 25-W CFL. | Ceramic good for color critical lighting. Produce high levels UV. Sensitive to position. Dimming expensive. Some problematic for occupancy sensors. | Primarily street lighting. | Few standards are available. Research manufacturers' credibility and claims, such as lamp/fixture life; efficacy ratings; and color characteristics. High initial cost. |

the lamp followed by a number that describes the diameter of the lamp in eighths of an inch. For example, in reviewing a lamp manufacturer's catalog, a designer will find an A19 listed in the incandescent lamp section. The A is the code for an "arbitrary" shape, and the lamp is 2⅜-inches (¹⁹⁄₈) wide at its widest point.

To improve the efficacy and directional qualities of the incandescent lamp, engineers developed the reflector (R) lamp, which includes the parabolic aluminized reflector (PAR) and the ellipsoidal reflector (ER). The PAR lamp has a heat-resistant glass that enables the lamp to be used outdoors. The ER lamp has a narrow light beam and is more energy efficient than parabolic reflectors when used in recessed luminaires.

The R lamp replaced the standard incandescent lamp in tracks, recessed downlights, and accent luminaires. However, guidelines developed by the U.S. Energy Policy Act (EPAct) in 1992 imposed limitations on lamp energy consumption. To comply with the standards, some of the incandescent R and PAR (parabolic aluminized reflector) lamps are no longer manufactured. This includes the incandescent R30, R40, and PAR38 lamps. The world's focus on sustainability has prompted even more attention to specifying energy-efficient lamps. Most recently, the Energy Independence and Security Act of 2007 and EPAct 2005 mandate several new phased-in energy-efficiency standards for specific lamps, and some fixtures and ballasts (see Chapter 4).

Lamps with optical control systems are available in a variety of beam spreads ranging from **spot (SP)** to **flood (FL)** (Figure 3.13). Codes for descriptors of incandescent lamps are shown in Table 3.2. Lamps that are designed with a spot beam provide a very focused area of light. The size of the area illuminated is dependent upon the type of spot used. The traditional spot will illuminate a small area. An area will become more focused by using a narrow spot (NSP) or a very narrow spot (VNSP). Flood lamps are designed to illuminate a large area. A traditional flood illuminates the smallest area. Wide flood (WFL), medium wide flood (MWFL), and very wide flood (VWFL) lamps illuminate larger areas.

## HALOGEN LAMPS

As a member of the incandescent family, the halogen lamp has the same positive and negative qualities that other incandescent lamps have; however, the **halogen regenerative cycle** produces a much-improved lamp in which the halogen gas and the compact size of the tube cause tungsten to be reapplied to the filament. This halogen regenerative cycle significantly reduces the amount of black sediment that accumulates on the inside of the glass. As a result, halogen lamps have a longer life than other incandescent lamps, and are 20 to 30 percent more efficient. The halogen lamp will emit more luminance using the same amount of electricity. Lumen maintenance is also improved because of the reduction or elimination of the bulb blackening. One of the most popular halogen lamps is the MR16 (multifaceted reflector) (Figures 3.14). The MR16 is ideal for accent lighting because of the lamp's compact size (2 inch or 51mm diameter), excellent beam control, and bright white color.

To increase the efficacy of the halogen lamp, the halogen infrared reflecting (HIR™) lamp was developed. With a coating on the glass,

**TABLE 3.2 Selected Codes for Descriptors of Lamps**

| LAMP CODE | DESCRIPTION | SHAPE | LAMP CODE | DESCRIPTION | SHAPE |
|---|---|---|---|---|---|
| A/* | Arbitrary shape | | MR/ | Multifaceted mirror reflector shape | |
| AR/ | Aluminum reflector shape | | /MWFL | Medium-wide flood | *** |
| B/ | Flame (smooth) shape | | P/ | Pear shape | |
| BT/ | Bulge tubular shape | | PAR/ | Parabolic aluminized reflector shape | |
| C/ | Cone shape | | PS/ | Pear; straight-neck shape | |
| CA/ | Candle shape | | R/ | Reflector shape | |
| CMH | Ceramic metal halide | *** | | | |
| ED/ | Elliptical shape | | /SP | Spot | *** |
| | | | S/ | Straight side shape | |
| F/ | Flame (irregular) shape | | T/ | Tubular shape | |
| **/FL | Flood | *** | | | |
| G/ | Globe shape | | | | |
| /H | Halogen | *** | | | |
| /HIR | Halogen infrared reflecting | *** | /VHO | Very-high output | *** |
| /HE | High efficiency | *** | /VWFL | Very-wide flood | *** |
| /HO | High output | *** | /WFL | Wide flood | *** |

*Letters before / represent a lamp shape
**Letters after / represent a descriptor of a lamp
***Characteristic-type lamps; no specific shapes

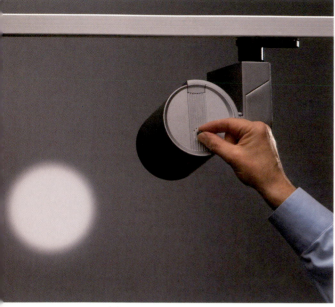
(a)

(b)

**FIGURE 3.13** Lamps with optical control systems are available in a variety of beam spreads ranging from (a) spot (SP) to (b) flood (FL). (Design Bruno Gecchelin. Images by kind permission of iGuzzini illuminazione.)

this lamp converts the infrared rays into visible light, resulting in an improved lpW rating. To improve the lamp's efficiency as well as the quality and quantity of light, manufacturers have developed new reflectors and have added a silver coating to the IR film. Compared to the standard halogen General Electric's HIR(tm) Silv-IR is up to 25 percent more efficient and has up to 50 percent longer life. In comparison to the standard halogen General Electric's HIR™ Plus (PAR38) has up to 36 percent in energy savings and up to 50 percent longer life.

An increase in the size of the filament of the incandescent lamp produced low-voltage lamps. Halogen and HIR(tm) lamps are available for line voltage and low-voltage systems. Line voltage in the United States is between 110 and 220 volts; a low-voltage application is between 6 and 75 volts. For a low-voltage application, a **transformer** is most often used to step down the electrical voltage. For luminaires with multiple fixtures, it is important not to exceed the maximum wattage permitted by a transformer; therefore, luminaires may require more than one transformer to accommodate high wattages. The low-voltage halogen lamp has excellent qualities including precise beam control, good resistance to vibration, high efficacy, high lumen output, and an extremely compact size.

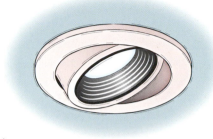

(a)

(b)

**FIGURE 3.14** A halogen MR16 lamp is used in this fixture. Examine the effect of (a) the fixture and lamp in (b) the room. (www.sistemalux.com.)

## FLUORESCENT LAMPS

The **fluorescent lamp** (linear and compact) is one of the discharge lamps. **Electric-discharge lamps** operate on low or high pressure and do not have the filaments that exist in incandescent lamps. Discharge lamps are made of glass, use mercury or sodium vapor, and require a **ballast** to start the lamp and control the electrical current. The majority of

these lamps have electrodes and maintain a fairly consistent color.

Fluorescent lamps are used extensively because they are energy efficient, have a high lumen output, have a long life, radiate less heat than incandescent lamps, have a moderate initial cost and low operating cost, and have a variety of color options. Fluorescent lamps use up to 80 percent less energy and can last thousands of hours longer than incandescent lamps. To conserve energy fluorescents are available in reduced-wattage, high-efficiency (HE), or high-performance versions. The light output levels of fluorescent lamps are standard, high-output (HO), and very high output (VHO). Of the three versions standard light output fluorescents are the most efficient and are the least expensive. Some fluorescent lamps are rated to last more than 40,000 hours.

As shown in Figure 3.15, the fluorescent lamp operates by having an electrical current pass through hot tungsten cathodes at either end of a long tubular shape (Benya, Heschong, McGowan, Miller, and Rubinstein, 2001; Coaton and Marsden, 1997; IESNA, 2000). The glass tube is filled with low-pressure mercury gas and other inert gases including argon, neon, and krypton. The cathodes emit electrons that excite the mercury gas, which produces radiant energy primarily in the form of invisible ultraviolet rays. The phosphorous coating on the inside of the glass tube reradiates the ultraviolet rays into the visible spectrum. As visible light is produced, the phosphor coating fluoresces. Because this glow occurs at a very low temperature, fluorescent lamps require very little electricity.

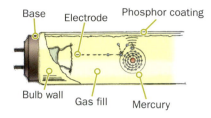

FIGURE 3.15 A florescent lamp operates by having an electrical current pass through hot tungsten cathodes at either end of a long tubular shape.

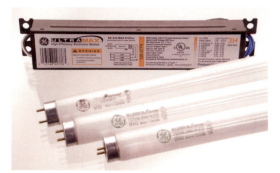

FIGURE 3.16 An example of a ballast and three fluorescent tubes. (Courtesy GE Appliance and Lighting.)

The phosphorous coating determines the color of the light produced. Initially, fluorescent lamps were manufactured with a chemical substance that limited the range of colors. The development of triphosphors made from rare-earth phosphors improved the color properties and efficacy ratings of fluorescent lamps.

Fluorescent lamps can operate only in a system that includes a ballast (Figure 3.16). The ballast starts the lamp and then regulates the flow of electrical current to it. Ballasts are designed for specific lamps (refer to the lamp manufacturer for requirements). The operating life of a ballast is approximately three times that of a fluorescent lamp. Ballasts are available in magnetic and electronic versions. The electronic ballast is preferred because it is more energy-efficient, is quieter, essentially eliminates lamp flicker, and weighs less than the magnetic ballast. EPAct 2005 has mandated efficacy standards for specific lamp-ballast systems. The phased-in requirements for the manufacture and sale of these systems began in 2009.

Fluorescent lamps are available in basically four lamp-ballast circuits, including instant-start, rapid-start, programmed-start (or programmed rapid-start), and universal-input. The instant-start lamp functions without a starter and has a high, open-circuit voltage that slightly reduces the life of the lamp, most notably when the lamp is turned on/off frequently. The rapid-start operates by continuously heating the cathodes and is the most common system used today. It can illuminate lamps at high wattages and has a longer life than the instant-start circuitry. A programmed-start lamp-ballast circuit fundamentally uses the technology of the rapid-start, but the filaments are preheated prior to applying the circuit voltage. This starting circuit is good for spaces where the lamps are frequently turned on/off. The universal-input fluorescent ballast functions in a range of voltages (120–277 volts). High-efficiency electronic ballasts are available, which can provide a 40 percent energy savings.

Fluorescent lamps are available in a variety of sizes, shapes, and wattages, but the most common specified today are the straight tubes—T8 and T5 (Figure 3.17).

One of the newest lamps is the very small T2 (¼ inch or 6mm diameter). These designations are derived from the industry's nomenclature for fluorescent lamps. For example, an F40T8/835 is the nomenclature for a fluorescent (F) lamp of 40 watts (40), with a tubular shape (T) that is 1 inch in diameter (⁸⁄₈), a CRI rating in the 80s (8) and with a chromaticity of 3500K (35). Nomenclature can vary among lamp manufacturers, so a designer must refer to the manufacturer's key to ascertain the nomenclature for that company.

T5 Fluorescent lamps

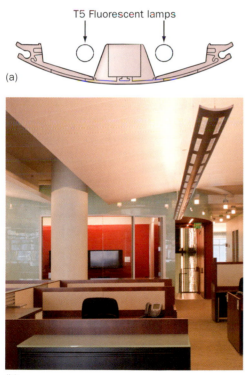

(a)

(b)

**FIGURE 3.17** Example of (a) a fixture with 2 T5 fluorescent lamps and (b) The fixture installed in a conference room. (Photograph: John Sutton Photography.)

The T8 has become very successful because of its high-efficiency, enhanced color, and small one-inch diameter (refer to Table 3.1). The smaller T5 lamp is as efficient as the T8, but the lamp poses retrofit problems. The T5 lamp is available only in metric sizes and its mini-bipin bases can be installed only in luminaires that are specifically designed for the lamp. In addition, when specifying very bright and small lamps pay close attention to their placement and the users of the space. A direct view to the bright light source could be very annoying as well as a potential safety concern.

The primary shapes of fluorescent lamps are the straight tube, U shape, and circle. Bending a straight tube makes the U shape and the circle. To comply with current energy legislation any fluorescent lamp that does not meet minimum performance standards can no longer be produced. (Chapter 4 discusses energy policies and legislation.)

## Compact Fluorescent Lamp (CFL)

As an energy-efficient alternative to the incandescent lamp, the **compact fluorescent lamp (CFL)** is the ideal choice (Figure 3.18). These lamps produce a high lumen output and can yield energy savings of up to 75 percent compared to the incandescent lamp, while lasting approximately ten times longer. One or multiple linear fluorescent tubes are folded to create a CFL. CFLs are available in twin, triple, and quadruple tubes. To maximize the light output while reducing the size of the lamp, manufacturers have developed the spiral-shaped CFL.

The ballast for the CFL lamp is either a separate control gear (pin-base), or is built into the unit (self-ballasted). The self-ballasted CFL (also known as screw-base and screw-in) has a screw base that replicates the base of an incandescent lamp. This lamp is an ideal replacement for fixtures that were originally designed for incandescent lamps, such as recessed downlights, wallwashers, sconces, and portable luminaires. Some CFLs are not designed to be dimmed and should not be used in a luminaire that has a dimming control. In this situation the lamp will not operate properly and there will be a significant reduction in the life of the lamp. In addition, specify a three-way CFL lamp for luminaires with three-way sockets.

## Hybrid Halogen–Compact Fluorescent Lamp

General Electric (GE) recently announced a new hybrid lamp that combines a halogen with a CFL. The halogen capsule illuminates first and then shuts off when the CFL is at full brightness. The lamp resembles a traditional incandescent lamp, but according to GE the 15- and 20-watt versions are equivalent to the 60- and 75-watt incandescent lamps, respectively. In addition to conserving energy, the hybrid lamp has a long life of 8,000 hours and only 1 milligram of mercury.

## HIGH-INTENSITY DISCHARGE LAMPS

Mercury, metal halide, and high-pressure sodium are **high-intensity discharge (HID) lamps** (Figure 3.19). These are electric-discharge lamps with a light-producing arc that is stabilized by the temperature of the bulb (IESNA, 2000). A **mercury (MV) lamp** uses radiation from mercury vapor for illumination and due to its inefficiency is being phased out. A **metal halide (MH) lamp** utilizes chemical compounds of metal halides and sometimes

(a)

FIGURE 3.18 Example of (a) a compact fluorescent lamp (CFL) and (b) the lamp installed in a room. (Photograph of lamp: Courtesy GE Appliance and Lighting. Photograph of room: Arcaid/Mark Bentley.)

(b)

(a)

**FIGURE 3.19** Example of (a) metal halide lamps and (b) the lamp installed in an interior setting. (Photograph of lamp: Courtesy Philips Lighting. Photograph of interior: Arcaid/Mark Bentley.)

(b)

metallic vapors such as mercury. A **high-pressure sodium (HPS) lamp** uses sodium vapor for illumination.

## HID Lamps: How They Work

HID lamps operate in a manner fairly similar to the fluorescent lamp. As with a fluorescent lamp, illumination from HID lamps begins with an arc between two electrodes, operates in a gas-filled cylindrical tube, requires ballasts, and uses radiant energy created by means of gases and metal vapors. Different lamps and wattages cannot be interchanged because HID ballasts are made for specific ones. Electronic ballasts are the best choice for HID lamps because they are more efficient than magnetic ballasts and can best control voltages.

HID lamps have been excellent choices for applications that require high efficacy, long life, high lpW performance, operation in a wide range of ambient temperatures, and positive long-term economics. Metal halide (MH) lamps have high efficacy, good color rendition, long life, good lumen maintenance, and a wide spectrum of colors and wattages. They are available in the shape of the arbitrary incandescent lamp and have warm and cool color renditions. Because of its excellent optical control and ability to be operated in a variety of temperatures, the MH lamp has many indoor and outdoor applications.

The high-pressure sodium (HPS) lamp has an extremely high lpW rating, exceptionally long service, and excellent long-term economics. HPS lamps can last 40,000 hours, but over-wattage can shorten the life of the lamps. Lamp life ratings are based upon ten hours per start.

Disadvantages of HID lamps include the required start-up time, color shifts during the life of the lamp, variations in color between lamps of the same type, strict ballast requirements, and the fact that they are not easily dimmable. Start-up times for some HID lamps are between two and ten minutes. The **restrike** time can be several minutes because the lamp must cool down before starting again. This is especially problematic in applications where safety and security are critical issues. Good restrike time is necessary when there is a power interruption or reduction in voltage in the system. Some instant-restrike HID lamps are available, but only at high wattages, and they must be used with special luminaires and ballasts. In applications that require illumination at all times, a designer should specify an additional luminaire that would illuminate the space during the restrike time, or specify an HID lamp with a built-in auxiliary unit that lights up when the lamp shuts down. Because of the warm-up and restrike characteristics of HID lamps, it is not advisable to use these lamps on units that have motion detectors.

The technology of MH and HPS lamps is continually improving. The compact MH lamp is available in lower wattages, making it an ideal solution for display and track systems. The pulse-start and the Ceramic MH lamps (CMH) are improvements on the standard quartz MH lamp. The CMH lamp has the best performance characteristics, including better color consistency over the life of the lamp. The newest CMH lamps have improved efficacy, lumen maintenance, color rendition, lamp life, and reduced warm-up and restrike times.

## REMOTE SOURCE ILLUMINATION SYSTEMS: FIBER OPTIC LIGHTING

**Fiber optic lighting** can be used for general, task, accent, and decorative applications. Fiber optics utilize a remote source for illumination, from which light is transmitted through a bundle of optical fibers. Fiber optic lighting is used in a variety of applications, including architectural, custom, landscape, and signage.

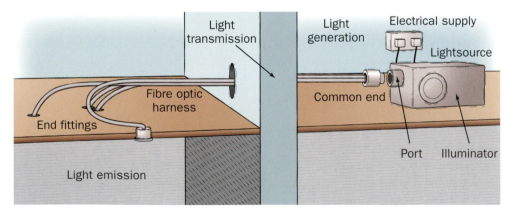

**FIGURE 3.20** A fiber optic lighting system.

The light source used for fiber optics is housed in a box called the **illuminator**, and the directional lamp is usually metal halide or halogen (low voltage) (Figure 3.20). Metal halide lamps are used for applications that require long lamp life, though some systems are starting to use LEDs as the light source. The optical fibers are bundled together at the "port" or opening in the side of the illuminator. They are made from glass or plastic, and hundreds of optical fibers can be used in the system. Glass is the preferred material because it transmits excellent color, transmits light well, lasts long, requires minimum maintenance, and bends easily.

Light produced from fiber optics is a result of internal reflection; in an **end-emitting system**, light is visible at the end of the fibers (Figure 3.21), while in a **side-emitting** system, light is visible along the sides of the entire length of the fibers (Figure 3.22).

End-emitting fiber optic systems produce directional illumination and are made from glass. End fittings are available in a variety of finishes and styles. The most common interior end fittings are fixed or adjustable downlights (Figure 3.21). The fittings are small, approximately 2 inches in diameter; crystal-end are made from glass or plastic and produce an even distribution of illumination over the length of the fibers. The longest optical fibers are made from plastic and can be 100-feet long. A variety of special effects are available that are housed in the illuminator. Wheels can be installed to provide color changes or twinkling. The twinkling wheel provides a touch of animation to the light. Fiber optic systems can also be dimmed.

End fitting: ajustable recessed eyeball

(a)

(b)

**FIGURE 3.21** Details of the (a) painting are highlighted by an (b) end-emitting fiber optic system. (Photograph of fiber optic system: Image of Wallace Collection, © Universal Fiber Optics. Photograph of end fittings: Arcaid/Mark Bentley.)

## Advantages to Using Fiber Optic Lighting

There are many advantages to using fiber optic lighting; these include safety, ease of maintenance, low transmission of heat to objects being illuminated, and very small amounts of the infrared (IR) and ultraviolet (UV) wavelengths. Because the light source in fiber optic systems is located in the illuminator, the fibers only transmit light and do not carry an electrical current. This makes it possible for a designer to place the fibers in wet spaces such as swimming pools, ponds, saunas, spas, steam rooms, showers, and steps while the illuminator is installed at a remote dry location (Figure 3.22).

Fiber optic lighting is easy to maintain because there are few lamps to replace and the illuminator can be mounted in a location that is easily accessible. Fewer lamps also result in energy savings. Because of the intense heat produced by some lamps, fans should be installed in the illuminator. Installing the lamp at a remote site eliminates the detrimental effects of heat and IR and UV rays

on objects being illuminated. Thus, fiber optic lighting is an excellent choice for heat-sensitive products, artwork and other decorative objects, and fragile museum artifacts.

## SOLID-STATE LIGHTING AND INDUCTION LAMPS

In 1907 Henry Joseph Round discovered the phenomenon of electroluminescence. **Electroluminescent lamps** operate through an interaction between an electrical field and a phosphor (Benya, Heschong, McGowan, Miller, and Rubinstein, 2001; Coaton and Marsden, 1997; IESNA, 2000). Electroluminescent lamps include **light-emitting diodes (LEDs)** and lamps used for instrument panels and liquid crystal displays. These lamps are lightweight, have long life, require high-voltage drivers, and use very little electricity. Currently, a tremendous amount of research is being conducted to improve LED

(a)

(b)

FIGURE 3.22 Example of (a) a side-emitting fiber optic system and (b) the fibers installed at the edge of steps. (Photograph of fiber optic system: Side Sparkle Fibre from Universal Fiber Optics. Photograph of steps: Photograph of Melrose Square © Universal Fiber Optics.)

lighting for the built environment. According to the U.S. Department of Energy (2009), "No other lighting technology offers as much potential to save energy and enhance the quality of our building environments, contributing to our nation's energy and climate change solutions."

LEDs are the first **solid-state light (SSL)** source for general lighting, and the technology has improved dramatically since first developed in the early 1960s. An LED is a semiconductor in the form of a chemical chip embedded in a plastic capsule (Figures 3.23). A volt from a direct current energizes the chip, making visible light. The minimal amount of heat that is produced is emitted to the bottom of the unit, which should be a heat-absorbing material, or what is referred to as a **heat sink** (Figure 3.24). A **driver** or transformer is needed to operate the LEDs with a direct current. The light is focused by lenses or scattered by **diffusers**. To produce adequate illumination for an area in a room or surface requires several LEDs in one fixture.

The chemicals contained in the chip determine the color of the light. The first colors were red, green, and amber; the development of blue in the 1990s enabled lamp manufacturers to produce white, significantly improving the application of LEDs for general illumination. One method used to produce the color white is through color mixing by combining red, green, and blue LEDs in one unit. This approach is not very successful because the white produced is altered as the individual LEDs deteriorate. The preferred way to create a white light is to use an LED with phosphors that absorb blue and hence produce a white color. Some individuals may perceive that the white light has a "cool" appearance. However, LEDs have a wide range of color temperatures, but they are not always consistent. To help resolve color inconsistencies manufacturers **bin** or sort LEDs according to their color properties.

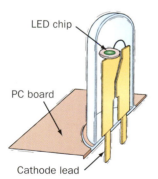

LED chip

PC board

Cathode lead

FIGURE 3.23 An LED is a semiconductor in the form of a chemical chip embedded in a plastic capsule.

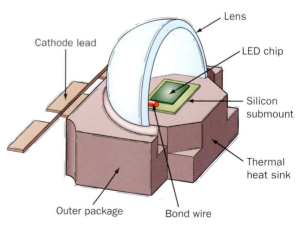

Lens

Cathode lead

LED chip

Silicon submount

Thermal heat sink

Outer package

Bond wire

FIGURE 3.24 LEDs that are used to heat an area should have a heat absorbing material, or what is referred to as a heatsink.

Scientists and engineers are continuing to improve color inconsistencies, color quality, as well as the color-rendering properties of LEDs. Based upon testing results the CIE (International Commission on Illumination) technical committee (2007) has determined that the traditional CRI ratings are not reliable for LEDs. The committee recommends that in situations where accurate color-rendering properties are important, individuals should view the light source in person.

LEDs are available in stand-alone, LED luminaires, and networked applications. Solar LEDs are also available. To ensure that any of these newly developed products perform as stated by their manufacturers a designer should contact independent testing organizations, such as the Department of Energy, IES, ANSI, and the Lighting Research Center.

Many LED stand-alone applications are similar in shape and configuration to incandescent, halogen, fluorescent, and neon lamps. For example, LEDs have been installed in a unit that allows a drop-in replacement for a halogen flood or accent light. A tube LED system that resembles the tube systems in neon lamps provides colored illumination throughout the element.

### LED Luminaires

LED luminaires are complete lighting systems in a **housing** that includes the LED light, a heat sink, a driver, and potentially reflectors and surfaces that help to reduce glare (Figure 3.25). The DOE's ENERGY STAR LED lighting program has a list of recommended commercial and residential luminaires that have met the agency's standards. Their testing procedures examine brightness, uniformity of brightness, consistency of light output over time, color excellence, efficacy that is equivalent or better than fluorescents, instant illumination, flickering, power used when off, and length of product warranties (ENERGY STAR, 2010).

Even though there are several incandescent replacement LED lamps on the market as of 2010 ENERGY STAR has not endorsed any of these lamps because the products tested have not complied with the standards of their program. Designers can monitor ENERGY STAR's website for new updates and developments (www.energystar.gov). Another resource for SSL product testing results is the DOE's Commercially Available LED Product Evaluation and Reporting (CALiPER) program. CALiPER reports are available online: http://www1.eere.energy.gov/buildings/ssl/caliper.html.

Networked arrangements include several luminaires and one controller. Digitally controlled LEDs provide flexibility in colors, brightness, and special effects such as twinkling or synchronization with music. These systems are especially effective for specialty architectural lighting and in retail stores, restaurants, and nightclubs (Figures 3.26a–c). Software and hardware LED systems allow a user to manage, design, and control large-scale installations. For example, LED systems are available that use a series of tiles, or panels, to create scenes. Computer graphics programs can be used to create images from the tiles; a programmable controller creates synchronous color that changes the LED light in each tile. This same technology is also available for tube lighting systems.

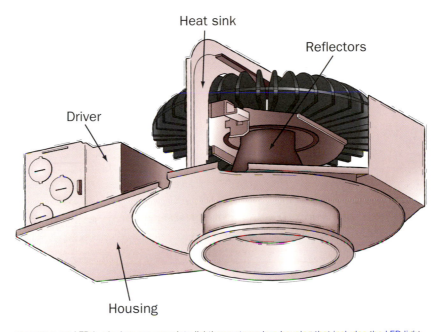

Heat sink

Reflectors

Driver

Housing

FIGURE 3.25 LED luminaires are complete lighting systems in a housing that includes the LED light, a heat sink, a driver, and potentially reflectors and surfaces that help to reduce glare.

## LEDs: Advantages, Disadvantages, and Development of Standards

As an illumination source in a development stage, LEDs have advantages and disadvantages, including high initial costs (Table 3.1). LED lamps are durable and small, have a long life, use minimal electrical power, have a directional source, and do not emit UV or IR radiation. Their efficacy is better than that of incandescent, halogen, and some CFL lamps. Their long life reduces maintenance costs and disposals in landfills. In addition, LEDs do not contain mercury and do not have glass or filaments that can break. As an indirect benefit LEDs' lack of heat helps to reduce the quantity of energy required to cool a building.

The tremendous potential of LEDs as a sustainable lighting solution has prompted many manufacturers to quickly develop and produce a wide variety of LED products. Unfortunately, many of these products were developed during a time period without appropriate standards or requirements. Consequently, many claims advertised by manufacturers were exaggerated or false, such as the lifetime of the fixture, lumens emitted, and consistency of color. Organizations have been developing standards that will improve LEDs and they are working on providing data that will allow product comparisons. These initiatives will help to create confidence in the reliability of the technology.

(a)

(b)

(c)

FIGURE 3.26 Digitally controlled LEDs (a) provide flexibility in colors, brightness, and special effects (b and c). (Photograph of LEDS: Photo courtesy of Philips Color Kinetics. Photographs of interiors: Colin Vincent Photography.)

Some of the standards associated with LEDs include the Alliance for Solid State Illumination Systems and Technologies (ASSIST) metric for the rated service life. In differing from conventional electrical sources, the life of LED commercial products is based upon the number of hours that have been expended when the fixture produces 70 percent of its initial lumen output. For residential products the number is reduced to 50 percent of the initial lumen output.

IES developed LM-80-2008 (LM-80) and LM-79-2008 (LM-79) for the purpose of establishing testing conditions for lumen depreciation as well as other measurements. To address color temperatures for SSL products, ANSI created the C78.377- 2008 standard. Designers should stay apprised of future standards, products, and technologies. LEDs have the potential to revolutionize interior lighting and hopefully new designs will be cost effective and will reflect the unique characteristics of this innovative technology.

## ORGANIC LIGHT-EMITTING DIODES (OLEDS)

In addition to monitoring LED technologies designers should watch closely technological developments associated with **organic light emitting diodes (OLEDs)** and **induction lamps** (Figure 3.27). OLEDs are a SSL technology and are extremely thin sheets of carbon-based compounds that illuminate when their electrodes are stimulated by an electrical charge. OLEDs are a diffused light source that is dimmable. The paper-thin technology can be envisioned as an illuminated wallcovering or window shade. Researchers are developing

OLEDs that can be adhered to surfaces, such as walls, windows, and ceilings. OLEDs thinness and its flexibility will enable the technology to cling to a variety of shapes and sizes. The potential with the technology is enhanced by being mercury-free and its ability to have holes inserted or sections cut away without destroying the light.

Induction lamps are able to produce a high quantity of light from a relatively small unit and they have a very long life. Induction lamps are also known as **electrodeless** because the source does not have electrodes. Because electrodes deteriorate over time eliminating electrodes helps to extend the life of the lamps. Currently, the lighting system is very expensive and is generally used for street lighting and industrial applications.

## Natural and Artificial Light Sources and LEED Certification

For a checklist of how you can apply natural and artificial light sources in creating a LEED-certified building, see Box 3.1.

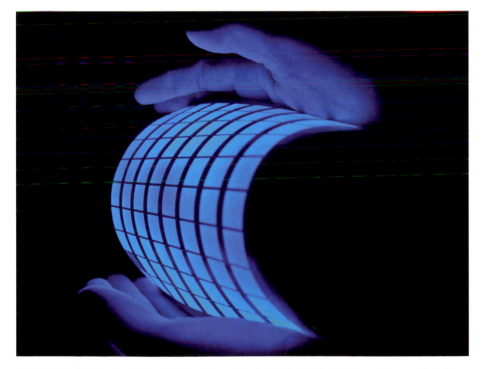

**FIGURE 3.27** OLEDs are a SSL technology and are extremely thin sheets of carbon-based compounds that illuminate when their electrodes are stimulated by an electrical charge. (Courtesy of GE Global Research.)

You can put the content of this chapter to work for you to create LEED-certified buildings by considering the following strategies:

- Monitor the directional attributes of lamps that are located close to windows in order to reduce light pollution.

- Minimize and optimize energy performance by optimizing daylighting and controlling for direct sunlight.

- Maximize users' connection to the outdoors by optimizing daylighting and controlling for direct sunlight.

- Maximize users' thermal comfort related to solar energy by optimizing daylight and controlling for direct sunlight.

- Minimize and optimize energy performance by selecting lamps (high lpW) that are the most energy-efficient for a specific application and produce minimal heat.

- Minimize and optimize energy performance by replacing and recycling inefficacious lamps and auxiliary equipment.

- Minimize and optimize energy performance by selecting ballasts that are the most energy-efficient for a specific application.

- Minimize and optimize energy performance by selecting the lamp-ballast circuit that is appropriate for how often lamps are turned on/off.

- Minimize and optimize energy performance by specifying illuminance levels that are efficient as well as appropriate for a given task and the characteristics of the users.

- Optimize energy performance of lighting controls by controlling for daylight, and selecting lamps and luminaires that direct the light where it is needed without spill to other areas or to the outdoors.

- Optimize users' ability to control lamps, window shades, and controls.

- In the fundamental/enhanced commissioning of the building energy systems monitor the installation, operation, and calibration of lamps as well as the controllability of lighting.

- Measure and verify the efficiency of daylighting, lamps, controls, and thermal comfort.

- Monitor new developments in lamps and auxiliary equipment to ensure the most efficient and cost effective lighting systems.

**TABLE BOX 3.1** LEED Categories Related to Natural and Artificial Light Sources

LEED CREDIT CATEGORIES RELATED TO CONTENT IN CHAPTER 3

| |
|---|
| SS (Sustainable Sites) Credit 1 Option 2 |
| Path 6: Light Pollution Reduction |
| EA (Energy and Atmosphere) Prerequisite 1 Fundamental Commissioning of Building Energy Systems |
| EA Prerequisite 2 |
| Minimum Energy Performance |
| EA Credit 1.1 |
| Optimize Energy Performance—Lighting Power |
| EA Credit 1.2 |
| Optimize Energy Performance—Lighting Controls |
| EA Credit 2 |
| Enhanced Commissioning |
| EA Credit 3 |
| Measurement and Verification |
| IEQ Credit 6.1 |
| Controllability of Systems—Lighting |
| IEQ Credit 6.2 |
| Controllability of Systems—Thermal Comfort |
| IEQ Credit 7.1 Thermal Comfort—Design |
| IEQ Credit 7.2 |
| Thermal Comfort—Verification |
| IEQ Credit 8.1 |
| Daylight and Views—Daylight |
| IEQ Credit 8.2 |
| Daylight and Views—Views for Seated Spaces |
| ID (Innovation in Design) Credit 1 |
| Innovation in Design |

Source: USGBC (2009). *LEED reference guide for green interior design and construction*. Washington, D.C.: U.S. Green Building Council.

# Fundamental Projects

**1. Research Design Project**

Select two types of lamps from the following categories: fluorescent, HID, and LED. Locate the lamps in the catalogs of three different lamp manufacturers. In a summary essay, compare and contrast the performance of the lamps.

**2. Research Design Project**

Identify several commercial and residential applications for end-emitting and side-emitting fiber optic systems. Write an essay that identifies the applications and discusses the advantages and disadvantages of using the two major types of fiber optic lighting.

**3. Research Design Project**

Write an essay that provides examples of how fiber optics and LEDs could be used for general, task, accent, and decorative lighting.

# Application Projects

## 1. Research Design Project

Write an essay that provides examples of how fluorescent, metal halide, and high-pressure sodium lamps could be used for general, task, and accent lighting. In this essay, discuss how daylight can be successfully integrated with these electrical light sources.

## 2. Human Factors Research Project

Developing observation and problem-solving skills is critical to the success of a designer. Find installations of incandescent, fluorescent, and HID lamps in residential or commercial interiors. For each installation:

a. Identify the purpose of the space.

b. Identify the purpose of the lighting, including an identification of general, task, and accent lighting.

c. Evaluate the appropriateness of the illumination level.

d. Based upon the definition of quality lighting environments described in Chapter 1, evaluate the overall quality of lighting in each space.

e. Based upon your observations and reflections, provide recommendations for improving the lighting environment.

# Summary

o It is essential to distinguish between sunlight and daylight. Direct sunlight can produce glare, excessive heat, and fading of materials. Daylight is the term that describes the desirable natural light in a space.

o Advantages to integrating daylight into interiors include energy savings resulting from a reduction in electrical lights and from passive solar energy penetration in the winter. Another advantage of daylighting is the even distribution of light that appears to reveal the true colors of objects and surfaces. Daylight enhances visual acuity by providing better light for reading and writing.

o Designing buildings that maximize penetration of daylight begins with an understanding of solar geometry and the variability of sunlight.

o Factors that influence the level and quality of daylight entering a space include clouds, weather, atmospheric pollution, orientation, landscaping, and surrounding structures.

o An understanding of electrical light sources and their advantages and disadvantages requires a review of a lamp's light output, efficacy, lamp life, color, maintenance factors, and cost.

o An incandescent lamp operates by having an electrical current heat the tungsten filament until incandescence is reached. A standard incandescent lamp uses argon with some nitrogen to prevent arcing.

o Use of a halogen, either iodine or bromine gas, improves the performance of an incandescent lamp by redistributing the oxidizing tungsten on the filament rather than allowing it to accumulate on the glass. These lamps are halogen and are available in line and low voltage.

o The fluorescent lamp is a discharge lamp. Discharge lamps are made from glass, use mercury or sodium, and require a ballast to start the lamp and control the electrical current.

o Fluorescent lamps are available in basically four lamp-ballast circuits including instant start, rapid start, programmed-start (or programmed rapid-start), and universal-input. Fluorescent lamps are available in a variety of sizes, shapes, and wattages, but the most common specified today are the straight tubes T8 and T5.

o Compact fluorescent lamps (CFL) produce a high lumen output and can achieve up to 75 percent energy savings compared to the incandescent lamp.

o The three basic types of high-intensity discharge (HID) lamps are mercury vapor (MV), metal halide (MH), and high-pressure sodium (HPS).

o HID lamps have been excellent choices for applications that require high efficacy, long life, high lpW performance, operation in a wide range of ambient temperatures, and positive long-term economics.

o Fiber optic lighting utilizes a remote source for illumination. The light source is housed in a box called the illuminator, and the directional lamp is usually metal halide or tungsten-halogen. The fibers are made from glass or plastic, and hundreds of optical fibers can be used in the system.

o There are many advantages to using fiber optic lighting, including safety, ease of maintenance, low transmission of heat to objects being illuminated, and very small amounts of the infrared (IR) and ultraviolet (UV) wavelengths.

## KEY TERMS

aperture
ballast
bin
candela (cd)
candlepower
circadian rhythm
compact fluorescent lamp (CFL)
daylight (skylight)
daylight harvesting
daylighting
diffuser
driver
efficacy

electric-discharge lamp
electrodeless (induction lamp)
electroluminescent lamp
end-emitting system
fiber optic lighting
flood
fluorescent lamp
halogen regenerative cycle
heat sink
high-intensity discharge (HID) lamp
high-pressure sodium (HPS) lamp
housing

illuminator
incandescent carbon-filament lamp
induction lamp (electrodeless)
lamp
lamp life
light-emitting diodes (LEDs)
light output
light shelf
lumens per watt (lpW)
mercury (MV) lamp
metal halide (MH) lamp
modeling

organic light-emitting diodes (OLEDs)
restrike
side-emitting system
sidelighting
solar geometry
solid-state lighting (SSL)
spot
sunlight
toplighting
transformer
tungsten
tungsten-halogen lamps
watt (w)

o LEDs are the first solid-state light (SSL) source for general lighting. An LED is a semiconductor consisting of a chemical chip embedded in a plastic capsule. A volt from a direct current energizes the chip, making visible light. A driver or transformer is needed to operate the lamps with a direct current. The light is focused or scattered by using lenses or diffusers.

## References

CIE Technical Report (2007). Color Rendering of White LED Light Sources 177.

ENERGY STAR (2010). *Learn about LEDs*. Retrieved on July 21, 2010 from www.energystar.gov/index .cfm?c=lighting.pr_what_are#all_equal

Heschong Mahone Group (HMG) (2003). *Windows and offices: A study of office worker performance and the indoor environment—CEC PIER 2003*. For the California Energy Commission's Public Interest Energy Research (PIER) program.

Heschong Mahone Group (HMG) (2003). *Daylight and retail sales*. For the California Energy Commission's Public Interest Energy Research (PIER) program.

Heschong Mahone Group (HMG) (2001). *Re-analysis report: Daylighting in schools, additional analysis—CEC PIER*. For the California Energy Commission's Public Interest Energy Research (PIER) program.

## Resources

Benya, J., Heschong, L., McGowan, T., Miller, N., & Rubinstein, F. (2001). *Advanced lighting guidelines*. White Salmon, WA: New Buildings Institute.

Gordon, G. (2003). *Interior lighting for designers* (4th ed.). New York: John Wiley & Sons.

Illuminating Engineering Society of North America (IESNA) (2011). *IESNA lighting handbook* (10th ed.). New York: Illuminating Engineering Society of North America.

Phillips, D. (2000). *Lighting modern buildings*. Oxford: Architectural Press.

Steffy, G. R. (2002). *Architectural lighting design* (2nd ed.). New York: Van Nostrand Reinhold.

Veitch, J. (2000, July). Lighting guidelines from lighting quality research. CIBSE/ILE Lighting 2000 Conference. New York, United Kingdom.

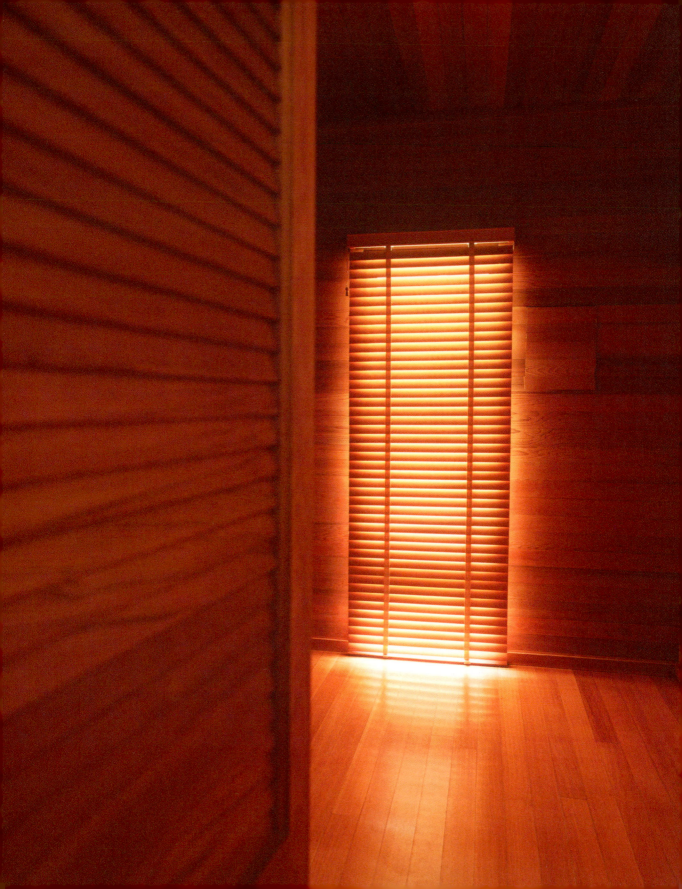

# 4 Energy, the Environment, and Sustainable Design

Interior designers have an ethical responsibility to safeguard the health, safety, and welfare of the occupants of the interiors they specify. As our planet experiences growth in population and the depletion of natural resources, protecting the environment has become increasingly essential for the health and welfare of future generations. As global citizens, interior designers can play an active role in educating consumers and making a conscious effort to specify products and materials that minimize the impact on the environment.

During the past several years, the field of interior design has become more focused on the environment than it had been previously. This is made evident by the popularity of sustainable designs and the rapidly increasing number of buildings that have LEED certification (Figure 4.1). Sustainable design focuses on products and processes that protect the environment while conserving energy for future generations. Whenever possible, lighting specifications should reflect the principles embodied in sustainable design, including energy conservation and compliance with standards, codes, and regulations. Such design will involve incorporation of the information reviewed in chapters of this textbook, including daylighting, characteristics of lamps, directional effects of lighting, design of luminaires, electricity, and

**OBJECTIVES**

o  Describe international energy requirements through 2030

o  Analyze the energy required for lighting, including consumption by type of building and practices described by producers, conveyors, and consumers

o  Define sustainable design and apply an understanding of it to lighting systems

o  Identify the factors that should be considered when specifying a sustainable lighting system

o  As prescribed by energy codes and standards, understand minimum requirements for energy-efficient design of new and existing buildings

o  Determine the factors that should be considered in an economic analysis

FIGURE 4.1 The Exelon Headquarters in Chicago received LEED platinum certification. Sustainable features include direct-indirect lighting system with daylight dimming, controllable task lighting for each employee, and an automated system that controls the lighting. (Steven Hall for Hedrich Blessing.)

controls. These areas and the principles of sustainable design should also be considered in a lighting system's energy and maintenance management plan.

## Energy

A quality lighting environment requires luminaire systems that protect the environment and conserve energy.

### GLOBAL ENERGY CONSUMPTION

The Energy Information Administration (EIA) is an independent statistical and analytical agency that issues the annual International Energy Outlook (IEO) publication. In projecting international energy consumption, the EIA indicates "world consumption of marketed

energy is projected to increase by 49 percent from 2007 to 2035" (IEO, 2010, 1). The EIA further examines world energy consumption specifically for the purpose of generating electricity, and projects increases in consumption of all primary energy sources, including coal and natural gas.

Increases in the consumption of fossil fuels deplete nonrenewable resources, while the associated combustion process increases world carbon dioxide emissions. Specifying energy-efficient lighting systems can assist in reducing future international energy consumption and subsequent emissions.

According to the EIA (2010), by the year 2035 world energy consumption will be 739 quadrillion British thermal units (Btu). The developing countries, primarily those in non-OECD (Organisation for Economic Co-operation Development) Asia (led by China and India) and Central and South America, will experience the greatest demand for energy (Figure 4.2). In reviewing energy consumption by type of fuel, the EIA reports that the greatest increase in demand is for natural gas. Most of the increase in the consumption of natural gas is attributed to the use of gas turbine power plants for the generation of electricity. This technology is appealing to producers and consumers because natural gas has many environmental and economic benefits. Natural gas burns more cleanly than other fossil fuels, thus reducing the ill effects derived from gas emissions.

Figure 4.3 illustrates recent history and projections for electrical generation by fuel. The EIA postulates that electrical consumption for non-OECD countries will continue to increase

Key
- North America
- OECD Europe
- OECD Asia
- Middle East
- Africa
- Central and South America

FIGURE 4.2 Map of members and non-members of the Organisation for Economic Co-Operation and Development (OECD).

even beyond 2035. Currently, some areas in developing countries do not have electricity. For example, in sub-Saharan Africa, 75 percent of the people do not have access to power; therefore, the EIA anticipates that the increase in electrical usage will be derived primarily from improvements in the standard of living in non-OECD countries. From a positive perspective, the report indicates that solar power is one of the fastest-growing sources of energy worldwide.

## ENERGY CONSUMPTION FOR LIGHTING

The EIA report does not provide a historical profile or projection of electrical demand by specific use, such as lighting. However, some

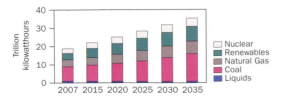

FIGURE 4.3 World electricity generation by fuel, 2006–2030.

of this information is available from the U.S. Environmental Protection Agency (EPA) and the International Association of Energy-Efficient Lighting (IAEEL). The EPA has determined that lighting consumes approximately 35 percent of the electricity used in commercial buildings and 20 percent of the electricity that is consumed in residences. In addition, approximately 20 percent of the electricity used for air conditioning is required as a result of the heat generated by lamps. Most of the need for lighting occurs during weekdays, which is the time of peak demand for electricity.

The purpose of a building affects the percentage of the electricity it uses for lighting. For example, a large percentage of the electricity consumed by a retail store is dedicated to lighting. In contrast, the percentage of electricity used for lighting by a factory is very small because the highest demands are for operating machinery. The design of a building also affects the percentage of electricity used for lighting. Generally, buildings whose interiors have relatively little exposure to daylight require more electricity for lighting. Effective daylight integration can conserve energy; the amount of illumination from a window approximately 3 feet × 5 feet (.9 meters × 1.5 meters) is equivalent to 100 incandescent 60-watt lamps.

A critical component to reducing energy consumed for lighting is daylighting. Software, such as Radiance, is available to generate a simulation of daylighting and the electrical needs for lighting in proposed buildings (Figures 4.4a and 4.4b). Radiance is a ray-tracing software that was developed from support primarily from the U.S. Department

**FIGURE 4.4A** Radiance software used to simulate daylighting. Image rendered and values computed by the Radiance system. (Courtesy Greg Ward and the Lawrence Berkeley National Laboratory.)

**FIGURE 4.4B** Radiance software used to simulate daylighting and to generate illuminance contours. Image rendered and values computed by the Radiance system. (Courtesy Greg Ward and the Lawrence Berkeley National Laboratory.)

of Energy. Radiance is an excellent program for analyzing and visualizing lighting and is licensed at no cost in source form (http://radsite.lbl.gov/radiance/framew.html).

To analyze lighting practices and attitudes, the Smithsonian National Museum of American History is collecting a written history of responses from those who make, sell, and use lighting (Figure 4.5). Questions and responses are available on the museum's website (http://americanhistory.si.edu/lightproject/introduction/intro.htm). You may refer to the museum's website to record your responses to the questions. The questions focus primarily on issues related to energy conservation. For example, one of the questions addressed to producers is: "Has your involvement with energy-efficient lighting led you to consider energy issues when you

think about other products? Can you give examples?" (2010, p. 1 updated 2004 and retrieved 2010). One conveyor question is: "Efficient lighting is increasingly seen as a system involving many integrated components. From your experience, how has this affected adoption of the technology?" (2010, p. 1). Consumers are asked: "Have you replaced entire lighting fixtures in order to use more efficient bulbs? If not, would you consider doing so?" (2010, p. 1).

The website includes selected responses to the questions. Because this is an ongoing study, findings and conclusions are not yet available; however, by reading the responses from producers, conveyors, and consumers, an interior designer can gain insight into problems associated with making and distributing efficient lighting systems. For example, in

and sophisticated technologies" (2010, p. 1). An understanding of the issues can facilitate discussion with industry representatives and lead to the design and use of more energy-efficient lighting systems.

An understanding of the perspectives of consumers can be invaluable in developing strategies to convince people to purchase energy-efficient lighting systems. For example, in response to being asked about using energy-efficient lighting equipment, a consumer commented, "Unfortunately, as a consumer I have no economic incentive to purchase energy-efficient fixtures. The premium for these types of bulbs is usually such that it is very hard to rationalize [buying them] as you are in the aisle of your local hardware store or Wal-Mart" (2003, p. 1). A homeowner responded, "It's a good idea, but how much of our energy budget is consumed by lighting?" (2003, p. 2).

# Environment and Sustainable Design

Interior designers are in a unique position to encourage sustainable design because they specify millions of products and materials each year. According to the Department of Energy (DOE) Energy Information Administration (EIA), in 2008 greenhouse gas emissions from commercial buildings were primarily from using lighting, heating, and cooling. Moreover, commercial buildings were the only sector examined by the EIA to have a positive increase in emissions in 2008. The other sectors reviewed were residential, industrial, transportation, and electric power.

**Lighting the Way: Collecting History with the World Wide Web**

**FIGURE 4.5** The Smithsonian National Museum of American History is collecting a written history of responses from those who make, sell, and use lighting. (http://americanhistory.si.edu.)

response to the conveyor question identified in the previous paragraph, one respondent who is a designer and specifier noted, "This is a great concept that has only begun to crawl. I am currently working on a very complex project where we [lighting, HVAC, security, and IT designers] have integrated wide and local control of all systems with cross-compatibility. The various industries involved have yet to recognize the complexity of cross-compatibility and many say they have gone there, but have [actually] only scratched the surface. Once the walls are broken down and the various disciplines truly work together in development, only then will we see some highly efficient

Sustainable designs focus on the interactions of the earth, society, the economy, and the built environment by conserving resources, minimizing waste, and creating healthy environments for current and future generations. The Environmental Protection Agency (EPA) (2001) has determined that the issues related to sustainable design include pollution prevention, multiple and systematic effects, an environmental life-cycle assessment (LCA), magnitude of impact (local and global), and specification of environmental attributes.

An LCA, or cradle-to-grave analysis, is a process that examines the complete impact of a product on the environment, beginning with raw material extraction, refining the materials, and continuing with manufacture, delivery, consumer use, recycling, and waste disposal. Embodied energy is the energy that is consumed throughout the life cycle of a product. Recently, there has been a focus on the embodied energy used to produce aluminum heat sinks in light-emitting diode (LED) luminaires.

All these areas are important when an interior designer specifies a lighting system. The manufacturing process, operations, and the disposal required for lighting systems consume resources, use energy, and cause pollution. In specifying lighting systems, the goals should be to:

o **Maximize daylighting**

o **Reduce the use of nonrenewable resources**

o **Control the use of renewable products**

o **Minimize air, water, and soil pollution**

o **Protect natural habitats**

o **Eliminate toxic substances**

o **Recycle lamps**

o **Reduce light pollution and light trespass**

**Light pollution** is due to excessive illumination in the sky from electrical sources. **Light trespass** occurs when an unwanted light source from one property directs light to adjacent properties.

The many public and private energy and sustainable programs currently in operation are valuable resources (Table 4.1). The EPA, DOE, National Wildlife Federation (NWF), and the National Science Foundation (NSF) all sponsor programs that encourage environmental conservation, minimization of waste, and maximization of energy.

Internationally there are several green building certification programs, including Building Research Establishment's Environmental Assessment Method (BREEAM) in the United Kingdom (www.breeam.org/), Comprehensive Assessment System for Built Environment Efficiency (CASEBEE) in Japan (www.ibec.or.jp/CASBEE/english/index.htm), Green Star in Australia (www.gbca.org.au), and LEED in the U.S. (www.usgbc.org) (Figure 4.6). BREEAM has an international program for buildings located outside the United Kingdom.

In addition to rating systems for buildings, voluntary labeling programs help to identify sustainable products. In the United States, the eco-label and other labels developed by businesses and government-sponsored programs designate such products. Many countries throughout the world have created similar labels, which are used on lamps, materials, equipment, appliances, and floor coverings (Figures 4.7a and 4.7b).

**TABLE 4.1 Energy and Sustainable Programs**

| RESOURCES | INTERNET ADDRESS |
|---|---|
| *Agencies* | |
| U.S. Department of Energy | www.energy.gov |
| U.S. Environmental Protection Agency | www.epa.gov |
| *Offices* | |
| Office of Energy Efficiency and Renewable Energy | www.eere.energy.gov |
| National Fenestration Rating Council (NFRC) | www.nfrc.org |
| *Programs and Research Laboratories* | |
| Advanced Buildings | www.advancedbuilding.net |
| ASHRAE/IESNA 90.1-2007 (American Society of Heating, Refrigeration, and Air Conditioning Engineers/ Illuminating Engineering Society of North America) | www.ashrae.org |
| Building America Program | www.eere.energy.gov/buildings/building_america |
| Building Industry Research Alliance | www.bira.ws |
| Consortium for Advanced Residential Buildings (CARB) | www.carb-swa.com |
| Dark Sky International | www.darksky.org |
| DesignLights Consortium | www.designlights.org |
| Energy Star | www.energystar.gov |
| Environmental Energy Technologies Division (EETD) | www.lbl.gov |
| Energy Information Administration | www.eia.doe.gov |
| Integrated Building and Construction Solutions (IBA-COS) | www.ibacos.com |
| International Association of Energy-Efficient Lighting (IAEEL) | www.iaeel.org |
| General Service Administration and the Public Building Services (GSA/ PBS) | www.gsa.gov |
| Lawrence Berkeley National Laboratory | www.lbl.gov |
| Leadership in Energy & Environment Design | www.usgbc.org |
| Lighting Systems Research Group | http://lighting.lbl.gov |
| MEC (Model Energy Code) | www.energycodes.gov |
| NFPA (National Fire Protection Act) 5000 | www.nfpa.org |
| National Renewable Energy Laboratory (NREL) | www.nrel.gov |
| National Science Foundation | www.nsf.gov |
| National Wildlife Federation (NWF) | www.nwf.org |
| Oak Ridge National Laboratory | www.ornl.gov |
| Rebuild America | www.rebuild.org |
| U.S. Green Building Council | www.usgbc.org |

FIGURE 4.6 An office in London that earned a BREEAM award. Sustainable features include abundant daylight and all electricity is purchased from renewable sources. (Photo by Philip Vile, courtesy of Morgan Lovell.)

FIGURE 4.7A The label that is used on products or practices that have met the energy efficiency guidelines established by the EPA and U.S. Department of Energy. (http://www.energystar.gov/.)

Successful sustainable practice requires teamwork in developing systems and procedures that maximize the overall efficiency and effectiveness of an entire building's system. For existing buildings, an assessment of daylighting and the lighting system should be conducted, including an inventory of lamps, ballasts, luminaires, portable fixtures, and controls. A record should be made of the number of hours during which elements are turned on as well as the specific times of the day and week when this is the case. Effective sustainable practice recognizes the interdependency of lighting and all the other elements of the interior and the architecture. Thus, the assessment should include the purpose of luminaires, human factors, room finishes, colors, materials, architectural

FIGURE 4.7B The label that is used on products and services that have meet the environmental and performance standards established by the European Commission. (EU Ecolabel.)

features, electrical usage, air-conditioning loads, maintenance, and disposal policies.

## DAYLIGHTING

Sustainable design emphasizes the importance of incorporating daylight in spaces. Daylighting not only reduces energy consumption but helps to improve the overall health of the atmosphere in buildings and the productivity of people. The National Institute of Building Sciences has estimated that effective daylighting can reduce approximately one-third of the total building energy costs. Moreover, a reduction in electricity results in fewer emissions of greenhouse gases. Chapter 2 provides an introduction to daylighting by reviewing solar geometry, the variability of sunlight, and advantages and disadvantages of natural light. This section expands upon the information presented in Chapter 2 by analyzing sustainable strategies for daylighting.

### Strategies for Daylighting

Daylighting strategies focus on creating the most effective means to provide the optimum quantity of natural light while controlling for glare, veiling reflections, and excessive heat gains (Table 4.2). Many examples of excellent daylighting strategies are found in buildings that were designed prior to the invention of electricity (Figure 4.8). Without the availability of electrical light sources architects were required to design structures that maximized daylight while controlling for direct sunlight. To learn how natural light affected the spaces in these structures an important resource is paintings; most notable is the works of Jan Vermeer, Hendrick van Steenwyck, Pieter Jansz

White arches

Placement of windows

**FIGURE 4.8** The Baroque Würzburg Residence (1720–1744) in Würzburg, Germany is an excellent example of an interior that maximizes daylight by limiting the width of spaces, having numerous recessed windows adjacent to white surfaces, and high-arched ceilings. (© Bildarchiv Monheim GmbH/Alamy.)

Saenredam, and Pieter Neeffs (elder and younger) (Figures 4.9a and 4.9b).

Maximizing the quantity of daylighting requires an analysis of the orientation of a building, the design of the building's façade, adjacent buildings, the ground close to windows, and characteristics of toplighting and sidelighting. Successful daylighting requires the proper control of sunlight by using devices on the exterior, interior, and effective plans for switching, dimming, and integration

**TABLE 4.2 Summary of Daylighting Strategies**

MAXIMIZING DAYLIGHTING

| Built Environment | Criteria |
|---|---|
| **Building Location** | **Urban vs. rural setting**—Adjacent buildings in an urban setting may block the sun. **Orientation**—Preferred direction of main façades is south and north; correspond to placement of windows. **Warm vs. cold climate**—A focus on shielding sunlight in warm climates; aim with cold climates is to provide passive solar energy during the winter months whereas providing shade during the summer months. |
| **Building Footprint** | **Shape/size**—Sidelighting generally easier with rectangular-shaped and U-shaped buildings. Sidelighting may be difficult with large, square-shaped buildings. Interior rooms may need toplighting. Other options include atria, courtyards, and lightwells. |
| **Building Façade** | Deep reveals. Splayed surfaces. Light shelves. Fins. **Light colors**—Minimize glossy finishes to avoid glare. |
| **Rooms** | **Size**—Narrow depths (daylight can penetrate ~1.5x height of window—farther with a light shelf). Tall ceilings (high reflectance and matte finish). Sloped ceilings. To balance light distribution: illuminate wall across from windows. Windows on multiple walls. Glazed interior walls extend daylight distribution. |

CONTROLLING DAYLIGHT

| Options/ Considerations | Criteria |
|---|---|
| **Exterior Shading** | Deep overhangs, recesses, balconies, double walls, fixed screens, arcades, louvers, fins, brise soleil, shutters, light shelves (reflect light and provide shade). Use horizontal elements on south/north and vertical on east/west windows. Sun tracking/reflecting systems. Movable units preferred to fixed elements. Exterior shading more effective than interior shading. Vegetation over windows. Deciduous trees. |
| **Interior Shading** | Accessible to users **Shades**—Light color and open weave to allow illumination. **Vertical blinds**—East and west. **Horizontal blinds**—North and south. **Shutters.** |
| **Integration Electrical Sources** | Effective means to conserve energy. Supplement daylighting with task specific luminaires. Indirect/direct luminaires compliment daylighting. To avoid glare and maximize illumination adhere to manufacturers recommendations. **Lamps**—4000K/4100K with electronic dimming ballasts. Use lamps that can be dimmed—HID difficult. |
| **Controls and Sensors** | Daylight controls that are integrated with electrical sources and shades if necessary. Dimming hardware or stepped controls. **Sensors**—Proper placement to register daylight—avoid obstructions. Dual-level switching in multiple lamp luminaires. Users access to controls. Use zoning based upon use, rows of luminaires, and type of shade. Proper calibration and commissioning. |

| | |
|---|---|
| **Windows** | **Glazing** |
| Orientation—Most windows on north and south. Limited on west and east. <br> Splay surfaces adjacent to windows. <br> Views—Avoid glare and solar heat gain with shading and glazing (low-transmission). <br> Outdoors reflectance—Light colors (snow, sand, concrete, bricks, etc.) increase light levels. <br> Shape—Strip windows even distribution of light. <br> Placement on walls—High on ceilings (clerestories) and close to other walls. <br> Size—Glare and solar heat gain a problem with large windows. <br> Light shelves—Reflect light and provide shade. Painted white/matte finish. Ideal on south side. <br> Purpose—Visual acuity tasks close to daylight. Short-term and visually undemanding activities farther away. <br> Reflectance—Ceilings (90+ %), Walls (70+ %), Floors (20–40%), & Furniture (25–45%). <br> Avoid obstructions—Furniture, walls, equipment/lighting on ceilings. | Low Visible Transmittance ($T_{vis}$). <br> Low Ultraviolet Transmittance. <br> U-Factor—Lower U-values have the greatest resistance to heat transfer and the greater insulation value (for ratings see the National Fenestration Rating Council (NFRC). <br> Solar Heat Gain Coefficient (**SHGC**)—Lower values = lower solar gain. <br> Color—Dark might prevent too much light. <br> Sound—Select glazing that reduces sound emission. Affects heating/cooling loads. |
| **Toplighting** | **Occupant Considerations** |
| Sheds <br> Monitors <br> Sawtooths (vertical and sloped apertures) <br> Skylights <br> Domes <br> Light Pipes | **Solar heat gain**—Glazing and shading required. <br> **Glare**—Glazing and shading required. |
| **Glazing** | **Maintenance** |
| High Visible Transmission ($T_{vis}$) <br> **Solar Heat Gain Coefficient (SHGC)**—Lower values = lower solar gain. <br> **Spectral selectivity**—Optimizing visible light while reducing solar heat gain. Photovoltaic glass. <br> **Color**—Consider impact on interior. Dark reduces visible light and can increase solar heat gain. <br> Consider single pane for temperate climates. <br> Dual pane preferred in most climates. | Calibrating—Coordination between daylight level detected and lamp output. <br> Commissioning before occupancy—Entire lighting system operates as designed. <br> Group relamping. <br> Cleaning—Lamps, luminaires, windows, surfaces O&M manuals. <br> Analyze costs and benefits. |
| **Maintenance** | |
| Cleaning—Windows and surfaces. <br> Operations and Maintenance (O&M) manuals. <br> Analyze costs and benefits. | |

FIGURE 4.9A The interior of the Antwerp Cathedral painted by Pieter Neeffs (the elder) in the seventeenth century is an excellent example of how natural light affects surfaces, colors, architectural details, and volumetric space. To examine how changes in daylight affect an interior, compare this painting to the illustration in Figure 4.9b. (Scala/White Images/Art Resource, NY.)

FIGURE 4.9B The interior of the Antwerp Cathedral painted by Pieter Neeffs (the younger) in the seventeenth century. To examine how changes in daylight affect an interior, compare this painting to the illustration in Figure 4.9a. (Scala/White Images/Art Resource, NY.)

with electrical sources. New developments in glazing have improved problems associated with glass (Figures 4.10a–e). For example, anti-reflective coatings applied to glass reduce reflections to just one percent while allowing for a high-visible transmission ($T_{vis}$) and reduced-UV transmission (Figure 4.10a). Installing windows with an efficient U-factor rating can control heat gain or loss through windows. The lower the U-value, the greater the resistance to heat transfer and the greater the insulation value. The National Fenestration Rating Council (NFRC) provides U-value ratings for windows. New films and coating technologies can cause glass to transition from transparent to translucent, an especially useful application for transmitting daylight through interior partitions (Figures 4.10b and c).

## LAMPS

As reviewed in Chapter 3, sustainable design requires the use of lamps that have a high efficacy rating, excellent light output, long life, high lumen maintenance, high color rendering, color stability, low mercury levels, and flexible disposal options. All lamps should be recycled, contain no additives, and they should be TCLP- (toxicity characteristic leaching procedure) compliant.

Lamps with high efficacy are often advertised as "high efficiency," "ultra energy-saving," "ultimate performance," "energy cost savings," or "long life." Discharge lamps, including fluorescent, metal halide (MH), and high-pressure sodium, are the most efficient white light sources, whereas incandescent lamps have low efficacy and should be used only for special applications. Compact

(a)

**FIGURE 4.10A** Anti-reflective glass used to help eliminate window glare. (Schott.)

**FIGURES 4.10B AND C** Note how the (b) laminated glass can be (c) clouded to create privacy. (Shtiever/WikiMedia/ Creative Commons 3.0.)

**FIGURE 4.10D** Electrochromic windows can darken the room. (Gallop Studio, Minneapolis.)

**FIGURE 4.10E** Electrochromic windows can lighten the same room illustrated in Figure 4.10d. (Gallop Studio, Minneapolis.)

(b)

(c)

(d)

(e)

fluorescent lamps (CFLs) are a good substitute for incandescent lamps because they consume approximately 70 percent less electricity and last six to ten times longer. For applications that require excellent color rendition and precise optical control, such as accent lighting, halogen or halogen infrared (HIR) are good choices because they are more efficient than incandescent lamps. Halogen compact PAR lamps (PAR20 and PAR30) can be substituted for R20 and R30 lamps.

Compared to incandescent lamps, linear fluorescent lamps produce the same light output while using 80 percent less energy. Fluorescent lamps also last approximately 10 to 20 times longer than incandescent ones and utilize less hazardous materials.

T8 and T5 fluorescent lamps are very popular because they are energy efficient, have improved color properties, and are small in size. The F32T8 that operates with a high-efficiency electronic ballast has been used as a retrofit system for the banned F40T12 with a magnetic ballast because it reduces the number of ballasts and lamps required for an installation in addition to saving considerable energy. Eliminating magnetic ballasts for electronic units will further reduce the watts required for operation.

High-intensity discharge (HID) lamps are efficacious sources and generally produce more lumens per watt in higher wattages. High-pressure sodium (HPS) is the most efficacious, followed by metal halide, and then mercury vapor. HPS or metal halide lamps should be substituted for mercury vapor lamps. Standard metal halide lamps should be replaced with energy-efficient ones. Compared to the conventional MH, the pulse-start metal halide (PSMH) lamp is more energy efficient, lasts longer, and has better color consistency. For some applications, HID lamps are being replaced with T5HO.

## LUMINAIRES

Energy-efficient lamps *require* a luminaire that maximizes the operating function that is unique to each lamp. Sustainable design includes proper placement of luminaires, as well as the use of colors and materials that maximize the reflectance of illumination (Figure 4.11). Luminaires should be located so as to provide effective lighting for specific tasks; layouts characterized by a uniform "blanket" distribution of light often waste energy. Specifying too many luminaires wastes energy and causes unnecessary consumption of natural resources involved in manufacturing and delivery. The lighting layout must be appropriate for the purpose of the luminaires and must control glare. The coefficient of utilization (CU) is an important calculation in determining how room

FIGURE 4.11 Sustainable design includes luminaires that maximize the reflectance of illumination. (Siteco Beteiligungsverwaltungs GmbH.)

proportions and the reflectances of walls, ceiling, and floors affect the quantity of lumens on a task (CU is discussed in Chapter 8). Colors of ceilings and walls should be light in value and should have a reflectance of at least 90 percent and 70 percent, respectively. Textures should be carefully chosen to avoid glare while enhancing reflectance.

The focus on sustainable design has encouraged luminaire designers to create fixtures made from recycled products. Using recycled products stimulates new designs for luminaires that also conserve resources. In addition to environmentally friendly material composition, a sustainable fixture is designed for energy efficiency.

To maximize lumen output interiors of luminaires should be semi-specular, low iridescent, or white. The luminaire efficacy ratio (LER) can be used to compare the efficiency and effectiveness of different luminaires, with high LERs corresponding to high efficiency. To reduce the accumulation of dirt and dust on lamps, which reduces light output, luminaires should also be sealed.

Luminaires in existing buildings should be evaluated to determine whether the fixtures should be replaced or retrofitted. A common retrofit strategy is to insert a reflector into the interior of a luminaire. The reflector can improve the lumen output by 20 to 30 percent. To enhance the optics of a luminaire, diffusers should be replaced with prismatic lenses made from either plastic or glass. In addition, "egg crate" louvers should be replaced with parabolic louvers because the contour parabolic shape maximizes lumen output and helps to control glare.

## CONTROLS AND MAINTENANCE

A quality energy-efficient lighting system requires a comprehensive plan for controls that meet the mandatory provisions in codes while addressing the needs of the users of the space (Figure 4.12). Energy consumed in a space is based upon wattage and duration. Controls are the elements of a lighting system that can affect the length of time electricity is used. Controls should be installed with a thorough **commissioning** process, which ensures that a building system performs according to the specifications. Controls conserve energy by switching lights off when not in use and dimming lamps that do not have to be operated at full intensity.

Lights can be controlled by manual switches, stepped switching, occupancy sensors, or a time switch. **Stepped switching** turn lights on/off by controlling each lamp within a luminaire. Ideally, as controls are operating in a space, users should not notice changes in the illumination levels. Dimming is the best application for this purpose, but dimming ballasts are expensive; especially continuous dimming systems that can reduce the full output down to only 1 percent. Dimming is the preferred strategy for daylighting because these control systems can continuously and gradually adjust electrical light sources according to the ever-changing daylight levels.

Many studies have been conducted to examine practices relating to controls and to determine the energy savings obtained through their use (Leslie et. al., 2004; Moore et. al., 2003; Wah Tong To et. al., 2002; Pacific Gas and Electric Company (PG&E), 2000). Research studies provide support

FIGURE 4.12 A quality energy-efficient lighting system requires a comprehensive plan for controls. Multiple photosensors are used in this interior to monitor daylight and control electrical sources. (Photograph © Sam Fentress.)

special consideration. Users of a space become very frustrated when lights are automatically turned off during times when they need illumination. Consequently, to keep lights on, people have deactivated sensor devices, which often results in lights remaining on when they are not needed. Specifying appropriate controls and sensors as well as other important considerations related to these devices are reviewed in Chapters 5 and 7.

### Energy-Efficient Maintenance Plans

A thorough maintenance plan that includes cleaning instructions, a relamping program, lamp recycling, and disposal guidelines is another element of sustainable practice. Dirt, dust, and age affect lumen output. The IESNA reports, "the combined effect of equipment age and dirt depreciation can reduce illuminance by 25 to 50 percent depending on the application and equipment used" (2000, p. 28-1).

Luminaires should be easily accessible to allow maintenance workers to clean and relamp fixtures. Cleaning instructions should specify the proper detergent and the intervals at which luminaires, lamps, ceilings, walls, and windows should be cleaned. Abrasive detergents can scratch reflectors, causing a decrease in lumen output; manufacturers' product literature will indicate the proper cleaning detergent and method. Generally, the most energy-efficient time to relamp is when 70 percent of the lamp's rated life has elapsed, as lamps burning beyond this point generally consume a high amount of electricity for the lumen output. To save labor costs, group relamping should be specified.

for saving energy by installing individual controls and people tend to demonstrate more satisfaction with a lighting system that allows flexibility (Jennings, Rubenstein, DiBartolomeo, and Blanc, 2000; Boyce, Eklund, and Simpson, 1999; Rea, 1998).

Using controls to conserve energy requires a detailed analysis of the factors that affect daylighting, the interior environment, space planning, schedules, activities, and characteristics of the users. Based upon the unique characteristics of a project, an interior designer must determine the most appropriate controls for reducing and turning off electrical light sources. Establishing the time when lights are turned off requires

# Energy Codes, Economics, and Disposal Regulations

To promote energy efficiency and sustainable development, standards, codes, and regulations have been established worldwide. Because standards, codes, and regulations are continuously being updated, an interior designer must always refer to the most current versions as well as examining the long-term economics of investing in energy-efficient lighting systems.

## ENERGY STANDARDS AND CODES

Standards delineate minimum energy efficiency for lighting equipment and limit power for special interior applications, whereas codes are the laws enacted to apply these standards; in the United States, state and local communities must enact laws that comply with federal standards. Many communities simply adopt the federal standards as their codes with no modifications; however, some states, such as California, have codes that exceed federal standards.

Interior designers must always refer to the state and local codes that regulate their clients' buildings. This is especially important when designers have a project located in a different state or country from their own. Most standards and codes prescribe requirements according to the type of structure and whether it is an existing or a new construction.

Important energy standards and codes that affect lighting efficiency are ASHRAE/IESNA 90.1-2007 (American Society of Heating, Refrigerating, and Air-Conditioning Engineers/Illuminating Engineering Society

of North America), approved by the American National Standards Institute (ANSI), Energy Independence and Security Act (EISA) of 2007, MEC (Model Energy Code), IECC-09 (International Energy Conservation Code), and NFPA (National Fire Protection Act) 5000.

Energy standards for lighting started in 1974 with a publication titled *Energy Conservation Guidelines for Existing Office Buildings*, developed by the General Service Administration and the Public Building Services (GSA/PBS). During this time period, the ASHRAE worked with the IESNA to write a chapter on lighting in its standards document, ASHRAE 90-75. The chapter focuses on lighting-power budget-determination procedures and energy standards for specific applications. This standard has had several revisions, the most current editions being ASHRAE/IESNA 90.1-2007 for commercial buildings except low-rise residential buildings, and ASHRAE/IESNA 90.2-2007 for low-rise residential buildings (Figure 4.13).

The standard specifies minimum requirements for the energy-efficient design of new buildings, as well as for additions or alterations to existing buildings. Established in 1978 **Title 24** is California's energy efficiency standards for residential and nonresidential buildings, and includes requirements for lighting (http://www.energy.ca.gov/title24/). Compared to other states, California's standards are the most stringent. According to the California Energy Commission (2010) the standards are responsible for saving more than $56 billion in electricity and natural gas since 1978, and it is anticipated that an additional $23 billion will be saved by 2013.

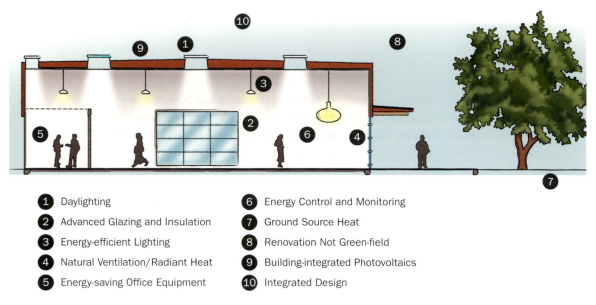

1  Daylighting
2  Advanced Glazing and Insulation
3  Energy-efficient Lighting
4  Natural Ventilation/Radiant Heat
5  Energy-saving Office Equipment
6  Energy Control and Monitoring
7  Ground Source Heat
8  Renovation Not Green-field
9  Building-integrated Photovoltaics
10 Integrated Design

FIGURE 4.13 Sustainability features illustrate how this zero-energy use and zero-carbon emissions building exceeds ASHRAE 90.1 standards. Integrated Design Associates (IDeAs) estimates energy consumption approximately 60 percent below ASHRAE 90.1.

The Energy Conservation Standard for New Buildings Act of 1976 mandated lighting efficiency standards. As a result of this legislation and ASHRAE 90-75, the Model Code for Energy Conservation in New Building Construction (MCEC 77), was developed by several professional organizations; in 1983, the title was changed to Model Energy Code.

The International Code Council is the organization responsible for the IECC, mentioned earlier. This code includes electrical power and lighting systems requirements for energy-efficient residential and commercial buildings. The National Fire Protection Association 5000 Building Code is NFPA's complete building code and includes ASHRAE/IESNA 90.1 and 90.2 as the standard for energy provisions.

Because most lighting codes and regulations are based upon ASHRAE/IESNA 90.1, an interior designer should know this document well. Section 9 of the document is dedicated to lighting. Section 9.1 reviews general lighting applications, whereas Section 9.2 encompasses compliance paths. Section 9.3 is not used, and Section 9.4 delineates lighting controls, tandem wiring, exit signs, and exterior building lighting.

Interior lighting power allowances (ILPA) using the Building Area Method and Space-by-Space Method are described in Sections 9.5 and 9.6, respectively. The former involves the entire building and is determined by multiplying the gross lighted area by allowances provided in the standard's table of **lighting power density (LPD)**. LPDs for common buildings are:

restaurants (1.3–1.6), hospital (1.2), hotels (1.0), offices (1.0), retail stores (1.5), and schools (1.2). These allowances are based on maximum watts per square foot for a given type of building. Thus, given the purposes of merchandising, the maximum watts per square foot for a retail store are higher than for an office.

The space-by-space method is a more flexible and accurate means to calculate the ILPA because each area of a building is identified. The ILPA is determined by adding up all the lighting power allowances room by room. For example, in a school building, the ILPA would include the lighting power for classrooms, hallways, offices, restrooms, cafeteria, and gymnasium. The sum of all the installed interior lighting power cannot exceed the ILPA for a specific building.

Compared to previous versions of the standard, ASHRAE/IESNA 90.1-2007 has more stringent interior lighting power requirements and mandatory control requirements. Lighting power calculations for installed interior lighting systems include lamps, ballasts, and controls for all permanent and portable luminaires.

Except for safety and security lighting, controls must be accessible and mounted in a location that can be seen by users. Control devices are restricted to an area of 2,500 square feet (232.3 square meters) in spaces less than 10,000 square feet (929 square meters). In spaces greater than 10,000 square feet (929 square meters), control devices are limited to an area of 10,000 square feet (929 square meters). Automatic shutoff controls are required for spaces greater than 5,000 square feet (464.5 square meters).

To simplify energy code compliance, the Department of Energy (DOE) has free software designed to perform the necessary calculations. REScheck and COMcheck are the compliance tools for residential and commercial buildings respectively (http://www.energycodes.gov). DOE also has a web page that features future webcasts on energy-related topics, such as IECC and Standard 90.1 that is free to individuals who register (http://www.energycodes.gov/training/onlinetraining/videos.stm). Archived webcasts (Windows Media and YouTube videos) are also included on the website.

The U.S. Energy Policy Act of 1992 (EPAct92) and EPAct 2005 have significantly affected energy-efficient lighting. The EPAct focuses on standards for lighting, energy-efficiency rating systems for windows, and demand-side management (DSM) programs. (DSM programs focus on strategies to reduce the consumption of energy by the customers of utilities providers.)

The EPAct mandates that all states must have codes meeting or exceeding the standards in ASHRAE/IESNA 90.1. The EPAct energy code also requires lamp manufacturers to stop producing many lamps that are not energy-efficient. Lamps for special applications, such as emergency, safety, and cold temperature service, are excluded from meeting efficiency standards. The Federal Trade Commission (FTC) developed a labeling program that must be used by all lamp manufacturers to indicate the energy efficiency of their products. The label includes energy ratings for lamps and the estimated operating costs per year.

EPAct 2005 is the first major energy efficiency standard in the United States since EPAct 1992. Requirements related to lighting are summarized in Table 4.3. Most noteworthy is the inclusion for the development of a SSL research program. Table 4.3 also includes a summary of the EISA 2007 as related to lighting systems. This legislation includes energy efficiency standards for general service lamps (common incandescent lamps) (Section 321), incandescent reflector lamps (Section 322), and ballasts for metal halide lamp fixtures (Section 324).

EISA 2007 has energy requirements for buildings, including a phased-in initiative to have **zero-net-energy** commercial buildings. By using energy-efficient technologies and on-site renewable energy generation systems, such as solar power, these buildings will be able produce as much energy as they consume. EISA 2007 also has a research and development component that includes daylighting systems, solar light pipe technology, and a lighting prize for the development of solid-state lighting that can replace 60-watt incandescent lamps, 38-PAR halogen, and the development of a "Twenty-First Century Lamp."

In addition to standards and codes, there are voluntary programs, such as those sponsored by the EPA and DOE that include recommendations for energy-efficient lighting practices. The EPA supports the ENERGY STAR Commercial Buildings Program, and the DOE has established the Building America programs. ENERGY STAR's program is an energy management strategy that allows a business to benchmark the energy use of their facility by using EPA's Portfolio Manager Software.

The purpose of the Building America research program is to "accelerate the development and adoption of advanced building energy technologies in new and existing homes" (www1.eere.energy.gov/ buildings, p. 1). The program also includes research to "support energy-efficient affordable housing for low-income homeowners" (www1 .eere.energy.gov/buildings, p. 1).

## ENERGY AND ECONOMICS

An economic analysis of lighting should include all expenses associated with an installed system, including lamps, luminaires, ballasts, transformers, controls, electricity, maintenance, disposal, and labor. A lighting system accounts for approximately 5 percent of the total cost of a building. These capital costs are generally distributed over a ten-year period. Factors that affect the operation of a lighting system include the daylight factor, lamp life, maintenance, and the efficiency of lamps and luminaires.

A lighting economic analysis can be conducted by examining simple payback or the life-cycle cost-benefit analysis (LCCBA). The LCCBA is complex and beyond the scope of this textbook. Chapter 25 in IESNA *Lighting Handbook,* 9th edition, provides a detailed illustration of how to conduct an LCCBA. Calculations include initial costs, annual power, maintenance costs, and the time value of money. IESNA recommends that LCCBA be used for large and complex projects (Figure 4.14).

# TABLE 4.3 Summary of EPAct 2005 and the Energy Independence and Security Act (EISA) 2007

## EPACT 2005 (EXCEPTIONS APPLY)

**Lamps CFLs (medium screw-based)**—Must comply with ENERGY STAR Program Requirements for CFLs including minimum efficacies, CRI minimums, specific CCT designations, and lumen maintenance.

**Ballasts**

**Mercury vapor ballasts**—No longer manufactured after January 1, 2006.

**Electromagnetic ballasts** (operate specific fluorescent lamps)—For use in new fixtures not sold after October 1, 2009.

**Electromagnetic replacement ballasts**—Sold until July 1, 2010, but must be labeled replacement only.

**T12 fluorescent ballasts**—Power factor of 0.90 or greater and shall have specific ballast efficacy factors.

**Fixtures**

**Illuminated exit signs**—Must comply with ENERGY STAR Program Requirements including maximum 5 watts and product reliability standards.

**Torchiere fixtures** —Shall consume not more than 190 watts of power and shall not be capable of operating with lamps that total more than 190 watts.

**Residential ceiling fan light kits**—Airflow efficiency standards and maximum power consumption without lights.

**Controls**

New buildings must comply with ASHRAE/IESNA 90.1 control provisions, including automatic lighting shutoff in buildings greater than 5,000 square feet (465 m²).

Bi-level switching (two levels of power)—required in all spaces (exemptions apply).

Separate controls for special lighting applications.

**Research and Development**

**Section 975** Solid-State Lighting: Conduct a program of fundamental research on solid state lighting in support of the Next Generation Lighting Initiative carried out under section 912.

**Section 931** The Secretary shall conduct a program of research, development, demonstration, and commercial application for solar energy, including—(iv) lighting systems that integrate sunlight and electrical lighting in complement to each other in common lighting fixtures for the purpose of improving energy efficiency.

## EISA 2007 (EXEMPTIONS APPLY)

**General Service Lamps (Section 321)**
Minimum rated lifetime of 1,000 hours 80 CRI

| | Current/Maximum Wattages (W) | Lumen Ranges | Effective Date |
|---|---|---|---|
| | 100W/72W | 1490–2600 | 1/1/2012 |
| | 75W/53W | 1050–1489 | 1/1/2013 |
| | 60W/43W | 750–1049 | 1/1/2014 |
| | 40W/29W | 310–749 | 1/1/2014 |

**Incandescent Reflector Lamps (Section 322)**

| Minimum Average Efficacy (lpW) | Wattages |
|---|---|
| 10.5 | 40–50 |
| 11.0 | 51–66 |
| 12.5 | 67–85 |
| 14.0 | 86–115 |
| 14.5 | 116–155 |
| 15.0 | 156–205 |

**Metal Halide Luminaires (Section 324)**

Metal Halide lamp luminaires manufactured after 1/1/2009 must have a ballast efficiency that ranges from 88% to 94%.

**Building Efficiency**

**Section 323**—Public Building Energy Efficiency and Renewable Energy Systems

**Section 421**—Commercial High-Performance Green Buildings

**Section 422**—Zero-Net-Energy Commercial Buildings Initiative

**Sections 431 and 436**—High-Performance Federal Buildings

**Research and Development**

**Section 605**—Daylighting Systems and Direct Solar Light Pipe Technology

**Section 655**—Bright Tomorrow Lighting Prizes

EPAct 2005 Sources: http://www.epa.gov/oust/fedlaws/publ_109-058.pdf and http://www.energystar.gov.
EISA 2007 Source: http://thomas.loc.gov/cgi-bin/bdquery/z?d110:HR00006:@ @@L&summ2=&

(a)

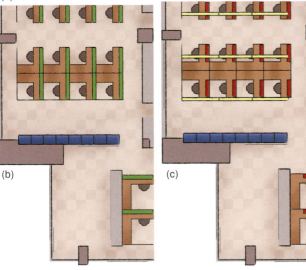

(b)                    (c)

Furniture mounted task ambient        Suspended indirect with task lights

FIGURE 4.14 A life-cycle analysis was performed to examine the cost benefits of lighting using (a) furniture-mounted luminaires, also shown in green on the (b) first drawing, and suspended indirect light fixtures with task lighting, shown in red on the (c) second drawing. This analysis found that the annual life cycle cost for the first seven years was less for the furniture-mounted luminaires. (Photograph: Courtesy of The Lighting Quotient.)

Many software tools are available to determine the costs and benefits of proposed energy conservation projects. The simple payback method is a quick estimate of the number of years required to pay back the money invested in a lighting system and is convenient for comparing different lighting systems. For example, the payback period is five years for a lighting system that saves $3,000 in energy costs per year and costs $15,000 to purchase and operate.

Payback = cost of system/savings per year

5 years = $15,000/$3000

## DISPOSAL REGULATIONS

The primary goals of sustainable disposal practices are to decrease the amount of waste and reduce its environmental impact. Commercial and residential lamp recycling is the first step in reducing waste. The EPA recommends LampRecycle (www.lamprecycle .org) as a source of information about lamp recycling.

To improve solid-waste disposal methods, the Solid Waste Disposal Act (SWDA) was enacted in 1965. In 1976, this act was amended to establish the Resource Conservation and Recovery Act (RCRA), whose objective was to: (1) protect human health and the environment; (2) reduce and/or eliminate the generation of hazardous wastes; and (3) conserve energy and natural resources (Department of Energy, 2003, p. 1).

The RCRA regulates hazardous waste associated with mercury, lead, and sodium. Several agencies have responsibilities associated with the RCRA, including the EPA, whose guidelines and regulations significantly affect the field of lighting. The EPA regulates the "proper management of solid and hazardous wastes, oversees and approves the development of state waste management plans, and provides financial aid to agencies and firms performing research on solid waste" (Department of Energy, 2003, p. 1). The Toxic Substances Control Act (TSCA) and the Superfund Law (the Comprehensive Environmental Response, Compensation and Liability Act or CERCLA) regulate proper disposal of **PCBs (polychlorinated biphenyls)** at the federal level.

To test the mercury content of lamps with a view to avoiding contamination of landfill sites, the EPA developed the **toxicity characteristic leaching procedure (TCLP)** in 1990. To pass the TCLP test, the range of mercury content in a lamp should be between 4 mg and 6 mg without additives. Some lamp manufacturers whose products have mercury levels exceeding the TCLP test include additives in the lamps in order to alter their material composition in a manner that allows them to pass the test regardless.

Local laws and regulations specify the maximum levels of mercury in lamps. Some states, such as California, have laws that mandate lower mercury levels than the TCLP. The Land Disposal Program Flexibility Act of 1996 is a law that addresses adjustments to land disposal restriction and water monitoring at solid-waste landfill units.

As a result of this legislation, there are many regulations that affect handling, removal, storage, transport, and disposal of lighting devices. Environmental regulations exist at the federal, regional, state, and local levels. The most current regulations should always be reviewed when lighting systems need to be removed, as a building owner can be held liable for failing to comply with environmental regulations. An interior designer should encourage a client to maintain records of lamps and ballasts operating in a building and keep track of subsequent disposal processes.

Primary concerns related to removing lighting systems are toxic leaks and lamp breakage. When a lighting system has been determined to contain toxic materials, removal requires strict handling procedures, including the wearing of special protective clothing, gloves, and goggles. The equipment must be contained in special packaging, labeled as prescribed, and transported by means that will help ensure safe delivery with no breakage. Materials can be transported to recycling facilities, hazardous waste landfills, or incinerators. Each method of disposal presents various cost options, which should be included in the price of lighting systems. Contact the EPA to obtain information on the most current methods for hazardous waste disposal.

Many companies specialize in lamp and ballast disposal. Appendix A provides a list of firms associated with recycling and processing lamps and ballasts. In selecting a disposal company, research should be conducted to ensure that the company has updated permits, good standing with the EPA, proper training in hazardous waste handling, and adequate liability insurance.

The environmental impact of the components of lighting systems includes the type of materials used for the products, the manufacturing process, delivery, use, and disposal practices. Information related to materials and delivery modes are available from manufacturers. Some manufacturers have made a conscious effort to create sustainable products and to be sustainable companies. Unfortunately, some manufacturers only appear to be sustainable; their claims prove to be superficial. Until formal standards have been developed that clearly define sustainable products and practices, interior designers must apply their own knowledge of sustainable design to information provided by manufacturers.

Ideally, materials used for the components of lighting systems should be derived from renewable resources, reused products, or recycled materials (Figure 4.15). In addition, the materials should have little or no toxic content. A primary area of concern is the use of mercury in fluorescent, HID, and neon lights. Currently, light for these lamps cannot be produced without mercury. Mercury is

**PBT (persistent, bioaccumulative, toxic)**, meaning that it is poisonous, remains in water or land indefinitely, and accrues in the world's ecosystems. For example, when a fluorescent lamp is deposited in a landfill and breaks, mercury leaks into the ground. Water from rain can transport mercury to the air, lakes, and rivers. After the mercury is in the water system, fish ingest the mercury, plant life is affected, and eventually people can develop high levels of mercury by eating fish. To reduce the environmental impact, lamps should be specified that have long life and low mercury content, both of which can be determined by consulting the information available from lamp manufacturers. Federal and state laws regulate the disposal of lamps containing mercury.

The European Union has broadened restrictions on mercury as well as other hazardous substances. Effective in 2006 the European Union (EU) banned in the EU marketplace any "new electrical and electronic equipment containing more than agreed levels of lead, cadmium, mercury, hexavalent chromium, polybrominated biphenyl (PBB) and polybrominated diphenyl ether (PBDE) flame retardants" (http://www.rohs.gov.uk/). This regulation is the **Restriction of the use of certain Hazardous Substances (RoHS)** and applies to some ballasts, controls, and lamps, including LEDs.

Another item of concern is the toxic substance polychlorinated biphenyls (PCBs). This chemical was used in ballasts before it was banned in 1978. Ballasts without PCBs are labeled "No PCBs." Federal and state laws also regulate the disposal of ballasts with PCBs. In addition to lamps, ballasts, and luminaires, other components of lighting systems should be examined with reference to the materials used to make them. These components include the housing unit, transformers, and controls. All products should be made from renewable resources, reused products, or recycled materials, and should not contain toxic substances.

In addition to the materials used for lighting systems, sustainable design takes into account the manufacturers' production processes and delivery of goods. A sustainable manufacturing company will promote energy efficiency and sustainable development by reducing electrical usage, using renewable resources, recycling, and preventing toxic waste. These practices should be evident throughout the life cycle of the manufacturing process, packaging, and delivery.

Packaging should be made from recycled materials and on the smallest scale possible, minimizing the resources needed to create the packaging and the space required in delivery trucks. A sustainable focus on delivery is important because many nonrenewable resources are used for transportation. A sustainable manufacturer will focus on minimizing the number of trucks needed to transport products and the distances each vehicle must travel.

## Energy, Environment, Sustainable Design, and LEED Certification

For a checklist of how you can apply energy, environment, and sustainable design in lighting in creating a LEED-certified building, see Box 4.1.

BOX 4.1 **Energy, the Environment, Sustainable Design, and LEED Certification**

You can put the content of this chapter to work for you to create LEED-certified buildings by considering the following strategies:

○ Optimize the interdependent relationships among people, the built environment, the earth, and economics.

○ Reduce light pollution; employ strategies that help eliminate the spill of interior light to the outdoors.

○ Minimize and optimize energy performance by optimizing daylight and controlling for direct sunlight.

○ Maximize user satisfaction with an environment and productivity by optimizing daylighting, providing individual lighting controls, ensuring views to the outdoors, and individualizing thermal comfort.

○ Minimize and optimize energy performance by selecting lamps (high lpW) and auxiliary equipment that are the most energy efficient for a specific application and produce minimal heat.

○ Minimize and optimize energy performance by replacing and recycling inefficacious lamps and auxiliary equipment.

○ Minimize and optimize energy performance by selecting appropriate controls for daylighting, dimming, occupancy/vacancy, and schedules.

○ Whenever possible, reuse luminaires and any building materials that are used with lighting systems, such as ceilings, walls, and architectural elements.

○ Reduce construction waste; redirect any materials used with lighting systems that have recyclable content, especially lamps.

○ Help protect the environment; monitor any lamps, controls, or ballasts that are identified in the European Union's RoHS regulation.

○ Whenever possible, specify luminaires and other elements associated with lighting systems that have recycled content and have been produced regionally.

○ Whenever possible, specify luminaires and other elements associated with lighting systems that have been produced with rapidly renewable materials. Wood-based products should be certified by the Forest Stewardship Council.

○ To ensure a quality indoor environment, specify low-emitting paint that is used for any element of a lighting system. To maximize illumination specify paint colors with a high reflectance (> 85%).

○ In the fundamental/enhanced commissioning of the building energy systems, monitor the installation, operation, and calibration of the lighting system, including controls and the elements used to control daylight.

○ Measure and verify the efficiency of daylighting, electrical sources, controls, and thermal comfort.

○ Monitor new sustainable developments in lighting systems to ensure the most efficient and cost-effective lighting systems.

○ Monitor global energy codes and standards.

**TABLE BOX 4.1** LEED Categories Related to Energy, the Environment, and Sustainable Design

LEED CREDIT CATEGORIES RELATED TO CONTENTS IN CHAPTER 4

SS (Sustainable Sites) Credit 1, Option 2, Path 6: Light Pollution Reduction

EA (Energy and Atmosphere) Prerequisite 1: Fundamental Commissioning of Building Energy Systems

EA Prerequisite 2: Minimum Energy Performance

EA Credit 1.1: Optimize Energy Performance—Lighting Power

EA Credit 1.2: Optimize Energy Performance—Lighting Controls

EA Credit 2: Enhanced Commissioning

EA Credit 3: Measurement and Verification

MR (Material and Resources) Credit 1.2: Building Reuse—Maintain Interior Nonstructural Components

MR Credit 2: Construction Waste Management

MR Credit 3.2: Materials—Reuse—Furniture and Furnishings

MR Credit 4: Recycled Content

MR Credit 5: Regional Materials

MR Credit 6: Rapidly Renewable Materials

MR Credit 7: Certified Wood

IEQ (Indoor Environmental Quality) Credit 4.2: Low-Emitting Materials—Paints and Coatings

IEQ Credit 6.1: Controllability of Systems—Lighting

IEQ Credit 6.2: Controllability of Systems—Thermal Comfort

IEQ Credit 7.1: Thermal Comfort—Design

IEQ Credit 7.2: Thermal Comfort—Verification

IEQ Credit 8.1: Daylight and Views—Daylight

IEQ Credit 8.2: Daylight and Views—Views for Seated Spaces

ID (Innovation in Design) Credit 1—Innovation in Design

Source: USGBC. (2009). *LEED reference guide for green interior design and construction*. Washington, DC: U.S. Green Building Council.

# Fundamental Projects

**1. Research Design Project**

Research local state laws and regulations affecting sustainable design and energy-efficient lighting systems. In a written report, summarize the findings and discuss the implications for designing lighting systems.

**2. Research Design Project**

Research international policies and regulations promoting sustainable lighting systems. In a written report, compare and contrast policies, and provide suggestions for improving the regulations in your hometown.

# Application Projects

**1. Human Factors Research Project**

Locate the study of the written history of responses from lighting producers, conveyors, and consumers conducted by the Smithsonian National Museum of American History. Analyze and summarize the results in a written report. Show how the results of the study can influence energy-efficient lighting practices in the future.

**2. Human Factors Research Project**

Visit an office and a department in a retail store. For each space, conduct an analysis of the lighting systems from the perspective of sustainability and energy conservation. Develop recommendations for improving the lighting systems, including retrofit applications. Summarize the results in a written report and include illustrations, photographs, or sketches.

**3. Research Design Project**

Interview facility managers to determine sustainable and energy-conserving lighting practices. In a written report, summarize your findings and provide suggestions for improving energy efficiency and sustainability.

# Summary

- According to the EIA (2010), by the year 2035, world energy consumption will be 739 quadrillion British thermal units (Btu).

- The EIA postulates that electrical consumption for non-OECD countries will continue to increase even beyond 2035.

- The Environmental Protection Agency (EPA) has determined that lighting accounts for approximately 35 percent of the electricity used in buildings.

- The EPA has determined that the issues related to sustainable design include pollution prevention, multiple and systematic effects, an environmental life-cycle assessment (LCA), magnitude of impact (local and global), and specification of environmental attributes.

- In specifying lighting systems, the goals should be to: (1) reduce the use of nonrenewable resources; (2) control the use of renewable products; (3) minimize air, water, and soil pollution; (4) protect natural habitats; (5) eliminate toxic substances; and (6) reduce light pollution.

- Internationally there are several green building certification programs, including Building Research Establishment's Environmental Assessment Method (BREEAM) in the United Kingdom (www.breeam.org/), Comprehensive Assessment System for Built Environment Efficiency (CASEBEE) in Japan (www.ibec.or.jp/CASBEE/english/index.htm), Green Star in Australia (www.gbca.org.au/), and LEED in the United States (www.usgbc.org).

- To promote energy efficiency and sustainable development, standards and codes have been established worldwide. An interior designer must always refer to the most current standards and codes because they are continuously updated.

- Important energy standards and codes that affect lighting efficiency are ASHRAE/IESNA 90.1-2007, MEC, and IECC-09.

- The U.S. Energy Policy Act of 1992 (EPAct-92) has significantly affected energy-efficient lighting. EPAct focuses on standards for lighting, energy-efficiency rating systems for windows, and demand-side management (DSM) programs.

## KEY TERMS

commissioning
light pollution
light trespass
light power density (LPD)
PBT (persistent, bioaccumulative, toxic)

PCBs (polychlorinated biphenyls)
Restriction of the use of certain Hazardous Substances (RoHS)
stepped switching

Title 24
toxicity characteristic leaching procedure (TCLP)
zero-net-energy

o EPAct 2005 is the first major energy efficiency standard in the United States since EPAct 1992.

o An economic analysis of lighting should include all expenses associated with an installed system, including lamps, luminaires, ballasts, transformers, controls, electricity, maintenance, disposal, and labor.

o An economic analysis of lighting can be conducted by examining the simple payback, or the life-cycle cost-benefit analysis (LCCBA). Many software tools are available to determine the costs and benefits of proposed energy conservation projects. The simple payback method is a quick estimate of the number of years required to pay back the money invested in a lighting system.

o The primary goals of sustainable disposal practices are to reduce the impact on the environment and decrease waste.

o Sustainable design requires the use of lamps that conserve energy and have high efficacy ratings, excellent light output, long life, high lumen maintenance, high color rendering, color stability, low mercury levels, and flexible disposal options. They should also be TCLP-compliant without additives.

# Resources

Benya, J., Heschong, L., McGowan, T., Miller, N., & Rubinstein, F. (2001). *Advanced lighting guidelines*. White Salmon, WA: New Buildings Institute.

Gordon, G. (2003). *Interior lighting for designers* (4th ed.). New York: John Wiley & Sons.

Illuminating Engineering Society of North America (IESNA) (2000). *IESNA lighting handbook* (9th ed.). New York: Illuminating Engineering Society of North America.

Phillips, D. (2000). *Lighting modern buildings*. Oxford: Architectural Press.

Steffy, G. R. (2002). *Architectural lighting design* (2nd ed.). New York: Van Nostrand Reinhold.

U. S. Energy Information Administration (2010). *International energy outlook 2010*. Retrieved on August 18, 2010 from http://www.eia.doe.gov/oiaf/ieo/highlights.html

Veitch, J. (2000, July). *Lighting guidelines from lighting quality research*. CIBSE/ILE Lighting 2000 Conference. New York, United Kingdom.

# References

California Energy Commission (2010). *California's energy efficiency standards for residential and nonresidential buildings*. Retrieved on July 21, 2010 from http://www.energy.ca.gov/title24/

U.S. Energy Information Administration. *Emissions of greenhouse gases in the United States 2008*. Retrieved on July 21, 2010 from ftp://ftp.eia.doe.gov/pub/oiaf/1605/cdrom/pdf/ggrpt/057308.pdf

# 5 Illumination, Human Health, and Behavior

Research indicates that lighting can affect the health, behavior, and psychological well-being of people. The fundamental basis for this research is the concept of the interaction between people and their environment. According to Wapner and Demick, the person-in-environment system assumes that the individual is "composed of mutually defining physical/biological (e.g., health), psychological (e.g., self-esteem), and sociocultural (e.g., role as worker) aspects; and the environment is composed of mutually defining aspects, including physical (natural and built), interpersonal (e.g., friend, spouse), and sociocultural (rules of home, community, and culture) aspects" (2002, p. 5). An awareness of the interaction between a person and the environment is key to understanding how illumination can affect people. In designing a lighting system, the interior designer must know the users of the space within the context of the specific environment, an especially challenging endeavor in an era of globalization.

## OBJECTIVES

o Describe the results of research that indicate both negative and positive effects of lighting on a person's health

o Understand how light affects the body's circadian rhythm

o Understand the behavioral and psychological effects of light on people

o Apply the principles of universal design to a lighting environment

## Optimizing the Person-in-Environment System

A quality lighting environment is planned to optimize the person-in-environment system and reflect the principles associated with **evidence-based design (EBD)**. Such planning involves knowledge of current research, practice, and a thorough assessment of the project. An excellent resource for examining summaries of research studies is InformeDesign (http://www.informedesign .umn.edu/).

Early lighting research focused on visual aspects of illumination as it related to workplace performance and perceptions of the environment. Current research still explores behavioral and psychological effects of illumination, but emerging topics include how lighting affects biological processes in people.

An assessment of a project includes the purpose of the space and the characteristics of the users of the space. (Chapter 9 reviews the client and project assessment process.) Understanding the effects of illumination on people can assist an interior designer in fulfilling the purpose of the environment. By knowing the specific characteristics of people, through observation, the designer can specify lighting to accommodate special needs of individuals within the context of the environment.

The effect of illumination on people includes physiological and psychological factors. Physiological aspects are related to health, vision, circadian systems, and the needs of special populations. From a different perspective extremely tiny-scale technology that is associated with **nanotechnology**, and **smart textiles** is providing innovative

FIGURE 5.1A An experimental installation of 900 mirror-like OLEDs at the Pinakothek der Moderne in Munich, Germany illustrates how the panels respond to movement. Notice how the panels interpret the man's outstretched arms. (Photo: © Rainer Schmitzberger.)

FIGURE 5.1B A close-up of the OLED panels described in Figure 5.1a. (Stuart Wood random.)

approaches to the physiological interaction between people and light sources (Figures 5.1a and 5.1b). Many of these products and materials are in the development stages, but there are organizations and artists who are exploring the possibilities with interactive technologies. For example, Jason Bruges Studio created *Mirror Mirror* (2009) for an exhibition at the Victoria & Albert Museum in London (Figure 5.2). The LED dot matrix panels included cameras that captured people and other activities in the garden. Another project in the United Kingdom used an interactive railing that changed colors and produced sounds as people touched its surface.

To personalize the retail experience Philips is developing a device that someone would have embedded in something they are wearing, such as a ring. As the person walks through the store lights on displays would change according to the preferences of the individual, including his or her past purchases (Figure 5.3).

Illumination can affect the psychological well-being of people by altering behavior and eliciting subjective impressions of an environment. The lighting in the United States Holocaust Memorial Museum in Washington, D.C. was specifically planned to evoke simultaneous feelings of compassion, sadness, and outrage in the viewers. The permanent exhibit begins with two images that have an immediate impact on viewers (Figure 5.4). A large photograph of people who were killed is directly in front of visitors as they come off the elevator, while the words "THE HOLOCAUST" next to the photograph bring an immediate connection to the tragedy. High-contrast lighting emphasizes

FIGURE 5.2 Jason Bruges Studio created *Mirror Mirror* (2009) for an exhibition at the Victoria & Albert Museum in London. Notice the images in the LED dot matrix panels that were captured by cameras. *Mirror Mirror* by Jason Bruges Studio 2009 for Decode: Digital Design Sensations at the Victoria and Albert Museum, London, in association with onedotzero, sponsored by SAP.

FIGURE 5.3 To personalize the retail experience Philips is developing a device that illuminates merchandise according to an individual's preferences. (Philips Lighting North America.)

FIGURE 5.4 One of the first images seen in the permanent exhibition space of the United States Holocaust Memorial Museum in Washington, D.C. The high-contrast lighting emphasizes the images and enhances emotional responses from visitors to the museum. U.S. Holocaust Memorial Museum. The views or opinions expressed in this book and the context in which the images are used, do not necessarily reflect the views or policy of, nor imply approval or endorsement by, the United States Holocaust Memorial Museum.

the images and enhances the viewer's emotional response.

The physiological and psychological effects of lighting on people should be applied to the design of the environment. Considerations should include the design of a layered lighting system, layout, physical attributes of the space, and ergonomic factors.

The effects of illumination on vision are discussed in previous chapters in this textbook and should serve as background to the information covered in this chapter. An overview of the vision process is presented in Chapter 1, whereas Chapter 2 reviews the subjective experience of brightness. Generally, the effects of illumination are dependent

upon subjective responses, the context of the situation, personal vision attributes, type of light source, directional qualities of light, and characteristics of elements of the design.

## PHYSIOLOGICAL FACTORS

The person-in-environment system examines the interaction between an individual's health and the natural and built environments. Daylight and electrical light are elements of the natural and built environments, respectively, that can affect health. The health of the world's growing senior population and their age-related vision changes are growing concerns. According to U.S. Census Bureau's International Data Base, by the year 2050 the world will have three times the number of people 65 years and older.

### Lighting Effects on Health

**Photobiology** is the science that examines the interaction of light and living organisms (http://www.pol-us.net, 2003). Research indicates that lighting has negative and positive effects on a person's health. Some of the negative effects from bad lighting include eyestrain, headaches, dizziness, skin cancer, and premature aging of skin and eyes. Individuals with epilepsy may experience seizures when exposed to flickering lights. Only a very small percentage of the population can detect flicker in a properly operating discharge lamp, but some groups have difficulties with such lamps. Kleeman (1981) found that fluorescent lighting affected hyperactive children by causing nutritional problems and a reduced attention span.

Autistic children have been found to be sensitive to variances in light output, especially when the changes are abrupt. The rapidly growing increase in the number of children diagnosed with autism presents a very serious analysis of the lighting that is used in classrooms. According to the U.S. Department of Education from 2001–2002 to 2006–2007 autism in children three to 21 years old rose from 0.2 to 0.5 percent of enrollment.

Some diseases or medications can cause an individual to be more sensitive to high illumination levels. Research is exploring the effects of lighting on the growth, weight gain, and development of infants (Figueiro, M. G., Applemen, K., Bullough, J. D., Rea, M. S., 2006; Quinn, Shin, Maguire, and Stone, 1999; Reynolds, Hardy, Kennedy, Spencer, van Heuven, and Fielder, 1998; Phelps and Watts, 1997).

## Photomedicine

Photomedicine is the science dedicated to using light to improve human health. Some of the positive effects of light on people are derived from the body's production of Vitamin D, which aids in the absorption of calcium. This can help to prevent osteoporosis and rickets. Ultraviolet light is used to cure jaundice in infants. In addition, the medical profession is using light therapy as a means of curing certain forms of cancer, leukemia, skin conditions, and sleep disorders and depression in older adults.

Light is also being used to regulate hormones, improve growth in children, and enhance the immune system. Research is examining the possibility that light can even affect biological functions through means other than just vision. A newly discovered photoreceptive mechanism in the eye could lead to a better understanding of the effects of illumination on biological and psychological functions.

Light therapy has been successful in helping to regulate the biological clock associated with the body's circadian rhythm (Rea, Bierman, Figueiro, & Bullough, 2008; Rea, Rea, & Bullough, 2006; National Mental Health Association, 2003; Rea, 2002; Rea, Bullough, and Figueiro, 2002; Rea, Figueiro, and Bullough, 2002). The circadian rhythm coordinates bodily functions for waking and sleeping, and affects hormone levels and metabolic processes. High levels of illumination are required to initiate the circadian process, and lower light levels trigger the production of melatonin, a hormone required for sleeping.

People who experience jet lag or work night shifts often have difficulty regulating their circadian rhythms. The role of light on disrupting or maintaining circadian rhythm is a research area at the Lighting Research Center (LRC). Other topics include human cancer development, productivity, core body temperature, alertness, and jet lag (Figueiro, September 2005; Figueiro, May 2005; Figueiro, 2003; Figueiro and Stevens, 2002; Lockley, 2002; Stevens, 2002).

Dr. Mariana G. Figueiro of the Lighting Research Center at Rensselaer Polytechnic Institute (May 2005) reported that exposure to blue light for two hours (4:30 p.m. to 6:30 p.m.) could be a viable treatment for improving sleep consolidation and efficiency in individuals with Alzheimer's disease as well as older adults. Figueiro (September 2005) also found that poorly designed night-lighting disrupted people living in senior health care facilities. Fluorescent lamp fixtures located above their beds were a problem when the nurses turned the lights on during the evening checks.

To eliminate the bright light source, which disrupted the circadian system, Figueiro conducted a study that modified the lighting plan. In four bedrooms motion-sensor-controlled amber-colored LEDs were installed under their beds, around doorways, above the bathroom sinks, and next to the toilets (Figure 5.5).

Figueiro selected LEDs due to their energy-efficiency, and the amber color was used because the color cost less than white LEDs and the hue resembled incandescent lamps. The study revealed that after the night-lighting installation all of the residents reported that the colored lights did not wake them up when the nurses came in their rooms, the color was comfortable when they went to the bathroom, and they liked the color. Most of the staff (81 percent) believed the lighting was adequate for bed checks and all of the staff thought it was convenient to have the lighting on motion sensors.

For the most part, problems associated with regulating circadian rhythms did not exist prior to electrical lighting because people functioned with the earth's natural clock of daylight and evening hours. Electrical lighting allows people to maintain high levels of illumination 24 hours a day, every day of the year. Most of the effects resulting from this are still unknown.

(a)

(b)

(c)

FIGURE 5.5A–C Dr. Mariana G. Figueiro of the Lighting Research Center at Rensselaer Polytechnic Institute conducted a study in a senior health care facility that involved modifying lighting by eliminating bright light sources and replacing them with motion sensor controlled amber-colored LEDs. (Rensselaer Polytechnic Institute's Lighting Research Center.)

## Light Therapy and SAD

Problems related to circadian rhythms are associated with **seasonal affective disorder (SAD)**, which is a condition associated with an individual's inadequate exposure to sunlight. Some of the effects of SAD are depression, weight gain, lack of concentration, and sleeplessness. Many people experience SAD during the winter months when the days are shortest. This is especially problematic for people living in the northern region of the northern hemisphere because of the few hours of sunlight. Research indicates that females are more likely to experience SAD than males. People with SAD are encouraged to spend more time outdoors, preferably on sunny days, early in the day.

Some physicians will prescribe light therapy to alleviate SAD. This treatment consists of exposure to high levels of illumination at the start of the day. Light therapy has also been helpful in regulating sleep patterns with dementia patients (Mishimia, Okawa, Hiskikawa, Hozumi, Hori, and Takashi, 1994; Satlin, Volicer, Ross, Herz, and Campbell, 1992). People who have a severe case of SAD need a professional diagnosis of the disease because medication may be needed. SAD can be very serious, in extreme cases even resulting in suicide.

## PSYCHOLOGICAL FACTORS

Wapner and Demick (2002) indicate that the person-in-environment system includes the effect of the environment on the psychological well-being of individuals as well as its effect on interpersonal relations. Lighting research has focused on the role of illumination in these factors, including characteristics of natural and electrical light sources and their behavioral and psychological effects on people. For example, Park and Farr (2007) conducted a cross-cultural comparison of "The Effects of Lighting on Consumers' Emotions and Behavioral Intentions in a Retail Environment." The study revealed that with respect to color rendering and color temperatures there were perceptual differences between American and Korean customers. Warm lighting encouraged Americans to enter a store and the Koreans in the study preferred cool lights.

Chapter 3 of this book discusses research studies that found positive effects of daylight on activities in hospitals, schools, and retail stores (Mistrick & Sarkar, 2005; Heschong, 2003; Boyce, 2003; Wu and Ng, 2003; Heschong, 2001; Heschong, 1999; Heschong, 1997) (Figure 5.6). In addition, Beauchemin and Hays (1996) found that individuals in psychiatric units who had rooms with natural daylight stayed approximately three days less than patients living with electrical light sources.

Researchers have been interested in understanding which characteristics of electrical light sources affect people. The topics investigated include specific lamps, color-rendering index, color temperature, quantity and intensity of light, spectral composition, and distribution patterns. Some studies have explored lighting effects on certain groups, such as people with Alzheimer's disease, cancer, and AIDS, as well as infants and the elderly (Figueiro, Rea, & Eggleston, 2003; Boyce, 2003; Figueiro, Eggleston, and Rea, 2002; Graham and Michel, 2003; Miller, 2002; Noelle-Waggoner, 2002).

FIGURE 5.6 The Morgan Library and Museum in New York City by Renzo Piano Building Workshop (RPBW) is an excellent example of daylighting in a study environment. (© Michel Denance.)

In examining the effects of lighting on behavior, research has focused on the performance of office workers, on cognitive processes, and on wayfinding. The types of psychological effects studied include attitude, stress, satisfaction, interpersonal communication, perception of space, motivation, control, and stimulation. The following two sections provide a summary of the effects of lighting on the behavior and psychology of people. For additional research studies, refer to the "References" and "Resources" lists at the end of this chapter.

## LIGHTING EFFECTS ON BEHAVIOR

Some of the earliest lighting research investigated the effects of quantity of light on productivity in the workplace (Blackwell, 1946; Boynton and Boss, 1971; Boyce, 1973; Hughes and McNelis, 1978; Simonson and Brozek, 1948; Weston, 1962) (Figure 5.7). At that time, electrical light sources were relatively

new, and the lighting industry was trying to persuade employers to invest in lighting systems. The cost–benefit approach served as a rationale; research studies demonstrated that quality lighting improved worker productivity, and the increase in performance offset the cost of the lighting system.

Owing to the interdependence of the many factors that can affect performance, including noise, stress, ambient temperature, and daylight, current research regarding the effect of lighting on productivity is inconclusive. Some studies have demonstrated that improved performance may be the result of a higher level of satisfaction with working conditions, rather than a direct relationship between lighting and productivity (Boyce, Akashi, Hunter, & Bullough, 2003; Ducker, 1999; Isen, Daubman, & Nowicki, 1987). Research has indicated that control over one's environment, including lighting, is a significant factor in employee

FIGURE 5.7 The platinum-certified LEED USGBC headquarters in Washington, D.C., is an excellent example of daylighting in offices. Notice how the glass partitions enable daylight to illuminate the entire office. The colored glass provides visual interest and from a safety perspective alerts people to the glass partitions. (Courtesy of U.S. Green Building Council/Photographer: Eric Laignel.)

satisfaction (Moore et al., 2004; Boyce, 2003; Boyce, Eklund, & Simpson, 2000; Hedge, Erickson, & Rubin, 1992; Sherrod and Cohen, 1979; Veitch & Newsham, 1998; Veitch & Newsham, 1999). Moreover, research has suggested that when individuals can control their lighting, they tend to lower the illumination to levels that are below established foot-candle levels, thus conserving energy.

In an attempt to determine the direct effect of illumination on performance, research studies have examined specific characteristics of lighting systems, including fluorescent lamps, ballasts, types of luminaire, and controls.

Extensive research on the effect of full-spectrum fluorescent lamps generally indicates that there is no effect on performance or mood (Berry, 1983; Boray, Gifford, & Rosenblood, 1989; Food and Drug Administration, 1986; Veitch, 1997; Veitch & McColl, 1995; Veitch, Gifford, & Hine, 1991). However, some studies do suggest that fluorescent light flicker can increase headaches and stress (Jaén et el., 2005; Boyce, 2003; Veitch & McColl, 2001; Kuller & Laike, 1998; Wilkins, Nimmo-Smith, Slater, & Bedocs, 1989). Veitch & Newsham (1998) found that the performance of clerical workers was improved by using electronic, rather than magnetic, ballasts in the workplace. Moreover, the use of electronic ballasts reduced headaches (Wilkins et al., 1989).

In addition to eliminating light flicker, electronic ballasts are preferred because they operate more quietly than magnetic ones. Many studies have shown a significant relationship between noise and quality of worker performance (Boyce, 2003; Banbury, Macken, Tremblay, & Jones, 2001; Evans &

Cohen, 1987; Gawron, 1982; Hygge, 1991; Hygge & Knez, 2001; Nelson, Nilsson, & Johnson, 1984). Certain types of luminaires might also contribute to noise in an environment because fixtures made from hard materials and having relatively large flat surfaces can reflect sound.

Generally, research indicates that worker performance is unaffected by type of luminaire and light distribution patterns (Eklund, Boyce, & Simpson, 2000; Veitch & Newsham, 1998). However, a study conducted in an office building in Albany, New York revealed that employees were most comfortable with direct/indirect luminaires, wallwashing, and control of the lighting above their workstation (Light Right Consortium, 2004) (Figures 5.8 a–e). Under these lighting conditions employees also were more satisfied with their work and the office environment.

Studies have also demonstrated that the elimination of glare reflected from glossy work surfaces and proper lighting for a computer **visual display terminal (VDT)** are required to enhance worker productivity (Japuntich, 2001; Clark, 2001; National Lighting Bureau, 1988). To reduce eyestrain and dry eyes, physicians recommend frequent eye movement. This can be accomplished by creating an interesting environment around the VDT screen and varying illumination levels.

## Universal Design

Lighting systems should be planned to accommodate all people, whenever possible, without modifications. This can be accomplished by specifying a lighting plan that meets the physical and psychological needs of the users of the space.

**FIGURE 5.8A** One of the lighting plans used in a study in Albany, New York to determine what type of lighting was most comfortable to employees. This plan focused on the array of parabolic-louvered luminaires. Compare this interior to the images in Figures 5.8b and c. (Photos a–e: The Light Right Consortium project is managed by Pacific Northwest National Laboratory, operated by Battelle for the U.S. Department of Energy.)

**FIGURE 5.8B** One of the lighting plans used in the study described in Figure 5.8a. This plan focused on direct/indirect luminaires and wall-washing. Compare this interior to the images in Figures 5.8a and c.

**FIGURE 5.8C** One of the lighting plans used in the study described in Figure 5.8a. This plan focused on direct/indirect luminaires, wall-washing, and portable fixtures on the desks. Compare this interior to the images in Figures 5.8a and b.

**FIGURE 5.8D** One of the lighting plans used in the study described in Figure 5.8a. This plan in the hallway focused on the array of parabolic-louvered luminaires. Compare this interior to the image in Figure 5.8e.

**FIGURE 5.8E** One of the lighting plans used in the study described in Figure 5.8a. This plan in the hallway focused on indirect luminaires. Compare this interior to the image in Figure 5.8d.

## PHYSICAL ENVIRONMENT

A quality lighting environment reflects the principles of **universal design**. To be able to design environments that meet the needs and abilities of all people, an interior designer should review the current literature. Research studies are invaluable in providing guidance and recommendations for effective environments.

There are many aspects of lighting that should be considered when applying the principles of universal design, including visual acuity, manual dexterity, controls, and the placement of luminaires, switches, and outlets. Visual acuity is affected by illumination level, type of lamp, distribution, color temperature, color rendering, ballast, and the ability to control lighting. The needs of individuals with visual impairments and diseases must be addressed in order to ensure visual acuity (Figures 5.9a and 5.9b). Specifying value contrasts—such as white/black—for tasks can also enhance visual acuity.

The operation of wall switches and luminaires should be intuitive and easy for users. Generally, rocker or touch switches are the easiest; devices that have to be pinched or twisted should be avoided. Switches and dimmers should be accessible and simple to operate. Avoid portable luminaires with switching mechanisms on the cord.

Luminaires that allow the user to change the direction of the light source should be weighted, and the shade should be designed to prevent burns from the heat from the lamp. Properly adjusted timed switches and occupancy sensor controls are important devices for universal design.

Luminaires, switches, and outlets should be placed so as to be accessible to people with

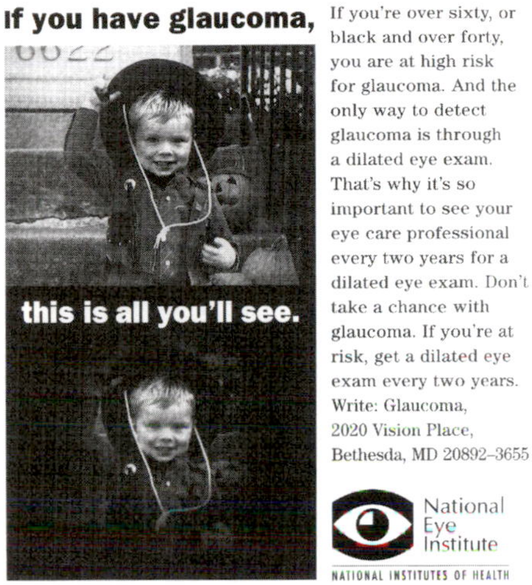

**FIGURE 5.9A** Vision that is impaired due to glaucoma. (National Eye Institute, National Institutes of Health.)

**FIGURE 5.9B** Vision that is impaired due to macular degeneration. (National Eye Institute, National Institutes of Health.)

disabilities, including individuals in wheelchairs. Luminaires should always be positioned to avoid shadows on work surfaces and direct views to lamps must be avoided from standing and seated positions. Portable luminaires designed to allow the user to adjust the direction or control the level of illumination should be

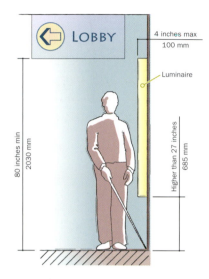

FIGURE 5.10 Elevation illustrating American Disability Act (ADA) (2003) guidelines for wall-mounted luminaires.

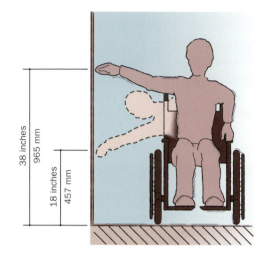

FIGURE 5.11 Elevation illustrating American Disability Act (ADA) (2003) guidelines for wall switches and outlets.

located within a convenient distance of the user; the average range of reach is 24 inches (610 mm).

The Americans with Disabilities Act (ADA) (2003) specifies that wall-mounted luminaires mounted between 27 inches and 80 inches (685 mm and 2030 mm) above a finished floor (AFF) should not extend more than 4 inches (100 mm) from the wall (Figure 5.10). Luminaires at or below 27 inches (685 mm) AFF may protrude any amount. The lowest element of a suspended luminaire should allow for 80 inches (2030 mm) of clear headroom. Freestanding luminaires mounted on posts may overhang 12 inches (305 mm) horizontally and 27 inches to 80 inches (685 mm to 2030 mm) AFF.

Wall switches and outlets should be mounted at a level accessible to people standing or sitting in a wheelchair (Figure

5.11). ADA specifies that electrical receptacles on walls shall be mounted no less than 15 inches (380 mm) AFF; however, in following the principles of universal design, a convenient location for wall switches and outlets is 38 inches and 18 inches (965 and 457 mm) AFF, respectively. With respect to intensity of illumination, the ADA requirements for signage are in the range of 100 to 300 lux (10 fc to 30 fc), and a minimum of 50 lux (5 fc) for elevator thresholds.

Designers should apply the results of research to lighting planning. Lighting research is a relatively new field of study and is continuously improving and expanding. Thus, to specify a lighting environment that addresses the health, behavior, emotions, and perceptions of people, an interior designer should always refer to the most current research. In analyzing the research, it is critical to scrutinize the specifics of a study. Each study is conducted with specific subjects and parameters, and can be applied to practice only when the conditions of the research study are similar to those of the interior project on which a designer is working. The material discussed in this chapter and the preceding chapters in this textbook should be applied to the lighting design process covered in Chapters 9 and 10.

# Illumination, Human Health and Behavior, and LEED Certification

For a checklist of how you can apply illumination and human health and behavior in creating a LEED-certified building, see Box 5.1.

---

**BOX 5.1 Illumination and Human Factors and LEED Certification**

You can put the content of this chapter to work for you to create LEED-certified buildings by considering the following strategies:

o To optimize user satisfaction and productivity, enhance the relationships between lighting and people, their health, behavior, physical characteristics, and the built environment.

o Maximize user satisfaction with an environment and productivity by optimizing daylighting, providing individual lighting controls, ensuring views to the outdoors, and individualized thermal comfort.

o Maximize user satisfaction by selecting appropriate controls for daylighting, occupancy, schedules, and thermal comfort.

o Monitor research related to the effects of daylighting and electrical sources on health, productivity, behavior, and well-being.

**TABLE BOX 5.1 LEED Categories Related to Illumination and Human Factors**

LEED CREDIT CATEGORIES RELATED TO CONENT IN CHAPTER 5

| |
|---|
| IEQ Credit 6.1: Controllability of Systems—Lighting |
| IEQ Credit 6.2: Controllability of Systems—Thermal Comfort |
| IEQ Credit 7.1: Thermal Comfort—Design |
| IEQ Credit 7.2: Thermal Comfort—Verification |
| IEQ Credit 8.1: Daylight and Views—Daylight |
| IEQ Credit 8.2: Daylight and Views—Views for Seated Spaces |
| ID (Innovation in Design) Credit 1: Innovation in Design |

Source: USGBC (2009). *LEED reference guide for green interior design and construction.* Washington, D.C.: U.S. Green Building Council.

# Fundamental Projects

**1. Human Factors Research Project**

Select five photographs of the interiors of public places. For each space identify the purpose of the space, the most frequent users, and the anticipated behavioral response to the lighting environment. Summarize your results in a written report and include photographs.

**2. Research Design Project**

Research a disease that affects the psychological and physical needs of the individuals who have it. Write an essay that includes specific lighting requirements for individuals with the disease. Illustrations of luminaires should be included.

# Application Project

**1. Human Factors Research Project**

Interview people in an office, restaurant, retail store, and health care facility to determine their perceptions of the interior. Analyze the results and determine the positive and negative attributes of each space. Summarize the results in a written report and include illustrations, photographs, or sketches.

# Summary

○ The person-in-environment system examines the interaction between an individual's health and the natural and built environments.

○ Research indicates that lighting can have both negative and positive effects on a person's health. Some of the negative effects from lighting include eyestrain, headaches, dizziness, skin cancer, and aging of skin and eyes.

○ Light therapy has been successful in helping to regulate the biological clock associated with the body's circadian rhythm.

○ Lighting research has focused on the characteristics of natural and electrical light sources and their behavioral and psychological effects on people. Topics studied include specific types of lamps, CRI, color temperature, quantity and intensity of light, spectral composition, and distribution patterns.

○ To determine the effect of illumination on performance, research studies have examined specific characteristics of elements of lighting systems, including fluorescent lamps, ballasts, and types of luminaire.

○ A quality lighting environment reflects the principles of universal design. Lighting systems should be planned to accommodate all people, whenever possible, without modifications.

# References

Boyce, P. R. (2003). *Human factors in lighting* (2nd ed.). New York: Taylor & Francis.

Figueiro, M. G. (2005). Research matters. The bright side of blue light. *Lighting Design and Application (LD+A), 35*(5), 16–18.

Figueiro, M. G. (2005). Research matters. The bright side of night-lighting. *Lighting Design and Application (LD+A), 35*(9), 18–20.

Figueiro, M. G. (2003). Research recap: Circadian rhythm. *Lighting Design and Application (LD+A), 33*(2), 17–18.

Figueiro, M. G., Applemen, K., Bullough, J. D., & Rea, M. S. (2006). A discussion of recommended standards for lighting in the newborn intensive care unit. *Journal of Perinatology, 26* (Oct. 1), S19–S26.

Figueiro, M. G., Rea, M. S., & Eggleston, G. (2003). Light therapy and Alzheimer's Disease. Sleep Review. *The Journal for Sleep Specialists, 4*(1), 1–4.

Heschong Mahone Group (HMG) (2003). *Windows and offices: A study of office worker performance and the indoor environment—CEC PIER 2003.*

## KEY TERMS

| | | |
|---|---|---|
| evidence-based design (EBD) | seasonal affective disorder (SAD) | universal design |
| nanotechnology | smart textiles | visual display terminal (VDT) |
| photobiology | | |

For the California Energy Commission's Public Interest Energy Research (PIER) Program.

Heschong Mahone Group (HMG) (2003). *Windows and classrooms: A study of student performance and the indoor environment—CEC PIER 2003*. For the California Energy Commission's Public Interest Energy Research (PIER) Program.

Heschong Mahone Group (HMG) (2003). *Daylight and retail sales*. For the California Energy Commission's Public Interest Energy Research (PIER) Program.

Heschong Mahone Group (HMG) (2001). *Re-analysis report: Daylighting in schools, additional analysis—CEC PIER*. For the California Energy Commission's Public Interest Energy Research (PIER) Program.

Jaén, M., Sandoval, J., & Colombo, E. (2005). Office workers visual performance and temporal modulation of fluorescent lighting. LEUKOS. *Journal of the Illuminating Society of North America 1*(4), 27–46.

Light Right Consortium (2004). *Albany Lab Study*. www.lightright.org/research/albany_study.htm

Mistrick, R., & Sarkar, A. (2005). A study of daylight-responsive photosensor control in five daylighted classrooms. LEUKOS. *Journal of the Illuminating Society of North America, 1*(3), 51–74.

Moore, T., Carter, D. J., & Slater, A. (2004). A study of opinion in offices with and without user controlled lighting. *Lighting Research Journal, 36*(2), 131–146.

Park, N., & Farr, C. A. (2007). The effects of lighting on consumers' emotions and behavioral intentions in a retail environment: A cross-cultural comparison. *Journal of Interior Design, 33*(1).

Rea, M. S., Bierman, A., Figueiro, M. G., & Bullough, J. D. (2008). A new approach to understanding the impact of circadian disruption on human health. *Journal of Circadian Rhythms, (6)*7.

Rea, M. S., Rea, J. D., & Bullough, J. D. (2006). Circadian effectiveness on two polychromatic lights in suppressing human nocturnal melaton. *Neuroscience Letters 4*(6), 293–297.

Smith F. K., & Bertolone, F. J. (1986). *iiii*. New York: Whitney Library of Design.

Steffy, G. R. (1990). *Architectural lighting design*. New York: Van Nostrand Reinhold.

Veitch, J., & Newsham, G. (1998). Lighting quality and energy-efficiency effects on task performance, mood, health, satisfaction, and comfort. *Journal of the Illuminating Engineering Society, 27*(1), 107.

Ward, L. G., & Shakespeare, R. A. (1998). *Rendering with radiance: The art and science of lighting visualization*. San Francisco: Morgan Kaufmann.

Watson, L. (1977). *Lighting design handbook*. New York: McGraw-Hill.

# Resources

Benya, J., Heschong, L., McGowan, T., Miller, N., & Rubinstein, F. (2001). *Advanced lighting guidelines*. White Salmon, WA: New Buildings Institute.

Boyce, P. N., Eklund, N., & Simpson, S. (2000). Individual lighting control: Task performance, mood and illuminance. *Journal of the Illuminating Engineering Society, 29*(1), 131–142.

Illuminating Engineering Society of North America (IESNA) (2011). *IESNA lighting handbook* (10th ed.). New York: Illuminating Engineering Society of North America.

Mistrick, R., & Sarkar, A. (2005). A study of daylight-responsive photosensor control in five daylighted classrooms. LEUKOS. *Journal of the Illuminating Society of North America, 1*(3), 51–74.

# 6 Lighting Systems: Luminaires

Earlier in this book, we saw how lamps are important elements of a lighting system. In this chapter, we review another major component of the system—luminaires. In addition to exploring the role of luminaires in an interdependent system, this chapter demonstrates how the selection and the placement of luminaires affect the consumption of energy, quality of lighting, quantity of illumination, and the directional effects of lighting.

Selecting efficient luminaires is essential to an energy-efficient lighting system. A significant amount of light can be blocked by the design of a luminaire. Some luminaires can prevent approximately 50 percent of the light that is produced by the lamps. An interior designer must understand all the interdependent elements of the lighting system and have a working knowledge of the products available to successfully plan a quality lighting environment. This chapter focuses on luminaires for installation in ceilings, walls, floors, architectural elements, or cabinetry as well as portable luminaires and innovative approaches to fixtures (Figure 6.1).

The design of luminaires blends science with art to resolve many of the contrasting characteristics of illumination, such as directing light up or down, flooding a space with light, or spotlighting a small art piece on a table. Many industrial designers, architects, and interior designers have

**OBJECTIVES**

o Identify primary ways to distribute light: direct, indirect, semi-direct, semi-indirect, and diffused

o Understand how luminaires are designed to distribute light

o Understand the advantages and disadvantages of the major categories of luminaires, including recessed, surface-mounted, suspended, track, structural, and furniture-integrated units

o Apply an understanding of luminaires to the specification and placement of fixtures in an environment

o Identify and apply selection criteria to the specification and placement of luminaires in an interior

FIGURE 6.1 Employees in an office building are aware of weather conditions by observing color changes in the suspended light globes. Designed by Jason Bruges, the globes in *Pixel Cloud* (2007) respond to environmental conditions in real-time. (*Pixel Cloud* by Jason Bruges Studio 2007 for Allen and Overy, Bishops Square, London.)

the primary ways in which light is distributed: (a) direct, (b) indirect, (c) semi-direct, (d) semi-indirect, and (e) diffused (Figures 6.3 a–e). In **direct luminaires**, distribution occurs when at least 90 percent of the illumination is downward. **Indirect luminaires** distribute at least 90 percent of the light toward the ceiling. **Semi-direct luminaires** distribute most of the illumination downward, and some of the light upward. **Semi-indirect** fixtures distribute most of the illumination upward, and some of the light downward. **Diffused luminaires** distribute illumination in all directions.

been challenged to design a luminaire that successfully addresses these issues. Two interior elements that often define a designer are luminaires and chairs. Charles Rennie Mackintosh is an excellent example of a designer who is well known for the design of his chairs and luminaires (Figure 6.2).

The primary factors affecting the distribution of illumination are the shape of the luminaire, its materials and finishes, the location and size of the aperture, and the mounting position. Chapter 2 provides examples of how the shape, materials, and finish affect the directional effects of lighting. The location of the aperture, materials, and mounting position determine

FIGURE 6.2 A bedroom in Hill House, Helensburgh, UK designed by Charles Rennie Mackintosh illustrates his custom-designed pieces, including the furniture and luminaires. (© Thomas A. Heinz/CORBIS.)

(a)

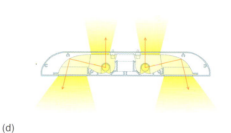

(b)

FIGURE 6.3A AND B The (a) suspended luminaires in this office provide direct illumination in the space. The (b) drawing illustrates how light is distributed from the fixtures. (Photo courtesy of Selux Corporation.)

(c)

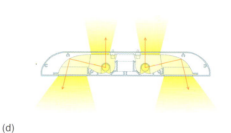

(d)

FIGURE 6.3C AND D An example of a (c) semi-indirect luminaire (80 percent uplight/20 percent downlight) and a (d) drawing that shows how light is distributed from the fixture. Design Studio & Partners. (Images by kind permission of iGuzzini illuminazione.)

FIGURE 6.3E Light is diffused through the mulberry paper used in the Akari luminaires by Isamu Noguchi. The fixtures are in the permanent collection of many museums. (The Isamu Noguchi Foundation and Garden Museum.)

# Luminaire Types

Major categories of luminaires include recessed, surface-mounted, suspended, track, structural, furniture-integrated units, and portable. These luminaires are designed primarily for incandescent, fluorescent, high-intensity discharge (HID) lamps, light-emitting diodes (LEDs), and they are available in a variety of sizes, shapes, and materials. Most of these luminaires can be used for general, task, and accent lighting. Some manufacturers design a luminaire for multiple applications, such as a pendant, ceiling mount, and sconce. Such luminaires make it possible to employ various lighting techniques while maintaining unity of design.

There are large manufacturers who mass-produce luminaires, but there are also numerous small companies that produce luminaires, some by hand (Figure 6.4). Italian

**FIGURE 6.4** An excellent example of luminaires made by hand is the glass rotunda chandelier (1999) by Dale Chihuly located in the Victoria and Albert Museum, London.

designers have a reputation for creating some of the most creative and classical pieces. The quality of construction and materials varies among manufacturers and product lines. To ensure a quality lighting environment, interior designers must be aware of the characteristics of the product they are specifying. This knowledge can be acquired by visiting manufacturer showrooms, discussing product attributes with manufacturer representatives, attending educational seminars, and reading current articles in trade journals.

As described in the previous chapter, surveying product updates should include

**FIGURE 6.5B** A textile woven with fiber optics. (Optic Fibres/Barbara Jensen/ Photo: Jan Berg.)

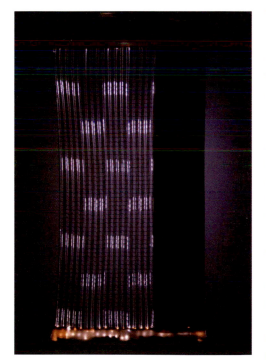

**FIGURE 6.5A** This *Energy Curtain* has solar cells that absorb energy during the day and then provide light in the evening. (Interactive Institute.)

nontraditional resources, such as innovative textiles. In addition to interactive textiles that illuminate in response to the touch or presence of people, there are textiles that are woven with extremely thin fiber optics, LEDs, and solar cells (Figures 6.5a and 6.5b). Woven shades have solar shades that collect energy during the day and then provide illumination during the evening. Niels van Eijk designed the Bobbin Lace Lamp that was made by interlacing fiber optics with traditional lace-making techniques (Figure 6.6). The possibilities are endless, and it is up to designers to be aware of new technological developments and understand how to apply the innovations to practice.

## RECESSED LUMINAIRES

**Recessed luminaires** are fixtures that are installed above a sheetrock or suspended-grid ceiling (Figure 6.7). Due to the variety of ceiling thicknesses and materials, refer to

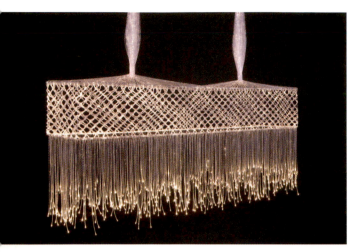

FIGURE 6.6 Niels van Eijk designed the *Bobbin Lace Lamp* by interlacing fiber optics with traditional lace-making techniques. (Design: Van Eijk & Van der Lubbe, www.ons-adres.nl; distribution: Quasar Holland, www.quasar.nl.)

FIGURE 6.7 A suspended-grid ceiling illustrating the installation of recessed luminaires. (© Bill Varie/Alamy.)

the luminaire manufacturers' specifications to make sure a specific recessed luminaire can be installed in the ceiling. **IC-rated (insulation contact) fixtures** are able to be in contact with insulation. **AT-rated (airtight) fixtures** are designed to reduce the

loss of heat or cold through a ceiling and attics. Recent developments in the design of recessed luminaires allow a flangeless installation, so that the ceiling surface is flush with the aperture of the recessed fixture. The installation has a clean appearance and helps to conceal the fixture (Figure 6.8). Recessed luminaires whose housing is partly above and partly below the ceiling are called **semi-recessed luminaires**.

FIGURE 6.8 Recessed fixtures with a clean appearance on the finished ceiling. (© Richard Bryant/Arcaid/Corbis.)

A recessed luminaire generally creates direct lighting in a space. The most common recessed luminaires are troffers, downlights, wall wash, and accent. Common sizes for recessed troffers are 6″ to 8″ × 4′ (15 to 20 cm × 122 cm), 1′ × 4′ (31 cm × 122 cm), 2′ × 2′ (61 cm × 61 cm), and 2′ × 4′ (61 cm × 122 cm). These sizes accommodate the various lengths of fluorescent lamps. The interior of a troffer is generally painted white or has a specular metal reflector, whereas the most common devices at the aperture are acrylic prismatic lenses and parabolic louvers. Parabolic louvers with large cell depths (1.5 to 4 inches or 4 to 10 cm) have higher luminaire efficiency than smaller cells because the large cells have more surfaces with high reflectance.

To improve the distribution of light emitted from small fluorescent lamps, such as the T5 HE, manufacturers have developed troffers that results in more illuminance on vertical surfaces, including walls (Figure 6.9). As discussed in Chapter 5, illuminating these surfaces was pleasing to office workers and luminaires that are able to illuminate multiple surfaces may reduce the number of fixtures that are required in an area.

## Downlights or High Hats

**Recessed downlights** are also referred to as **high hats** or cans. The most common shapes for recessed downlights are round and square. The size of a downlight aperture can be as small as 2 inches (5 cm). The finish applied to the rim affects the efficiency of the luminaire, with white and aluminum finishes providing the highest luminaire efficiency. Dark-colored and black rims have lower luminaire efficiency

**FIGURE 6.9** As shown with the bright wall in the back of the room these recessed fixtures illuminate the entire volume of space. (© Lithonia Lighting.)

ratings, but the reflectance values help to reduce glare. The efficiency of a downlight is also affected by the existence of a reflector in the luminaire. To maximize the lumens emitted from downlights without reflectors, reflector lamps should be specified.

The type of device used at the aperture affects the light distribution from downlights. In general, light emitted from a downlight with a bare opening will be dependent upon the type of lamp. For example, a narrow halogen spot lamp mounted in a recessed downlight will emit a narrow beam of light.

Recessed downlights with a bare opening can cause discomfort or disability glare because of the exposed lamp. There are many devices available for this purpose, including baffles, louvers, and specialized lenses. Special recessed luminaires are designed for floor installations. These recessed uplight luminaires include a floor-mount plate and are often used to enhance architectural details.

Recessed downlights may also be designed to direct light to a vertical surface. For grazing techniques, the distance from the downlight to the wall should be approximately 6 to 8 inches (15 to 20 cm). The distance between downlights depends upon whether a scalloped pattern on the wall is considered desirable; luminaires that are close together are less likely to create a scalloped pattern.

Recessed linear or round wall washers distribute light over a large area on a wall (Figure 6.10). In a recessed wall washer a reflector or an angled lens causes the light to strike the wall. Wall washer luminaires should be located at least 30 inches (76 cm) from the wall to prevent hot spots. To avoid scalloped patterns on the wall, the distance from the luminaire to the wall and between luminaires should be approximately one-third the height of the ceiling.

Recessed accent or spot downlights emit a narrow beam of light. Recessed accent downlights have an aiming angle of 30 to 45 degrees, can rotate at least 350 degrees, and are either fixed or adjustable. Common directional trims for recessed accent downlights include slotted, baffled, eyeball, and pinhole apertures (Figures 6.11a–c).

Multiple recessed luminaires have two to six spots in one rectangular opening (Figure 6.12), enabling them to spotlight three different points of emphasis with only one hole in the ceiling. Recessed fixtures are available that can be adjusted for multiple purposes, such as downlighting, wallwashing, or accent lighting. For interiors with angled ceilings, recessed, sloped-ceiling luminaires can be used to distribute light downward, provide a wall-wash effect, or spotlight objects.

## Recessed Luminaires: Advantages and Disadvantages

One advantage of recessed luminaires is that they can direct light to a variety of locations while maintaining the appearance of a clean ceiling line, often making a space appear larger. Recessed luminaires can provide task lighting for an area that has a decorative luminaire. Miniature recessed luminaires can be hidden to promote an element of mystery. Some disadvantages of recessed lighting include the clearance space required for

(a)

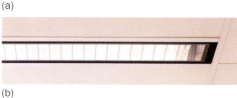

(b)

FIGURE 6.10 A recessed linear wall washer fixture illuminates the wall on the left side of this reception area. As shown in the (b) enlarged photograph of the fixture an asymmetric reflector system directs light to the wall. (Photo [reception area]: Peerless Lighting; photo [fixture]: Ron Solomon Photography.)

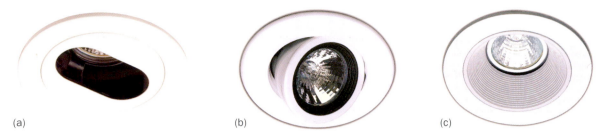

(a)        (b)        (c)

FIGURE 6.11A A slotted adjustable wall wash in a recessed accent downlight. Shown with a ceramic metal halide MR16 lamp. (Photographs courtesy Con-Tech Lighting.)

FIGURE 6.11B A surface adjustable eyeball with a black baffle in a recessed accent downlight. Shown with a ceramic metal halide MR16 lamp. (Photographs courtesy Con-Tech Lighting.)

FIGURE 6.11C An adjustable baffle in a recessed accent downlight. Shown with a ceramic metal halide MR16 lamp. (Photographs courtesy Con-Tech Lighting.)

FIGURE 6.12 Multiple recessed luminaires installed in the ceiling. (© Marc Gerritsen/Look Photography/Corbis.)

installation, the need for space allowances between insulation and the housing unit, and the need for ventilation to remove heat. Because of the mounting requirements, the need to accommodate a fire-rated ceiling, and the holes in the ceiling, recessed luminaires should always be planned early in construction.

In addition to the structural mounting requirements, there are other challenges related to recessed luminaires. They must be placed in the proper location to avoid problems associated with direct lighting, including glare and unflattering shadows on people. The fixed distance from the ceiling to an object or surface makes it very important to select a luminaire and lamp that can perform to suit the parameters of the specific site. The removal of recessed luminaires can be costly and disrupts the surface of a finished ceiling. Relamping can also be difficult, especially for rooms with very high ceilings; recessed luminaires designed for front relamping are easier to maintain.

## SURFACE-MOUNT LUMINAIRES

**Surface-mount luminaires** are fixtures that are installed on a ceiling, wall, or floor, or under a shelf or cabinet (Figure 6.13). They are designed for direct, indirect, semi-direct, and diffused lighting. Surface-mount luminaires for ceilings include troffers, downlights, wraparound lens luminaires, and **HID high/ low-bays**. Wraparound lens luminaires emit most of the light from the sides and bottom of the fixture. Close proximity to the ceiling can maximize luminance by reflecting from the ceiling; however, these luminaires can

Surface-mount luminaire installed on the kitchen ceiling. (Mark Dell'Aquila, Eagle Eye Images, Long Beach, CA.)

also cause glare on computer monitors. HID high/low-bay luminaires accommodate metal halide and high-pressure sodium lamps. The aluminum reflector has good optical control and is often used in commercial applications with high ceilings.

Sconces and whiteboard luminaires are some of the most common surface-mount luminaires for walls (Figure 6.14). Sconces are often decorative light sources that provide direct, indirect, semi-direct, semi-indirect, and diffused lighting. For safety purposes, and to comply with the Americans with Disabilities Act (ADA), sconces that are mounted less than 80 inches (203 cm) from the floor should project no more than 4 inches (10 cm) from the wall. The eye-level location of a sconce can easily create discomfort or disability glare. This is especially problematic when sconces are located at the bottom of stairways. An individual coming down the stairs can experience disability glare from viewing the exposed lamps. Exposed lamps can also be a problem when the shielding device for the sconce is a thin, translucent material and the illumination level is high. To help prevent glare, some sconces have diffusers, louvers, baffles, or lenses.

Whiteboard lighting is mounted on a wall and provides direct light on a whiteboard or chalkboard. Generally, fluorescent lamps are used for whiteboard lighting. The internal reflector emits a soft light on the vertical surface without shadows or glare.

Surface-mount luminaires also include fixtures that are installed under a shelf or cabinet. The most common shapes are linear, round, and square. Generally, these luminaires

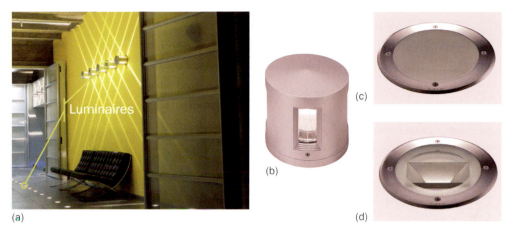

**FIGURE 6.14** Surface-mount luminaires create interesting light and shadow patterns on the wall. Notice the (a) in-ground fixtures that provide a decorative element on the floor and can serve as wayfinding. Note enlarged photographs of the (b) surface fixture and the two types of in-ground fixtures: (c) frosted glass and (d) semi-frosted glass. (Courtesy of Sistemalux http://www.sistemalux.com.)

have fluorescent, halogen, or incandescent lamps. There are also luminaires with LEDs. The punch of light emitted from miniature, surface-mount luminaires is an excellent way to highlight objects on a shelf.

## Surface-Mount Luminaires: Advantages

**Surface-mount luminaires** have the advantage of simultaneously being decorative and providing illumination. The potential to direct and diffuse light provides flexibility in addressing the multiple lighting requirements in an environment. Compared to recessed luminaires, surface-mount fixtures are easier to install. In specifying the location of a surface-mount luminaire, an interior designer generally does not have to consider clearances for insulation or mechanical and plumbing restrictions.

## Surface-Mount Luminaires: Disadvantages

Some of the disadvantages of surface-mount luminaires have to do with the location of the fixtures. Relamping at the ceiling level can be difficult, and removing the luminaire can result in severe damage to finishes and materials. Because a surface-mount luminaire can become a focal point in a room, selection and location of the fixtures must adhere to the principles of design. For example, luminaires should reflect the theme of the design concept, the scale must be appropriate for the shape and size of the room, and the placement of fixtures should be balanced on the ceiling. Some surface-mount luminaires cast a light and shadow pattern on a wall or ceiling, which could negatively distort the appearance of a patterned or textured surface.

## SUSPENDED LUMINAIRES

**Suspended luminaires** are fixtures that are installed on a ceiling and extend into the room by cords, chains, poles, or wires (Figure 6.15). Some luminaires have a mechanism that allows for easy cord-length adjustments. Suspended luminaires can emit direct, indirect, semi-direct, and diffused lighting. The most common suspended luminaires include pendants, chandeliers, ceiling fans, linear fluorescent fixtures (indirect and bidirectional), and luminaires forming an element of a track system. Some of these are for decorative purposes only.

Linear fluorescent luminaires are frequently designed for task lighting. Bidirectional (direct–indirect) luminaires for general or task lighting should have materials, reflectors, baffles, or louvers with reflectance values greater than 90 percent. To avoid hot spots, or glare, suspended luminaires giving indirect light should be mounted at least 18 inches (46 cm) from the ceiling; those in a circulation area should be at

least 80 inches (203 cm) from the floor. The distance from a dining table to the bottom of the luminaire should be 30 inches (76 cm) or more. The height of the ceiling and the scale of the room and the luminaire should determine an appropriate distance.

When the primary use of a suspended luminaire is decorative the design of the fixture must reflect the design concept of the interior and adhere to the principles of design. Because suspended luminaires are generally focal points in an interior and can visually divide the space, they can make an interior appear smaller depending upon the location, size, and material of the luminaire. Suspended luminaires can also be difficult to maintain because of their location and the high accumulation of dirt and dust.

Two important considerations for mounting suspended luminaires are avoidance of glare and prevention of collision with people moving through the space. To specify an appropriate location, an interior designer should consider

(a)

(b)

**FIGURE 6.15** (a) Linear suspended luminaires with two light sources: T5s and MR16s. Note (b) enlarged photograph of the fixture. (Illustration [reception area]: © Borotolotto/photo Tom Arban; photo [fixture]: Courtesy of Sistemalux, http://www.sistemalux.com.)

how the location affects people standing and sitting. Whenever possible, the location of the luminaire should not interfere with decorative focal points in an environment, such as artwork on a wall or a beautiful view from a window. When using multiple, suspended luminaires in rows, take care to ensure that the fixtures are hung in a perfectly straight line.

## TRACK LUMINAIRES

**Track luminaires** are fixtures that have multiple heads and are mounted on an electrical raceway (Figure 6.16). Tracks are available in a variety of lengths, and connectors are used to create shapes such as L, T, or X. Generally, one end of the track connects to the main circuit wiring whereas the other end is dead. Multitracks are available for separate switching arrangements, as are low-voltage track systems with remote transformers. Track systems can be suspended from a ceiling by cables, recessed into the ceiling plane, or surface-mounted on a ceiling or wall. Track-mounted luminaires, known as track heads, are available in a variety of styles, colors, sizes, lamp types, and materials; they also come with

FIGURE 6.16 Track luminaires installed in the Morgan Library in New York City. (Michel Denance.)

**FIGURE 6.17** A cable system installed over the island in a kitchen. The space also has under-cabinet fixtures. (© Andreas Von Einsiedel/View Pictures.)

built-in transformers. Some track heads are connected to the end of a long, flexible cable that can be shaped to aim light in numerous directions. A monopoint luminaire is used for installations that require only one track head. Track luminaires have evolved to designs that include low-voltage cable and rail systems (Figure 6.17). The heads on these systems are attached to a cable or rail, which can be adjusted and shaped at the site of installation. The flexibility of the system allows for designs in curves and soft angles.

Light distribution from the heads of a track system is direct, indirect, direct–indirect, or diffused. The most common applications for track systems are accent, wall wash, and downlight. Many heads are designed merely to hold the lamp and do not allow any adjustment or control; for these heads, it is critical to select the lamp that will have the desired beam spread and intensity. To control glare, heads are available with louvers, lenses, and solid or mesh shielding devices. Suspension kits for track systems, and extensions for each track head, are available for use on high ceilings.

## Track Luminaires: Advantages

The primary advantage of a track system is flexibility, in that it is relatively simple to re-aim and reposition the heads. This is why they are frequently used to highlight items on display in retail stores. Tracks also provide the flexibility of having different types of illumination from one fixture.

## Track Luminaires: Disadvantages

Disadvantages of a track system include difficulty in reaching the heads, a strong potential for glare, and a high accumulation of dirt and dust. When it is difficult to reach the track heads, they are seldom re-aimed or repositioned, negating the most important advantage of a track system and increasing the potential for glare. To reduce the potential for glare, avoid track locations where users can see the lamps, or add a shielding device to the heads.

In specifying a track system, it is important to be aware of the quality of the product. Some tracks are made of flimsy aluminum and are not suitable for applications that require frequent re-aiming and repositioning. There are also some safety concerns associated with track systems.

Generally, components are not interchangeable from one manufacturer to another, especially for track systems that are rated specifically for one manufacturer and one product line. In addition, the ease of adding heads to a track increases the likelihood of exceeding the maximum wattage for the system.

## STRUCTURAL LUMINAIRES

**Structural luminaires** are those that form an element of the architectural interior. Major types of structural luminaires are cove, valance, cornice, soffit, wallslot, and wall brackets (Figures 6.18a–c). **Cove lighting** is mounted on a wall, with the light directed up toward the ceiling. Cove lighting is especially effective in rooms with high ceilings, and can be integrated with crown molding. **Valance lighting** is mounted above a window, with the light directed up and down. **Cornice lighting**

can be mounted on a wall or above a window, with the light directed down. **Soffit lighting** is a built-in wall element close or next to the ceiling and extends 12 to 18 inches (31 to 46 cm) from the wall, generally directing the light down onto a task although some units can include indirect lighting. Soffit lighting is frequently used over work areas, such as kitchen counters, desks, and bathroom sinks.

**Wall bracket lighting** is mounted on a wall, with the light directed up and down. A **wallslot** is integrated in the ceiling system and distributes light down on vertical surfaces. They are sometimes used around the perimeter of a room. Seamless fluorescent systems and LEDs eliminate dark zones in continuous rows. This results in a continuous band of illumination on walls and ceilings.

The most common materials used for structural luminaires are wood, metal, and

(a)    (b)    (c)

**FIGURE 6.18A** Cove lighting in the center of the space. Notice the even distribution of light. (Jud Haggard Photography.)

**FIGURE 6.18B AND C** A wallslot installed in a reception area. Note the (b) close-up of the wallslot fixture. (Photo [reception area]: Charles Mayer Photography; photo [fixture]: Balthazar Korab.)

gypsum board. The board shielding the light source is called a fascia. To achieve the maximum amount of light from structural luminaires, the interior surfaces should be painted white and the fascia should have an angled cutoff. Generally, linear fluorescent lamps are used in these units. To ensure consistency in color and intensity level, all lamps installed in a unit should be from the same manufacturer. To reduce glare, some structural luminaires include a device that shields the light source, such as a baffle, lens, or louver.

The size of the unit and its location on a wall are also important to the success of structural luminaires. The unit must have the proper dimensions so as to maximize reflectance and adequately shield the lamps from multiple angles of view. The location on the wall affects reflectance, illumination levels, and the potential for glare.

The dimensions that follow are applicable for cove, valance, cornice, and wall bracket lighting. Structural luminaires should be mounted at least 18 inches (46 cm) from a ceiling. The distance from the wall should be 6 to 12 inches (15 cm to 31 cm). Lamps should be mounted at least 4 inches (10 cm) from the wall and 2 inches (5 cm) from the fascia. The height of the fascia should be 8 to 12 inches (20 cm to 31 cm). Soffit luminaires should be 6 to 12 inches (15 cm to 31 cm) high and mounted 12 to 18 inches (31 cm to 46 cm) from the wall.

Modifications to recommended dimensions may be necessary for rooms with high ceilings or for very large or small rooms. For example, in a large room, the dimensions of cove lighting may need to be modified in order to avoid dark areas in the center of the room. Some luminaires distribute light more evenly and avoid hot spots from the lamps. The integration of built-in reflectors assists in distributing the light along a surface.

## Structural Luminaires: Advantages

Structural luminaires have the advantage of enhancing the interior by being well integrated with the interior architecture. Outlining the shape and size of an interior can make a space appear larger and can serve as a means of following the rhythm of the structure. Another advantage of this type of lighting is that the even distribution imitates one of the positive qualities of daylight, making it excellent for general lighting purposes. Structural luminaires can also add an element of mystery to an environment, because the light sources are hidden from view and the light appears to be floating.

## Structural Luminaries: Disadvantages

Disadvantages of structural luminaires are the potential for glare, damage to ceiling and walls when removing the elements, and difficulties associated with cleaning the lamps and relamping. In the case of large rooms, structural applications may leave the center of the room in darkness. In addition, any cracks or imperfections in walls or ceilings can become very noticeable when the light grazes the surfaces, though this effect can be minimized by use of a matte finish paint.

## FURNITURE-INTEGRATED LUMINAIRES

**Furniture-integrated luminaires** are mounted in a cabinet and generally hidden from view. The most common furniture pieces that have integrated lighting are office systems, curio cabinets, breakfronts, and bookcases (Figure 6.19). Office-system integrated furniture has lamps for ambient and task lighting, whereas furniture designed for the purpose of highlighting objects generally has downlights or spots. Furniture-integrated luminaires can provide excellent light for their intended purpose. Concerns related to these luminaires focus on the amount of heat that can collect in the cabinets and the difficulties associated with relamping.

## PORTABLE LUMINAIRES

**Portable luminaires** include table and floor fixtures, and are used primarily in residential interiors, hotels, restaurants, and private offices. These fixtures are easy to install, provide instant illumination, have a wide range of lighting effects, and can have a relatively inexpensive initial cost. However, most portable luminaires have been designed for incandescent lamps; which should be replaced with compact fluorescent lamps (CFLs).

Portable luminaires are excellent for task lighting and sustainable designs because users can easily position and adjust the fixture to meet their needs. As an accent lighting technique, portable luminaires are ideal because small fixtures can be easily mounted in positions to highlight objects while they remain hidden from view. Portable luminaires also play an important role as decorative lighting (Figure 6.20).

FIGURE 6.19 An innovative approach to integrated lighting is the lack of electrical wires in this glass case. The light source is powered through a specialty glass that can conduct electricity. (Schott.)

Marble base

FIGURE 6.20 Shown arching over the sofa the marble and stainless steel Arco (1962) floor luminaire by Achille Castiglioni and Pier Goacomo Castiglioni is one of the most well-known portable fixtures. The luminaire is in the permanent collection of many museums. (Digital Image © The Museum of Modern Art/Licensed by SCALA/Art Resource, NY.)

Most portable luminaires have basic on/off switches for controls. Luminaires that are designed for three-way switching should have a three-way lamp to save energy and provide flexibility for the user. However, a three-way lamp should not be used in a luminaire that does not have a three-way switch because fixtures that operate the lamp at only the highest wattage waste energy.

Some portable luminaires have dimmers, timers, photosensors, or occupancy sensors. These are either built into the luminaire or are a separate device. For safety reasons the fixture should be physically balanced, and the cord should be kept away from walkways. To help conceal cords, floor outlets should be specified whenever possible.

In specifying portable luminaires, interior designers must consider the design of the fixture, the relationship of the fixture to other elements in the space, and the appropriate location for the intended purpose. Glare is an important consideration in analyzing the design of the fixture and where it will be located. Discomfort or disability glare can occur when an exposed lamp is in a direct line of view, or when a shade is too translucent. To determine problems associated with glare, the location of the fixture must be analyzed in relation to the users from various positions. For example, the location of a table luminaire might be perfect for people seated next to the fixture. However, people standing in the room might experience glare because they are able to see the top of the lamp. In contrast, an individual sitting next to a table fixture that is on a high table might experience glare, but people standing in the space may not be affected by the brightness.

Portable luminaires should be located to provide direct light on the task, with no shadows or glare. To accommodate an individual seated in a chair or on a sofa, the luminaire should be placed to the side and slightly behind the person. To avoid shadows on a task, the luminaire should be placed on the left side for right-handed individuals and on the opposite side for left-handed people. The bottom of the shade should be at about eye level, which generally translates to 38 to 42 inches (97 to 107 cm) from the floor. This height emits light directly on the task, and the individual does not experience glare from the lamp.

The location of a fixture for an individual working at a desk should be approximately 15 inches (38 cm) from the individual and 12 inches (30 cm) from the front edge of the desk. The bottom of the shade should be about 15 inches (38 cm) above the desk. The location of the luminaire might have to be adjusted to avoid reflections on a computer monitor.

## Specifying Luminaires

To specify luminaires, an interior designer must be knowledgeable about the products offered by various manufacturers of luminaires, lamps, and devices used to control fixtures.

### MANUFACTURERS' SPECIFICATIONS

The specification process begins with researching current products. The Internet is an excellent resource for identifying and comparing products because websites have specification-driven product categories. For example, some websites list several product categories, such as type of fixture, lamp, and applications. A user selects the desired categories, and the website locates the products that fit the specifications.

In reviewing various products, it is critical to locate specification data supplied by the manufacturer. These data include installation instructions, application guides, specification sheets, photometric information (explained in Chapter 8), and costs. An interior designer needs this information to select and specify luminaires and lamps. Data are also used to perform calculations and provide maintenance recommendations to a client.

## SELECTION CONSIDERATIONS

Selecting luminaires for a quality lighting environment begins with an analysis of the site and the users of the space. (Information about the lighting design process is provided in Chapters 9 and 10.) Ideally, lighting is considered at the beginning stages of a project; an essential time when seeking LEED certification. A major factor that can affect the lighting plan is whether the project is new construction or work being done on an existing structure. Both situations can present unique challenges that an interior designer must resolve before specifying the luminaires.

In reviewing the specifics of the project, it is important for the designer to prioritize criteria associated with luminaires. For example, when an existing building has significant structural limitations, the first priority would be to ensure that the luminaires specified can in fact be installed in the rooms. Economic considerations could be a major priority for a client who has a building in a community with high electrical costs. A priority for an expensive

jewelry store is to enhance the sparkle of jewels. Prioritized criteria are very helpful when specifying categories of luminaires.

Within the context of these priorities, the purpose of the luminaire must be identified (Figure 6.21). How will the luminaire be integrated with the layered lighting plan? Will the luminaire provide general, task, accent, or decorative lighting? An interior designer must also determine whether the luminaire should be the focal point of the space, blend into the interior, or be completely hidden.

After these decisions have been made, the next step in selecting luminaires involves evaluating specific characteristics of lighting systems, including quality of product, photometric data, lamp characteristics, economics, installation methods, operational considerations, maintenance, and design considerations.

FIGURE 6.21 The purpose of the luminaires in this space was to create uniform lighting in the dance studio. Daylighting contributed to creating an inspirational space. (Iwan Baan.)

The desired quality of the luminaire is often dependent upon the priorities of the client. However, to make informed decisions, it is the responsibility of the interior designer to know the quality differences between products. Well-constructed luminaires made from quality materials are a good sustainable investment. Quality luminaires are especially important for long-term installations and when durability is critical.

Photometric data should be reviewed to determine the light distribution of the luminaire; the designer should perform the calculations necessary to make this determination. Specification data will also indicate the suggested lamps for the luminaire. Characteristics of the suggested lamps should be reviewed to determine whether they meet the objectives of the lighting plan. Some of the considerations are efficacy ratings, color characteristics, life of the lamp, aiming qualities, operating position, wattages, heat accumulation, optical control properties, control features, and availability of lamps.

When searching internationally for luminaires, it is critical to know the plug and outlet compatibilities and the rating because different countries have different electrical systems and requirements. The economics associated with luminaires include the costs of the fixture, lamps, ballasts, controls, electricity, installation, and maintenance.

In selecting luminaires, there are many installation factors to consider. To determine the feasibility of installing a luminaire, the electrical, mechanical, plumbing, and structural components of the building must be surveyed.

This process includes reviewing local building and electrical codes. Historical buildings have strict renovation codes and regulations that must be followed throughout a project (Figure 6.22a and b). The interior must be surveyed to determine access for installation and maintenance. Space requirements may include ballasts, transformers, output boxes, and climate control. There must be adequate support in ceilings and walls for mounting luminaires. Materials such as sheetrock, plaster, wood, and acoustical tile are the most common surfaces for mounting luminaires. Masonry walls and irregular surfaces can pose installation difficulties. In addition, unusual surface configurations may require a luminaire that can be modified or adjusted at the field site.

The horizontal and vertical impact on the space must also be considered when installing a luminaire, as well as any effect on the placement of art on the wall. A review of installation considerations should also take into account the directional effects of lighting on the space and users.

Operational considerations are another aspect of specifying luminaires. Factors to examine include use of controls, adjustability, future requirements, ergonomics, environmental factors, and safety. An interior might require special controls, such as dimmers, occupancy detectors, and daylight photosensor systems. For a successful operation, a luminaire must be selected that is compatible with the specific requirements of the controls. (Controls for luminaires are covered in the Chapter 7.)

Adjustability of a luminaire could be critical for lighting that is used by a variety of users

(a)

(b)

FIGURE 6.22 (a) The Auditorium Theatre (1889), Chicago by Louis Sullivan and Dankmar Adler was one of the first buildings with electrical light sources. The 3,500 clear glass carbon-filament lamps emphasize the theatre's arched ceiling. Due to its historic landmark status, the (b) current lamps are replicas of the original Thomas Edison carbon-filament lamps. (Photo [auditorium]: James Steinkamp; photo [fixture]: 2010 © Chip Williams.)

and for a variety of tasks. It may be necessary to move luminaires to different locations or to completely remove the lighting system at a later date. For these situations, luminaires should be selected that allow for easy relocation and removal.

Ergonomic and environmental factors should always be considered when specifying luminaires and lamps. In addition, there are safety concerns: a luminaire with an exposed lamp poses the danger of someone being burned or a flammable material igniting on contact. Inadequate light to perform tasks may result in injury or damage due to an inability to see work materials properly. The stability of the luminaire should also be examined, especially when children, elderly people, and pets are users of the space.

Maintenance is another important consideration for specifying a luminaire. A luminaire that cannot be easily cleaned or relamped reflects badly on the reputation of an interior designer. The cost of labor is a critical expense related to maintenance. Luminaires mounted in a location that is easily accessed generally do not pose maintenance problems; for locations that are difficult to reach, such as 20-foot ceilings, the luminaire should relamp from the front and be equipped with a shield to reduce the accumulation of dirt or dust. Lamps that have long life should also be considered. A product that requires special tools can hamper luminaire maintenance. The material of the luminaire could also pose maintenance problems. For example, shiny aluminum scratches easily and shows fingerprints.

The luminaire must reflect the theme of the interior and reinforce the principles of design. Interior designers should approach

FIGURE 6.23 Designers are creating decorative luminaires as well as fixtures that can help communities without adequate electricity. Still in experimental stages the solar cells embedded in *Sonumbra*'s parasol by Loop. pH are intended to provide shade and collect energy during the day. In the evening the laced together strands emit light. (Wally Gobetz.)

the selection of a luminaire with the same aesthetic criteria they would use for other elements in the space. To select a luminaire

of a specific period often requires historical research. To be in concert with the theme of an interior, some interior designers have luminaires custom-made (Figure 6.23). This is frequently done for hotels and restaurants.

The principles of design should also be applied to locating luminaires in a space. Ceiling-mounted luminaires should be balanced with other elements on the ceiling, including diffusers, returns, smoke alarms, and emergency lights. Symmetrical or asymmetrical balance can be used depending upon the type of fixture and the purpose of the lighting.

Luminaires should be selected that reinforce the rhythm, emphasis, unity, proportion, and scale of a space and its furnishings. When high ceilings are emphasized in a room, luminaires should be selected that provide a vertical focus. Low-level lighting should be used in a space that is intended to be intimate.

The size of the luminaire should be proportionate to the size of the room and the installation area. In addition, for nonresidential projects, the number of different types of lamps should be limited so as to avoid confusion when maintenance people must relamp the fixtures. When there are many different types of lamps, it is very likely that the correct lamp will not be placed in the proper luminaire during relamping.

The proper selection and placement of luminaires is essential to a quality lighting environment. To conserve energy, designers should choose luminaires that emit as many lumens as possible. The key to success is having a thorough knowledge of the products, understanding the interdependence of the elements in a lighting system, and considering how luminaires affect the overall design of an interior. Controls are another important element of the system. A discussion of controls, and how they affect the performance of luminaires, is covered in the next chapter.

## Luminaires and LEED Certification

For a checklist of how you can apply luminaires in creating a LEED-certified building, see Box 6.1.

## BOX 6.1 Luminaires and LEED Certification

You can put the content of this chapter to work for you to create LEED-certified buildings by considering the following strategies:

o Help reduce light pollution select lamps and luminaires that direct the light where it is needed without spilling to other areas or to the outdoors.

o Minimize and optimize energy performance by selecting luminaires that maximize light output and produce minimal heat.

o Minimize and optimize energy performance by selecting air-tight rated fixtures.

o Minimize and optimize energy performance by replacing and recycling inefficacious luminaire-lamp systems.

o Minimize and optimize energy performance by installing devices in existing luminaires that are designed to redirect light that is wasted in the fixture to the unit's aperture.

o Minimize and optimize energy performance by replacing and recycling luminaires that are not compatible with controls, such as daylighting.

o Whenever possible reuse luminaires and any building materials that are used with lighting systems, such as ceilings, walls, and architectural elements.

o Reduce construction waste redirect any materials used in luminaires that has recyclable content.

o Reduce construction waste in the future by specifying quality luminaires that, whenever possible, are adjustable for future alternative purposes.

o Whenever possible specify luminaires that have recycled content and have been produced regionally.

o Whenever possible specify luminaires that have been produced with rapidly renewable materials. Wood-based products should be certified by the Forest Stewardship Council.

o To have a quality indoor environment, specify low-emitting paint for surfaces where luminaires are installed, such as ceilings and walls. To maximize illumination specify paint colors with a high reflectance (> 85 percent).

o Maximize user satisfaction with an environment and productivity by selecting luminaires that distribute light in the most optimum direction for a specific task and the characteristics of the users.

o Maximize user satisfaction with an environment and productivity by selecting luminaires that are appropriate for a task, eliminate glare, have individual controls, and do not negatively impact the thermal environment by emitting heat felt by the user.

o In the fundamental/enhanced commissioning of the building energy systems monitor the installation, operation, and calibration of the luminaires, include controls and elements used to control daylight.

o Measure and verify the efficiency of luminaires, controls, and thermal comfort.

o Monitor new sustainable developments in luminaires to ensure the most efficient and cost effective lighting systems.

**TABLE BOX 6.1** LEED Environmental Categories Related to Lighting Systems: Luminaires

| |
|---|
| SS (Sustainable Sites), Credit 1, Option 2, Path 6: Light Pollution Reduction |
| EA (Energy and Atmosphere) Prerequisite 1: Fundamental Commissioning of Building Energy Systems |
| EA Prerequisite 2: Minimum Energy Performance |
| EA Credit 1.1: Optimize Energy Performance—Lighting Power |
| EA Credit 1.2: Optimize Energy Performance—Lighting Controls |
| EA Credit 2: Enhanced Commissioning |
| EA Credit 3: Measurement and Verification |
| MR (Material and Resources) Credit 1.2: Building Reuse—Maintain Interior Nonstructural Components |
| MR Credit 2: Construction Waste Management |
| MR Credit 3.2: Materials—Reuse—Furniture and Furnishings |
| MR Credit 4: Recycled Content |
| MR Credit 5: Regional Materials |
| MR Credit 6: Rapidly Renewable Materials |
| MR Credit 7: Certified Wood |
| IEQ (Indoor Environmental Quality) Credit 4.2: Low-Emitting Materials—Paints and Coatings |
| IEQ Credit 6.1: Controllability of Systems—Lighting |
| IEQ Credit 6.2: Controllability of Systems—Thermal Comfort |
| IEQ Credit 7.1: Thermal Comfort—Design |
| IEQ Credit 7.2: Thermal Comfort—Verification |
| ID (Innovation in Design) Credit 1: Innovation in Design |

Source: USGBC (2009). *LEED reference guide for green interior design and construction*. Washington, D.C.: U.S. Green Building Council.

# Fundamental Projects

**1. Research Design Project**

For each major luminaire type (recessed, surface-mount, suspended, track, and structural), identify effective applications for general, task, and accent lighting. Summarize your suggestions in a written report; you may include illustrations and sketches.

**2. Research Design Project**

Create a product resource file. Search the Internet for 20 luminaire and 5 lamp manufacturers. The products should include all the types of luminaires. Locate all specification data for each product. Compile the resources in a file that is organized by types of luminaires and lamps. For each manufacturer, locate the photometric reports for three different luminaires.

# Application Projects

**1. Research Design Project**

Locate five different commercial or residential interiors. For each interior, respond to the following items: (a) identify the overall design theme of the space; (b) identify the luminaires; (c) evaluate the luminaires according to the principles of design, including balance, rhythm, emphasis, proportion, scale, variety, and unity. In a written report, summarize each interior and include illustrations.

**2. Research Design Project**

Interior designers must write specifications for lighting plans. Identify two interiors and write the lighting plan specifications for the luminaires and lamps. Specifications should include all the information needed to order the luminaires and lamps. Refer to manufacturers' product data for the specification details. Specifications may be presented in a table.

# Summary

o Primary ways to distribute light are: direct, indirect, semi-direct, semi-indirect, and diffused.

o Major categories of luminaires include recessed, surface-mounted, suspended, track, structural, and furniture-integrated units. These luminaires are designed primarily for incandescent, fluorescent, and HID lamps, and they are available in a variety of sizes, shapes, and materials. Most of these luminaires can be used for general, task, accent, or decorative lighting.

o The major types of structural luminaires are cove, valance, cornice, soffit, wall bracket, and wallslot.

o To specify luminaires, an interior designer must be knowledgeable about the products offered by various manufacturers of luminaires, lamps, and controls. It is critical to locate specification data supplied by the manufacturer.

o Selecting luminaires for a quality lighting environment begins with an analysis of the site and the users of the space. Within the context of established priorities, the purpose of the luminaire must be identified.

o To determine the feasibility of installing a luminaire, the electrical, mechanical, plumbing, and structural components of the building must be surveyed.

o Operational considerations include use of controls, adjustability, future requirements, ergonomics, environmental factors, and safety. Maintenance is another important matter when specifying a luminaire.

o A luminaire must reflect the theme of the interior and reinforce the principles of design.

## KEY TERMS

air-tight (AT) fixture
cornice lighting
cove lighting
diffused luminaire
direct luminaire
furniture-integrated luminaire
HID high/low-bay
high hat

indirect luminaire
insulation–contact (IC) fixture
portable luminaire
recessed downlight
recessed luminaire
semi-direct luminaire
semi-indirect luminaire
semi-recessed luminaire

soffit lighting
structural luminaire
surface-mount luminaire
suspended luminaire
track luminaire
valance lighting
wall bracket lighting
wallslot

# Resources

Benya, J., Heschong, L., McGowan, T., Miller, N., & Rubinstein, F. (2001). *Advanced lighting guidelines*. White Salmon, WA: New Buildings Institute.

Bernstien, A., & Conway, K. (2000, March). *The public benefits of California's investments in energy efficiency*. Prepared for the California Energy Commission by the RAND Corporation. MR-1212.0-CEC.

Bierman, A., & Conway, K. (2000). Characterizing daylight photosensor systems performance to help overcome market barriers. *Journal of the Illuminating Engineering Society, 29*(1), 101–115.

Boyce, P. N., Eklund, N., & Simpson, S. (2000). Individual lighting control: Task performance, mood and illuminance. *Journal of the Illuminating Engineering Society, 29*(1), 131–142.

Illuminating Engineering Society of North America (IESNA) (2011). *IESNA lighting handbook* (10th ed.). New York: Illuminating Engineering Society of North America.

Jennings, J. F., Rubinstein, R., & DiBartolomeo, D. R. (2000). Comparisons of control options in private offices in an advanced lighting controls test bed. *Journal of the Illuminating Engineering Society, 29*(2), 39–60.

Maniccia, D., Von Neida, B., & Tweed, A. (2000). Analysis of the energy and cost savings potential of occupancy sensors for commercial lighting systems. *Proceedings of the 2000 Annual Conference of the Illuminating Engineering Society of North America*.

Mistrick, R., Chen, C., Bierman, B., & Felts, D. (2000). A comparison of photosensor-controlled electronic dimming systems. *Proceedings of the 2000 Annual Conference of the Illuminating Engineering Society, 29(1), 66–80*.

Narendran, N., Yin, T., et al. (2000). A lamp life predictor for the frequently switched instant-start fluorescent systems. *Proceedings of the 2000 Annual Conference of the Illuminating Engineering Society of North America*.

Phillips, D. (2000). *Lighting modern buildings*. Oxford: Architectural Press.

Portland Energy Conservation, I. (1992). *Building commissioning guidelines* (2nd ed.). Portland, OR: Bonneville Power Administration.

Veitch, J., & Newsham, G. (2000). Exercised control, lighting choices, and energy use: An office simulation experiment. *Journal of Environmental Psychology, 20*(3), 219–237.

# 7 Lighting Systems: Controls

Controls are mechanisms designed to regulate a lighting system, and are especially important for energy-efficient lighting. In the past, controls were not a major consideration and were primarily used for decorative applications, but advancements in digital technologies have increased the performance and options available to an interior designer. As controls become even more sophisticated, interior designers will have many ways to improve the efficiency of lighting systems and provide flexibility for users. Constant improvements in the technology of controls require that interior designers routinely read product literature and articles in professional journals.

This chapter explores auxiliary and lighting controls and how they affect a quality lighting environment. Auxiliary controls include transformers and ballasts. Lighting controls include a broad category of techniques and equipment that are designed to conserve energy and enhance an environment. Lighting controls operate either manually or automatically and include switches, dimmers, timers, occupancy sensors, photosensors, and central controls.

## OBJECTIVES

o Describe the role of transformers and ballasts in a lighting system

o Differentiate between magnetic and electronic versions of transformers and ballasts

o Describe how lighting controls can conserve energy and enhance an environment

o Identify the primary ways in which controls can conserve energy, including scheduling, daylighting, monitoring lamp maintenance, and load shedding

o Describe the basic equipment for lighting controls, including switches, dimmers, timers, occupancy sensors, photosensors, and central units

o Understand how to specify auxiliary and lighting controls for a quality lighting environment

# Auxiliary Controls

Transformers and ballasts are devices that are essential in the operation of some lighting systems. These controls must be compatible with a lighting system, and they consume electricity. To accommodate smaller spaces some auxiliary controls are available in low-profile styling.

## TRANSFORMERS

A **transformer** is an electrical device that raises and lowers voltage in a system. Step-up transformers raise the quantity of voltage, and step-down transformers lower the voltage for specific commercial and residential applications. For lighting purposes, a transformer is either integral to the design of the luminaire, or it is a separate unit concealed under a ceiling or behind a wall (Figure 7.1). The vast majority of line-voltage lighting applications operate at 120 V. Low-voltage lighting applications usually operate at 12 V. Thus, for low-voltage lighting, a transformer is needed to step-down the line voltage to 12 V. Another type of transformer, a **driver**, converts alternating current to direct current for devices including LEDs.

Transformers are available in magnetic and electronic versions. Magnetic transformers have a steel core, are encased in copper wire, and are inexpensive and very reliable. However, they are also heavier, larger, and noisier than electronic transformers. Electronic transformers are composed of an electrical circuit. The advantages of electronic transformers include smaller size, less weight, and quieter operation. Since electricity is required to operate transformers, the energy consumed by the device must be included

Transformer

**FIGURE 7.1** A transformer that is integral to the design of a luminaire. Shown is a head for a track luminaire. (Philips Lightolier.)

in determining the watts-per-square-foot calculations in a space.

Each transformer is rated with a maximum wattage; manufacturers provide this information. For fire safety purposes and proper operation of the luminaire, it is critical to match lamps and the transformers to be used with them so that neither exceeds the maximum wattage. Also, the transformer should be installed as close as possible to the luminaire because there can be a noticeable voltage drop and reduced light output when the distance between the transformer and luminaire is too great. The maximum distance from a luminaire to a transformer is dependent upon the wattage and the wire gauge. For example, a single-fixture luminaire with a 16-gauge wire at 12 V can accommodate 150

W when the transformer is 50 feet (15 m) from the luminaire. A single-fixture luminaire with a 12-gauge wire at 12 V can accommodate 250 W when the transformer is 50 feet (15 m) from the luminaire. A 24 V system is available to help alleviate problems associated with distances between the transformer and luminaires. All these data are available from luminaire manufacturers.

Most transformers work with halogen and incandescent dimmers. There are some options available for transformers, including automatic reset, soft starting, resettable circuit breakers, thermal protection, and short-circuit protection. There are also special devices designed for unique installation requirements, such as expandable hanger bars that provide support for suspended fixtures. Very small transformers with dimmers can be used in cabinets or display shelves. Plug-in transformers are available for 12 V fixtures.

## BALLASTS

A **ballast** is a control device used with an electric-discharge lamp to start the lamp; it also controls the electrical current during operation (refer to Figure 3.16). Fluorescent and HID discharge lamps require ballasts to operate. The ballast for a lamp is either a separate control gear or an integral system and generally lasts longer than the discharge lamp itself. Ballasts are available in magnetic and electronic versions, but there are electronic replacements for every type of magnetic ballast. Moreover, as of July 2010 to comply with the Energy Policy Act of 2005, the sale of some magnetic ballasts have been banned. Magnetic ballasts are made with a steel core wrapped with copper or aluminum wire. They may produce a humming sound that can be a problem. Based on the level of sound in decibels, ballasts have been rated on a scale from A, the quietest (20 to 24 dB), to F, the loudest (greater than 49 dB). Electronic ballasts are produced with solid-state circuitry, and some are designed to operate on high-frequency power to improve the efficiency of lamp/ballast systems. Multiple-lamp ballasts are available to accommodate several lamps.

As with transformers, the electronic version is preferred over the magnetic because the unit is more energy-efficient, quieter, and weighs less. Also, electronic ballasts use less electricity for the light output and operate at cooler temperatures, thereby saving energy. The cooler operating temperature improves lamp life and helps to reduce the energy required for air conditioning. Electronic ballasts eliminate flicker and can accommodate multiple-lamp operations.

Ballasts are designed to operate in a parallel or series circuit. In a series circuit, lamps operate together as one system. If one lamp burns out, the remaining lamps do not work. Lamps operating with a parallel ballast circuit function independently and continue to operate when one of the lamps burns out.

Ballasts must always be considered as forming a system together with specific lamps (Figure 7.2). Generally, ballasts are designed to work with the specific characteristics of lamps, such as type of source, wattage, and controls. For example, there are ballasts made specifically for metal halide lamps operating at a designated wattage. Fluorescent lamp/ballast circuits are uniquely

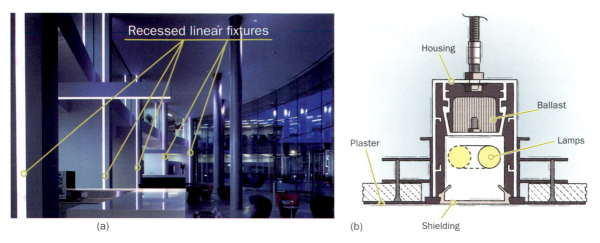

(a)  (b)

**FIGURE 7.2** (a) The integration of the ballast with the recessed luminaire is illustrated in (b) the cross section drawing of the fixture. (Courtesy of Selux.)

designed for rapid-start and instant-start systems. Moreover, variations among lamp manufacturers result in lamps and ballasts that may not be interchangeable.

Lamps and ballasts operate as an interdependent unit, and should be selected to maximize the performance of the system. For example, high-frequency electronic ballasts were developed to accommodate the efficacious T-8 fluorescent lamp. The union of a T-8 lamp and high-frequency electronic ballast results in low energy consumption, long lamp life, and improved maintenance.

High-intensity discharge (HID) lamps, on the other hand, are slightly more efficient operating at high frequencies than at low ones. Thus, to maximize the operating potential of a lamp/ballast system, all characteristics must be reviewed, including how the individual units affect one another. Ballast characteristics and operating factors are used in determining light

loss factors (LLF) and the watts-per-square-foot calculations for an interior. Maximizing a lamp/ballast system includes reducing the number of ballasts. **Tandem wiring** can reduce the number of ballasts by using one ballast for lamps in two or more fixtures (Figure 7.3). Reducing the number of ballasts conserves energy, resources, and costs.

The technology of ballasts is constantly improving in areas such as system efficacy,

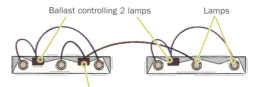

**FIGURE 7.3** Tandem wiring can reduce the number of ballasts and energy by using one ballast for lamps in two or more fixtures.

control abilities, and daylight integration. The goals are to provide greater flexibility, enhance control, improve light output, and conserve energy and natural resources. Energy-saving ballast/lamp systems, such as the T-8 or T5 lamps, reduce the consumption of watts. Circuits are being improved by allowing control of several lamp wattages on one circuit and reading input voltages and lamp types. These enhancements reduce the number of ballasts needed for an interior, facilitating specification and maintenance requirements. Improvements in controls include devices, such as smart circuitry, that regulate starts and restarts.

Circuits can also monitor the end-of-life of a lamp, dimming, and photocells. To protect the environment, materials used to fabricate ballasts have also been improved. Some ballasts produced prior to 1978 contained the toxic substance polychlorinated biphenyls (PCBs). Ballasts without PCBs are labeled "No PCBs."

## Lighting Controls

Lighting controls are available in manual, automated, or a combination of both. The newest integrated control systems allow access to interiors from anywhere. Lighting control systems can be monitored, programmed, and managed using building networks or Ethernet/Internet. System software features allow a user to customize a graphic depicting the lighting system on floor plans, elevations, or any other illustration that helps to visualize illumination throughout a space and building. For example, via the Internet, a person sitting in her office can view a floor plan of her home and learn which lights

are on or off. She can also review the status of any system integrated with the centralized control unit, such as security and fire alarms, and can control elements of any of these systems from the office.

A very important component of lighting control systems is commissioning (Figure 7.4). The focus on energy-efficient lighting systems has prompted attention to commissioning. As described earlier in this textbook commissioning ensures that a building system performs according to the specifications, space, and activities. Initial commissioning is performed after a lighting system is installed and before occupancy. When possible commissioning should be done after furniture and interior finishes have been installed.

Retro-commissioning should be performed periodically, especially after renovations to a space. Some of the key commissioning procedures include inspecting equipment, including automated window treatments, to make sure the correct systems have been installed in the specified locations. Sensors must be located in the optimum location to detect people and illumination levels for daylight harvesting. Commissioning should be performed during different times of the day and daylight conditions. Daylight harvesting controls must be calibrated to ensure that the electrical light sources and daylight are continuously providing the optimum light levels. Manufacturers have calibration instructions for their equipment. Commissioning and calibration reports should be provided to the operations and maintenance (O&M) staff as well as other product literature supplied by manufacturers.

(a)                                                 (b)

**FIGURE 7.4** Initial commissioning is performed after a lighting system is installed and before occupancy. (a) This individual is using technology to commission shades prior to occupancy of *The New York Times* headquarters building in Manhattan. Note the (b) closeup of the computer screen and the printed plan. (Courtesy of Lawrence Berkeley National Laboratory.)

## CRITERIA FOR SPECIFYING CONTROLS

There are many criteria an interior designer should consider when specifying lighting controls, including energy considerations, economics, and aesthetics. Controls can be used to conserve energy by turning lights off when they are not needed, daylight harvesting, monitoring lamp maintenance, and load shedding (Figures 7.5a and b). Conserving energy requires examining the activity patterns of the users of the space. Based upon an analysis of how people function in a space, controls can be programmed for various types of schedules. Predictable scheduling is used to control the lights in a space when there is a set routine. For example, many offices have a fixed schedule for people arriving at work,

**FIGURE 7.5A** To research the optimum lighting control system for the new headquarters building in Manhattan for *The New York Times*, the company involved the Lawrence Berkeley National Laboratory (Berkeley Lab) at the University of California. The Times Company desired daylight harvesting and a lighting plan that enabled them to easily reconfigure spaces. (© Michel Denance.)

FIGURE 7.5B The centrally located spaces also have daylight in *The New York Times* building. (© Michel Denance.)

maintaining an appropriate illumination level regardless of the weather conditions and time of year (Figures 7.6a–k). Controls can also be adjusted to ensure that areas located far from windows have adequate illumination for required tasks. Multiple switching plans, dimmers, and photosensors are excellent techniques for conserving energy by integrating daylight.

Technology has allowed very sophisticated daylight harvesting systems. For example, a centralized lighting control system in an office

taking lunch breaks, and leaving at the end of the day. A control system can be designed to turn lights on and off automatically according to the designated time and day of the week.

Unpredictable scheduling is designed to accommodate unusual activities in a space. For example, a local control could be installed in a private office to turn the lights off when a person is out sick or away on vacation. Unpredictable scheduling could also be used in spaces such as retail dressing rooms, washrooms, or stacks in a library. IES (2000) estimates that predictable and unpredictable scheduling can reduce energy by up to 40 percent and 60 percent respectively.

Controls can also conserve energy by orchestrating daylight, electrical light sources, and automated window-shade systems. Dimming and switching plans can be programmed to complement daylight by

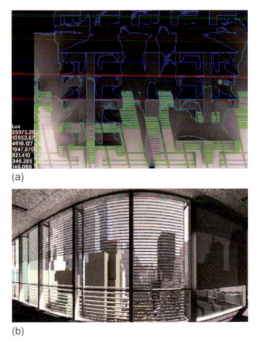

(a)

(b)

**FIGURE 7.6** To plan daylighting and the controls in *The New York Times* headquarters building the Berkeley Lab used radiance software. These simulations monitored shades, daylight, and work plane illuminance data. Other simulations of the building are shown in Figures 7.6c–h. (Courtesy of Lawrence Berkeley National Laboratory.)

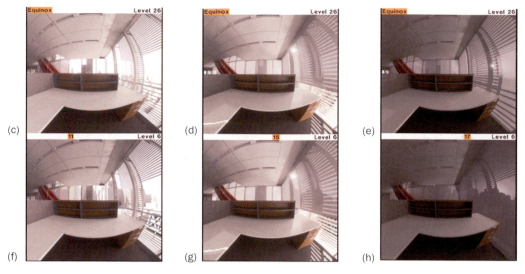

(c)　(d)　(e)

(f)　(g)　(h)

**FIGURE 7.6C–H** Berkeley Lab used radiance software to simulate the effectiveness of automated shades in controlling daylight, brightness, and illuminance distribution throughout the space. The (c–e) top row is level 26 (26th floor) and the (f–h) bottom row is level 6 (6th floor). Compare the differences in the six images. (Courtesy of Lawrence Berkeley National Laboratory.)

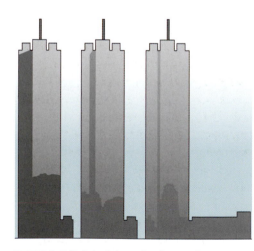

**FIGURE 7.6I** Berkeley Lab used radiance software to simulate shadowing patterns created by buildings surrounding *The New York Times* building.

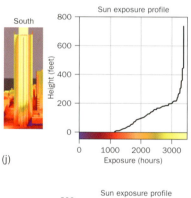

(j)

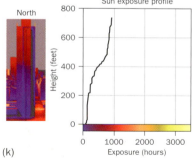

(k)

**FIGURE 7.6J AND K** Berkeley Lab used radiance software to simulate sun exposure profiles on the north and south side of *The New York Times* building.

can connect electrical sources, photosensors, and shade control. Automated window shades are installed in front of windows, and a small photocell is suspended close to the window to monitor the level of daylight illumination (Figures 7.7a and 7.7b). As the level of daylight increases, the translucent

FIGURE 7.7A To maximize daylight, control for glare, and maintain views automated roller shades were used in *The New York Times* building. Task tuning was also performed in these areas. (© Michel Denance.)

FIGURE 7.7B To control sunlight ceramic rods were installed on the façade of *The New York Times* headquarters building. (© Michel Denance.)

shades automatically come down and the light from electrical luminaires is dimmed. Throughout the day the lighting control system is constantly balancing the amount of light and glare in a room using window shades and electrical sources. This results in a consistent foot-candle level in the space and conserves energy by eliminating or dimming electrical sources when daylight is sufficient. In addition, to customize lighting requirements for users, the system will allow individuals to control the light level in their spaces.

Energy can also be conserved by programming controls to monitor lamp maintenance. For example, controls can notify users when lamps are operating at an unacceptable lumen output level. Lamps operating at less than optimum levels require more energy to function. The low lumen output could be the result of the lamp's end of life, or the accumulation of dirt and dust. Upon notice of lamp lumen depreciation, relamping procedures could be activated automatically.

Reducing the electrical needs of a space is known as load shedding. A load represents all the lights on one switch. Centralized lighting control systems will produce power consumption reports for every fixture in a building and indicate the foot-candle level for any surface or area in a space. This information can be used to carry out load shedding. One form of load shedding is to reduce illumination during peak times. For example, because of high air-conditioning requirements, summer is a peak electrical demand period. Thus, during the summer, one way to minimize electrical consumption could be to dim or turn lights off on sunny days. Another peak electrical period

**FIGURE 7.8** Scene controls are used in this room to create a relaxed atmosphere as well as other effects. (© David Zanzinger/Alamy.)

is during normal working hours. Any load shedding that can be done during the week on a regular basis will conserve energy and natural resources. **Task tuning** is another method of conserving energy in work areas. This is accomplished by having lighting systems that individualize luminaires for each person in the space (refer to Figure 1.13).

Using controls to conserve energy can result in long-term economic savings; of course, the cost of controls must be considered when calculating the cost of a lighting system. Control costs include the control unit itself, installation, electricity, and maintenance. Generally, proper specification,

installation, commissioning, and use of controls can offset these expenses. To conserve energy and reduce costs for existing lighting systems, there are retrofit control kits.

Controls are often specified for aesthetic purposes (Figure 7.8). General, task, accent, and decorative light sources should all have controls that will enhance the purpose of the light source. Controls can be adjusted to create the mood and atmosphere required by the environment and the activity taking place at a given time. They can also be used to create the perfect balance for accenting a piece of artwork, or they can establish the ideal levels between illumination zones in a space. Controls also enhance an interior by balancing natural and electrical light sources. For example, when illumination levels in an existing lighting plan are not balanced, controls can be added to lower or increase light levels for specific luminaires.

Controls provide the flexibility to accommodate a variety of activities in the same space (Figure 7.9a–c). A lighting system with properly designed controls can transform a working conference room into an evening dining area. Controls also enable individuals to take notes while watching a presentation on a screen or monitor, and can improve visibility and reduce eyestrain by providing gradual adjustments in light levels. The proper placement of controls can assist individuals with visual impairments or challenging visual tasks. In addition, programming lights either

FIGURE 7.9B A general meeting scene in a conference room. Notice the shades are down and task lighting illuminates the table. Presentation boards on the back wall are also illuminated. Compare this room to Figures 7.9a and c. (Photo courtesy of Lutron Electronics/ copyright 2010 Lutron Electronics.)

FIGURE 7.9A A morning scene in a conference room. Notice the shades are up and electrical sources are dimmed. Compare this room to Figures 7.9b and c. (Photo courtesy of Lutron Electronics/copyright 2010 Lutron Electronics.)

FIGURE 7.9C An AV presentation scene in a conference room. Notice the shades are partially down, low-level task lighting illuminates the table, and there is low-level lighting for walking through the room. Compare this room to Figures 7.9a and b. (Photo courtesy of Lutron Electronics/ copyright 2010 Lutron Electronics.)

to fade off or to delay switching off can help provide an element of safety to a space.

Planning for controls requires a thorough analysis of the current and future needs of the space in terms of users and their activities. Key to successful planning is providing a system that allows for flexibility and individual control. Unfortunately, sometimes an expensive, well-planned control system is turned off, or is not used to the greatest advantage because individuals do not know how to do so. To inform people of the proper operation and maintenance of controls, written documentation and training sessions are very helpful.

## EQUIPMENT

The basic equipment for lighting controls includes switches, dimmers, timers, occupancy sensors, photosensors, and central controls. In specifying equipment, designers must ensure that the controls are compatible with the entire lighting system, including the specific light source. Lighting controls operate manually, automatically, or by a combination of the two. The needs of the environment and users of the space should determine the type of control specified. (Chapters 9 and 10 discuss the process of designing a quality lighting environment.) The greatest flexibility for users is provided by automatic controls having a manual-off override.

Designers should also consider how easy it is for individuals with disabilities to use the equipment. It is important to keep in mind that, because of the ever-changing technological advancements, the industry related to lighting controls is expanding. To optimize a lighting plan, an interior designer must keep current in

the field and be knowledgeable regarding the interface among energy conservation, controls, and other elements of a lighting system.

### Switches

A **switch** is the easiest and oldest means of controlling lights. The function of an electrical switch is to stop the flow of electricity. A circuit is closed when a light is on and is open when the light is off. Relays, solenoids, or contactors are used for remote-control switching and for switching large lighting loads. The most common switch is a single pole that is operated manually. Switches are available in toggles, rockers, push buttons, rotary, or touch-plate mechanisms (Figure 7.10). Generally, they are mounted on a wall 48 inches (122 cm) above the floor, next to the opening side of a door.

Systems with more than one switch are known as multigang configurations. Multilevel or bilevel switching provides the flexibility of obtaining different levels of illumination from the same luminaires. Stepped switching is used for an entire circuit of lights. There are also hotel card-key switches that are activated

FIGURE 7.10 Switches and dimmers for residences are available in toggles, rockers, push buttons, or touch-plate mechanisms. (Courtesy of Leviton.)

by a guest or housekeeping staff. Inserting the key activates the circuits in the room and when the key is removed the circuits are turned off after a programmed time period, such as 30 seconds.

Switches can be localized or mounted in a central switching system. A double pole with a single throw operates two different electrical devices at the same time. A three-way switch operates a circuit from two different locations. A four-way switch will turn a light on or off from three different locations. When dimming a three-way switch, the dimming function will operate on only one of the switches. (For information on how to draw switching arrangements on electrical plans, see Chapter 10.)

**Dimmers** are used to conserve energy and enhance the aesthetics of an environment (Figures 7.10 and 7.11). Generally, reducing the power in a lamp conserves energy, affects color, and can extend the life of some lamps. Architectural dimming is the term describing a continuous dimming control system that can be reduced to a light output of 1 to 2 percent. To have gradual changes in light levels, continuous dimming should be used for daylight harvesting.

Using step-dimming ballasts can also reduce light levels. Less expensive than continuous dimming, step dimming uses bi-level or multilevel switching to turn off lamps. For example, in a luminaire with three lamps switch "A" controls one lamp and switch "B" controls the other two lamps. When only "A" is turned on one lamp is on; switch "B" turns two lamps on; and when both "A" and "B" are turned on three lamps are activated.

Dimmers have maximum wattages, indicated by manufacturers as part of their product information, that must be adhered to for proper performance and safe operation. Low-voltage lamps require a transformer designed for dimming. Generally, a rotary unit, toggle, linear slide, or touch plate operates dimmers. Plugs and adapters are available for dimming portable luminaires.

Dimming affects each light source in different ways. For incandescent and halogen lamps, dimming results in energy savings, longer lamp life, and a warmer color. To accommodate the halogen regenerative cycle, manufacturers may suggest that tungsten-halogen lamps be operated at full power

FIGURE 7.11 Commercial dimmers with different ways to control the level of light by using a preset slide or rotary device. (Courtesy of Leviton.)

periodically. Fluorescent and HID lamps are expensive to dim. Dimming these lamps requires special ballasts (a dimming ballast for each luminaire) and reduces lamp life. Also, some dimmers cause fluorescent lamps to flicker at low light levels. Typically, HID lamps do not perform well with dimmers because of the required warm-up and restrike times, increased flicker, and color shifting; however, step-dimming ballasts are improving the system.

### Dimming Equipment

There is a range of dimming equipment. Sophisticated dimmers will adjust the speed of raising or lowering light levels to accommodate the adaptive function of the eyes. For example, the eye takes longer to adjust from bright to dim than from dim to bright light levels. Thus, dimmers can be programmed to take a longer period of time to change the light level from bright to dark. This can be very useful in a conference room when lights need to be dimmed for events such as viewing audiovisual presentations.

### Timers

**Timers** control lighting systems by turning lights on and off at designated times. A timer can be a very simple device that a homeowner sets manually and plugs into a wall socket, or it can be a component in a very sophisticated computer program, including energy management systems (EMSs). Some of the computer programs include astronomical data that automatically adjusts the timer function according to the amount of daylight at a particular time of year in a specific geographical location. Many timers

have backup systems for power outages. Although they are most useful for predictable schedules in areas of high use, or for HID lamps that should not be switched frequently, timers can also be used in spaces that are not often occupied, such as restrooms or storage facilities. Unless there is supplementary lighting, they should not be used in areas where there is concern for safety or security.

### Occupancy (Vacancy) Sensors

**Occupancy sensors** (also termed **vacancy sensors**) are designed to turn lights on or off based upon whether there are people in a room (Figures 7.12a–d). Research indicates significant energy savings from the use of occupancy sensors (Jennings, Rubenstein, and DiBartolomeo, 2000; Maniccia, Von Neida, and Tweed, 2000). Generally, occupancy sensors are practical in spaces that are used sporadically or unpredictably, such as conference rooms and restrooms. They are also useful for security purposes.

Sensors detect the presence of people in a space by discerning sounds, movements, or body heat. Some sensors have sensitivity settings that allow you to program the level of detection. Ultrasonic sensors detect movement by analyzing changes in wave patterns, and are, therefore, not recommended for interiors with a high degree of air movement, which may interfere with their operation. For the same reasons they should not be installed close to ventilation diffusers.

Passive infrared (PIR) sensors detect body heat and require an unobstructed view of all areas of a room in order to function properly. The motion coverage range for PIR sensors is

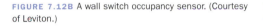

(a)                    (b) 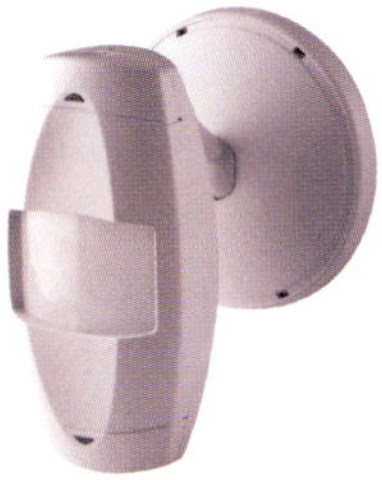              (c) 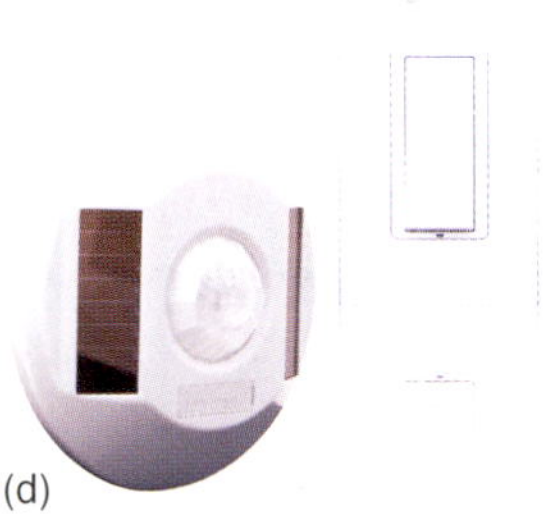              (d)

**FIGURE 7.12A** A ceiling mount occupancy sensor. (Courtesy of Leviton.)

**FIGURE 7.12B** A wall switch occupancy sensor. (Courtesy of Leviton.)

**FIGURE 7.12C** A wall mount occupancy sensor. (Courtesy of Leviton.)

**FIGURE 7.12D** A wireless occupancy sensor. (Courtesy of Leviton.)

less than ultrasonic sensors; therefore, the quantity of sensors needed for a space may be higher when using PIR sensors. Generally, ultrasonic sensors are more successful than PIR units. There are also dual-technology sensors that combine the functions of ultrasonic and PIR.

Occupancy sensors can be used with switches, dimmers, timers, photosensors, daylight harvesting, and central controls, providing maximum flexibility in designing a system for a variety of spaces and users. To facilitate installations, there are wireless occupancy sensors. As with photosensors and timers, occupancy sensors do not operate well with HID lamps because of their long restrike times. In addition, programmed-start electronic ballasts should be used in spaces where people may turn lights on and off several times per day, such as restrooms. The instant start fluorescent ballast should be installed in rooms where lights will remain on for long periods of time (three to ten hours), such as lobbies.

The success of occupancy sensors is dependent upon a thorough analysis of the interior and how people function in the space. Physical characteristics of the space and the users will determine the appropriate sensor and the ideal mounting location. Generally, PIR sensors are effective in open spaces that are free of obstructions, rooms with ceilings higher than 14 feet (427 cm), and remote areas. Ultrasonic or dual-technology sensors should be used in rooms with ceilings lower than 14 feet (427 cm), partitions, or large furniture.

Occupancy sensors can be mounted in a variety of ways—on the ceiling, on walls, or in the corners of a room (Figures 7.12a–d). There are units available for wall switches (**wallboxes**) and for plugging into electrical outlets, as well as portable units that can be located next to an individual. Each type of sensor has a designated angle of coverage and an effective range; manufacturers' literature provides these performance characteristics. In determining the location of the sensor, the most important consideration is to maintain an unobstructed view. The wrong type of sensor or an inappropriate location will cause lights to turn on or off at the wrong time. For example, when a PIR sensor is unable to detect a person working behind a high partition, the lights will automatically turn off. If this continues to happen, users of the space become frustrated and may eventually deactivate the system. To help avoid false readings, installations should include commissioning adjustments. This involves testing and adjusting the occupancy sensor to accommodate any nuances present in an interior.

**Photosensors** are devices that detect the amount of illumination in a space, and then send signals that control electrical light sources by switching lights on/ off or by adjusting illumination levels to reach the optimum point (Figures 7.13a and 7.13b). Photosensors adjust electrical light sources to accommodate fluctuations in the quality and quantity of daylight in a space or on a task, and research indicates the result is a savings in energy (Li & Lam, 2003; Jennings, Rubenstein, and DiBartolomeo, 2000; Pacific Gas & Electric Company, 1999; Rundquist, McDougall, and Benya, 1996). Photosensors are available as separate units or may be integrated in a luminaire or automated window coverings.

As with occupancy sensors, photosensors must be properly mounted. Photosensors can be mounted on a ceiling close to a task, directly on a work surface, or next to a window or skylight (Figure 7.14). Locating a photosensor close to exterior openings

(a)

(b)

FIGURE 7.13A An indoor photocell that can detect the amount of illumination in a space, and then send signals that control electrical light sources by switching lights on and off or by adjusting illumination levels to reach the optimum point. (Courtesy of Leviton.)

FIGURE 7.13B Photocells were used to detect illumination for the daylight harvesting system installed in this exhibition at the Liberty Bell Center in Philadelphia. (© Visions of America, LLC / Alamy.)

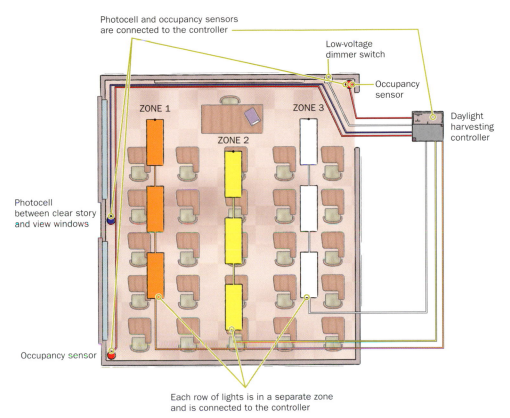

Photocell and occupancy sensors are connected to the controller

Low-voltage dimmer switch

Occupancy sensor

ZONE 1

ZONE 3

ZONE 2

Daylight harvesting controller

Photocell between clear story and view windows

Occupancy sensor

Each row of lights is in a separate zone and is connected to the controller

**FIGURE 7.14** In this small classroom a photocell is used to monitor illumination levels. A harvesting controller is used to coordinate information from the photocell and the rows of zoned fixtures. The occupancy sensors are also connected to the controller.

can be done with an indoor or outdoor mount. For the most accurate readings, a photosensor should not be mounted in direct view of electrical sources or sunlight. In addition, each photosensor should be connected to luminaires sharing one set of lighting requirements. For example, in a large classroom, the general perimeter lighting has a lower illumination level than the task lighting located above the desks; therefore, different individual photosensors should be connected to the general and task luminaires respectively.

A **central control system** uses a microprocessor to monitor, adjust, and regulate lighting in many areas or zones within a building. Some units are designed to integrate lighting with other electrical units, including mechanical, energy, and security systems. Electrical units can include motorized window treatments, whirlpool jets, ceiling fans, kitchen appliances, sprinkler systems, garage door openers, security systems, skylights, sound systems, and audiovisual equipment. Mechanical systems can include heating, ventilation, air-conditioning, and plumbing. Central control systems can be connected to switches, dimmers, timers, occupancy sensors, and photosensors. For flexibility and safety purposes, central control systems should always have manual options for operating the luminaires.

Central control systems can be programmed for preset "scenes." Each scene is designed for a specific space or activity and its illumination requirements, for example, energy savings, security, entertainment, exterior lights, relaxation, or work (Figures

(a)

(b)

(c)

(d)

FIGURE 7.15A A model illustrating a control system programmed for a "morning" scene. Lights are on in the kitchen and bathroom. Shades are closed in the front of the dwelling and open in the living area. Compare this model to the images in Figures 7.15b–d.

FIGURE 7.15B A model illustrating a control system programmed for an "away" scene. All lights are off and all shades are down. Lowered shades help to provide security and create a uniform appearance to the exterior of the dwelling. Compare this model to the images in Figures 7.15a, c, and d.

FIGURE 7.15C A model illustrating a control system programmed for a "summer" scene. To help keep the dwelling cool shade is provided on the south side. Lights are on in the kitchen and bathroom. Shades are closed in the front of the unit and open in the living area. Compare this model to the images in Figures 7.15a, b, and d.

FIGURE 7.15D A model illustrating a control system programmed for a "winter" scene. Shades are used to provide insulation as well as absorbing radiant heat. Compare this model to the images in Figures 7.15a–c.

7.15a–d). For example, if the button labeled "work" is pressed in a conference room, the central control system will adjust the luminaires to the programmed illumination levels for that activity in that space. Striking the "video" button will automatically adjust the luminaires for the task of viewing a video.

Central control systems have become very sophisticated in residential buildings. Someone driving home from work can telephone the system and direct it to start running the bath water to a specific level and temperature, warm the towel bars, heat the tile floor, close the blinds, play music, and dim the lights. A preset scene can be programmed to save energy by dimming lights, turning off lights in unoccupied rooms, controlling automated window treatments, and adjusting light levels and temperatures according to daylight.

Central controls are activated by keypads, touch screens, computers, telephones, and handheld infrared remotes. Keypad buttons and faceplates are available in a variety of finishes and can be custom engraved for labeling purposes (Figure 7.16). High-humidity and waterproof versions of control units can be specified to resist the effects of mild moisture and water.

Computer network control systems for lighting will continue to improve in the future. For digital lighting control, the focus is on the **digital addressable lighting interface (DALI)**. DALI is a means of communicating through low-voltage wires, allowing information to be distributed to the lighting system and allowing the luminaires to report back. DALI controls

FIGURE 7.16 A keypad with various scenes that are programmed for a kitchen. (©2010 Lutron Electronics, Inc.)

individual luminaires, groups of fixtures, occupancy sensors, dimmers, photosensors, timers, scenes, transition fades, and other networked systems. Luminaires communicate with the DALI when a lamp is close to burning out, has low lumen output, or has ballast irregularities.

Controls play a very important role in a quality lighting environment by fine-tuning the system. Effective use of lighting controls can conserve energy and natural resources, provide users with flexibility, vary illumination using the same fixtures, and create an atmosphere conducive to the purpose of a space. Controls can also help to support safety and security systems. The progressive nature of the technology associated with controls requires that interior designers stay abreast of developments in the field.

## Controls and LEED Certification

For a checklist of how you can apply lighting controls in creating a LEED-certified building, see Box 7.1.

---

**BOX 7.1 Sustainable Considerations Related to Controls**

You can put the content of this chapter to work for you to create LEED-certified buildings by considering the following strategies:

o Help reduce light pollution by selecting lamps and luminaires that direct the light where it is needed without spilling to other areas or to the outdoors.

o Reduce light pollution by employing controls that help eliminate the spill of interior light to the outdoors.

o Minimize and optimize energy performance by selecting efficient transformers and ballasts.

o Use tandem wiring to minimize and optimize energy performance as well as conserving resources.

o Minimize and optimize energy performance by selecting controls that monitor occupancy/vacancy, daylight, lamp maintenance, load shedding, and schedules.

o Minimize and optimize energy performance by using controls that optimize daylighting, coordinate electrical sources, and control direct sunlight.

o Minimize and optimize energy performance by selecting controls that can be adjusted according to activities, weather conditions, seasonal changes, decorative effects, and moods.

o Minimize and optimize energy performance and user satisfaction by updating inefficacious and/or ineffective control systems.

o Minimize and optimize energy performance by selecting appropriate controls for daylighting, occupancy, and schedules.

o To protect the environment, replace any ballasts that contain PCBs; always follow EPA disposal requirements.

o Maximize user satisfaction with an environment and productivity by enabling individuals to control their light and thermal comfort.

o Maximize user satisfaction with an environment and productivity by using controls for daylighting, dimming, and controlling the heat and glare from direct sunlight.

o In the fundamental/enhanced commissioning of the building energy systems, monitor the installation, operation, and calibration of the controls and elements used to control daylight, such as automated shades.

o Measure and verify the efficiency of controls, thermal comfort, and the effectiveness of sensors used to detect illumination levels and occupancy/vacancy.

o Monitor new sustainable developments in controls to ensure the most efficient and cost effective lighting systems.

**TABLE BOX 7.1** LEED Categories Related to Controls

LEED CREDIT CATEGORIES RELATED TO THE CONTENT IN CHAPTER 7

SS (Sustainable Sites) Credit 1, Option 2, Path 6: Light Pollution Reduction

EA (Energy and Atmosphere) Prerequisite 1: Fundamental Commissioning of Building Energy Systems

EA Prerequisite 2: Minimum Energy Performance

EA Credit 1.1: Optimize Energy Performance—Lighting Power

EA Credit 1.2: Optimize Energy Performance—Lighting Controls

EA Credit 2: Enhanced Commissioning

EA Credit 3: Measurement and Verification

IEQ Credit 6.1: Controllability of Systems—Lighting

IEQ Credit 6.2: Controllability of Systems—Thermal Comfort

IEQ Credit 7.1: Thermal Comfort—Design

IEQ Credit 7.2: Thermal Comfort—Verification

IEQ Credit 8.1: Daylight and Views—Daylight

IEQ Credit 8.2: Daylight and Views—Views for Seated Spaces

ID (Innovation in Design) Credit 1: Innovation in Design

Source: USGBC (2009). *LEED reference guide for green interior design and construction.* Washington, D.C.: U.S. Green Building Council.

# Fundamental Projects

**1. Research Design Project**

Review the literature for the past two years to identify the newest developments in transformers and ballasts. In a written report, summarize the results and identify how to apply the findings to lighting systems.

**2. Research Design Project**

Identify effective methods for applying controls to general, task, accent, and decorative lighting, and provide the suggestions in a written report. The report may include illustrations and drawings.

# Application Projects

**1. Human Factors Research Project**

Review current literature regarding lighting controls. For each major type of lighting control, including switches, dimmers, timers, occupancy sensors, and photosensors, provide recommendations for effective interior applications and human factor considerations. Write a report that includes your research and effective applications.

**2. Research Design Project**

Identify three commercial and two residential spaces that will use central controls. For each space, develop preset scenes that integrate lighting with other systems. In a written report, describe the preset scenes and indicate how the programming will enhance the quality of the lighting environment.

# Summary

o Magnetic and electronic transformers convert voltages in a system. For lighting purposes, a transformer is either integral to the design of the luminaire or is a separate unit concealed above a ceiling or behind a wall.

o Magnetic and electronic ballasts are control devices used with electric discharge lamps; they start lamps and control the electrical current during operation.

o Electronic transformers and ballasts are preferable to magnetic units because they are more energy-efficient, make less noise, and weigh less.

o Lighting controls operate either manually or automatically, and include switches, dimmers, timers, occupancy sensors, photosensors, and central controls.

o Controls can be used to conserve energy by turning lights off when they are not needed, integrating daylight, monitoring lamp maintenance, and load shedding.

o Generally, using controls to conserve energy will result in economic savings. The cost of controls includes the unit itself, installation, electricity, and maintenance.

o Controls can be adjusted to create the mood and atmosphere required for an activity or space.

o The function of an electrical switch is to stop the flow of electricity. A circuit is closed when a light is on and open when the light is off.

o Dimmers can conserve energy and enhance the aesthetics of an environment. Reducing the power to a lamp conserves energy, affects color, and can extend the life of some lamps.

o Timers control lighting systems by turning lights on/off at designated times.

o Occupancy sensors are designed to turn lights on/off based on whether there are people in a room.

o Photosensors are devices that detect the amount of illumination in a space and then send signals to control electrical light

## KEY TERMS

ballast
central control system
digital addressable
   lighting interface
   (DALI).

dimmer
driver
occupancy sensor
photosensor

switch
tandem wiring
task tuning
timer

transformer
vacancy sensor
wallbox

sources. Photosensors are often used for daylighting.

o Research indicates that the use of occupancy sensors and photosensors saves energy.

o Proper mounting location is key to the success of occupancy sensors and photosensors.

o A central control system uses a microprocessor to monitor, adjust, and regulate lighting in many areas or zones within a building. Some units are designed to integrate lighting with other electrical systems, including mechanical, energy, and security systems.

## References

Li, D. H. W.,& Lam, J.C. (2003). An investigation of daylighting performance and energy saving in a daylit corridor. *Energy and Buildings*, 35(4), 365–373.

## Resources

American History Museum of the Smithsonian Institute (2003). Lighting the Way: A Project at the Smithsonian. http://americanhistory.si.edu/

Benya, J., Heschong, L., McGowan, T., Miller, N., & Rubinstein, F. (2001). *Advanced Lighting Guidelines*. White Salmon, WA: New Buildings Institute.

Bernstien, A., & Conway, K. (2000, March). *The public benefits of California's investments in energy efficiency*. Prepared for the California Energy Commission by the RAND Corporation. MR-1212.0-CEC.

Bierman, A., & Conway, K. (2000). Characterizing daylight photosensor systems performance to help overcome market barriers. *Journal of the Illuminating Engineering Society, 29*(1), 101–115.

Boyce, P. N., Eklund, N., & Simpson, S. (2000). Individual lighting control: Task performance, mood and illuminance. *Journal of the Illuminating Engineering Society, 29*(1), 131–142.

Department of Energy (DOE) (2003). Resource conservation and recovery act. http://www.energy.gov

Energy Information Administration (EIA) (2002). *International Energy Outlook 2002*, Washington, D.C.: U.S. Department of Energy.

Erwine, B., & Heschong, L. (2000, March/April). Daylight: healthy, wealthy & wise. *Architectural Lighting Magazine*. http://www.archlighting.com/architecturallighting/al/index.jsp

Illuminating Engineering Society of North America (IESNA) (2011). *IESNA lighting handbook* (10th ed.). New York: Illuminating Engineering Society of North America.

Interlaboratory Working Group. (2000, November). *Scenarios for a Clean Energy Future* (Oak Ridge, TN: Oak Ridge National Laboratory and Berkeley, CA: Lawrence Berkeley National Laboratory), ORNL/CON-476 and LBNL-44029.

International Association of Energy-Efficient Lighting (IAEEL) (2000). Global lighting: 1000 power plants. *IAEEL Newsletter*, 1-2/00, 1–4.

Jennings, J. F., Rubinstein, R., & DiBartolomeo, D. R. (2000). Comparisons of control options in private offices in an advanced lighting controls test bed. *Journal of the Illuminating Engineering Society, 29*(29), 39–60.

Lee, E. S., DiBartolomeo, D. L., & Selkowitz, S. S. (2000, August). Electrochromic glazings for commercial buildings: Preliminary results from a full-scale testbed. *ACEEE 2000 Summer Study on Energy Efficiency in Buildings, Efficiency and Sustainability*. CA: Pacific Grove.

Lee, E. S., Selkowitz, S. E., Levi, M. S., Blanc, S. L., McConahey, E., McLintock, M., Hakkarainen, P., Sbar, N. L., & Myser, M. P. (2002, August). Active load management with advanced window wall systems: Research and industry perspectives. *ACEEE 2002 Summer Study on Efficiency in Buildings*. CA: Pacific Grove.

Lewis, I. (2000, April). *Light Trespass Research, Final Report: TR-114914*. Electric Power Research Institute.

Maniccia, D., Von Neida, B., & Tweed, A. (2000). Analysis of the energy and cost savings potential of occupancy sensors for commercial lighting systems. *Proceedings of the 2000 Annual Conference of the Illuminating Engineering Society of North America*.

Mistrick, R., Chen, C., Bierman, B., & Felts, D. (2000). A comparison of photosensor-controlled electronic dimming systems. *Proceedings of the 2000 Annual Conference of the Illuminating Engineering Society, 29*(1): 66–80.

Pacific Gas & Electric Company (2000). *Lighting Controls: Codes and Standards Enhancement (CASE) Study*. San Francisco, CA: Pacific Gas & Electric Company.

Phillips, D. (2000). *Lighting modern buildings*. Oxford: Architectural Press.

Rubinstein, F., & Pettler, P. (2001). *Final report on Internet addressable light switch. High Performance Commercial Building Systems*. CA: California Energy Commission.

U.S. Environmental Protection Agency (EPA) (2001). *Design for the Environment*. http://www.epa.gov/

Veitch, J. (2000, July). Lighting guidelines from lighting quality research. *CIBSE/ILE Lighting 2000 Conference*. New York, U.K.

Veitch, J., & Newsham, G. (2000). Exercised control, lighting choices, and energy use: An office simulation experiment. *Journal of Environmental Psychology, 20*(3), 219–237.

# 8 Quantity of Light

Reducing the quantity of lighting and creating flexible illumination levels is essential to sustainable interior environments (Figure 8.1). Managing the quantity of lighting used reduces the consumption of energy and natural resources, and decreases the amount of waste that is deposited in landfills. Interior designers must understand the factors that affect the quantities of illumination in a space and develop strategies for the management of lighting systems.

Unfortunately, often due to the required mathematical calculations, people tend to dislike the information reviewed in this chapter. The content has been simplified to help make the material more interesting. For example, calculations are described in a step-by-step manner, and examples are color-coded to correspond to the text, tables, and figures. Follow the colors to find information required for the calculations. All of the calculations are basic mathematics (addition, subtraction, multiplication, and division). Software programs are available to perform the calculations. However, to understand what the numbers represent and how they were obtained requires doing the calculations manually. This knowledge provides the background to know which conditions in a room and what characteristics of a lighting system could be changed in order to provide the optimum level of illumination where light is

**OBJECTIVES**

o Describe the basic units of measurement used in lighting, including luminous intensity, luminous flux, illuminance, luminance, and luminance exitance, and comprehend the relationships among them

o Understand candlepower distribution curves and how to apply the data they provide

o Identify key factors to consider when specifying illumination levels for a quality lighting environment

o Determine the average illuminance for an interior by using the lumen method

o Determine illuminance levels for a point in a space

FIGURE 8.1 Spaces should be analyzed to determine appropriate illumination levels. It is unlikely that this room for computers requires the high number of fixtures that are present or the quantity of light. (© Horizon International Images Limited/Alamy.)

needed, and to avoid wasting energy by using too many or the wrong fixtures and lamps.

# Units of Measurement
## INTERNATIONAL SYSTEM OF UNITS

Measuring the quantity of lighting in an environment is based upon the principles of radiometry and photometry. **Radiometry** is a scientific discipline dealing with the measurement of radiant energy in the form of electromagnetic waves. Radiant energy is heat energy transferred through space.

**Photometry** is a science derived from radiometry that includes the human response to a source of illumination. The worldwide standard for the units of measurement is the International System of Units (SI). The

properties measured include luminous intensity, luminous flux, illuminance, luminance, and luminous exitance.

In photometry, **luminous intensity** (abbreviated as **I**) is the intensity of a light source, measured in candelas (cd). One candela represents the luminous intensity from a source pointing in a specific direction on a solid angle called the **steradian** (Figure 8.2). Originally, a candle was used to measure luminous intensity, but it was impossible to arrive at a standard with so many types of candles; hence the international use of the candela, from which other units of measurement are derived. Candlepower and candela are considered interchangeable terms.

**Luminous flux** is the total amount of illumination emitted by a light source, measured in lumens (lm). The SI symbol or abbreviation is **F**. Lamp manufacturers provide this information about their products. As

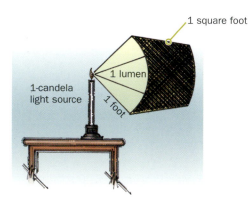

FIGURE 8.2 One candela from a source pointing in a specific direction on a solid angle, the steradian.

discussed in Chapter 3, the number of lumens produced by a lamp per watt of electricity consumed determines the lamp's efficacy.

The **luminaire efficacy ratio (LER)** is a ratio of the lumens per watts consumed for the entire luminaire system, which includes the total lamp lumens, ballast factor, and photometric efficiency.

The unit of measurement used to determine the total amount of light falling on a surface is **illuminance**. The abbreviation for illuminance is **E**, and it is measured in lux (lx) or foot-candles (fc) in the metric and customary systems, respectively. An illumination of 1 lux is produced by 1 lumen of light shining on an area of one square meter. Ten lux equals approximately one foot-candle. Thus, a recommendation for 400 lux of illumination on a work surface would be equivalent to 40 foot-candles.

By way of context for these measurements, the foot-candle levels for a full moon and for sunlight at noon are .01 fc and 10,000 fc, respectively. Many work areas in homes, offices, and conference rooms utilize 30 to 50 fc (300 to 500 lx). Other measurements suggested by the IESNA (2000) are: (1) simple visual tasks is 3 to 10 fc (30 to 100 lx); (2) important visual tasks is 30 fc (300 lx) for tasks with high contrast and large size; (3) important tasks with low contrast and small size is 100 fc (1,000 lx); and critical visual tasks is 300 to 1,000 fc (3,000 to 10,000 lx). As discussed in previous chapters, there are many factors to consider in determining illumination levels, including the lamp, design of the luminaire, maintenance procedures, reflectance values, and distance and angle from the light source to the task.

**Luminance** is a measure of the objective brightness of a light source. It indicates the amount of light in the eyes of users of the space after reflection or transmission from a surface. Thus, illuminance and reflectance affect luminance. The unit of measurement is candela per square meter (cd/m2), and $L$ is the abbreviation for the term.

Brightness is the term used to refer to an individual's perception of the light in a space and, being somewhat subjective, is not a measurable property. Luminance affects the apparent brightness of a surface or material and is dependent upon the location of the user as well as colors, textures, and interior architecture.

**Luminous exitance** is another term associated with luminance. This is a measure of the total quantity of light reflected and emitted in all directions from a surface or material. Luminous exitance is measured in lumens per square foot (lm/ft2).

## PHOTOMETRIC DATA

This section will focus on the photographs and photometric data provided in Figures 8.3a and b and Figure 8.4, respectively. Photometric data are especially important to sustainable designs because they provide the information that is needed to have the appropriate level of light where it is needed.

To determine the direction, pattern, and intensity of light from reflector lamps and luminaires, interior designers refer to **candlepower distribution curves**, as provided by lamp and luminaire manufacturers (see Figure 8.4). Interior designers often use the term "batwing graphs" to refer to specific curves that

(a)

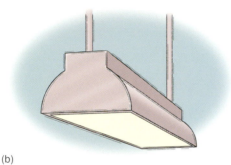

(b)

**FIGURE 8.3** (a) An installation example of the fixture associated with the photometric chart in Figure 8.4. Note the (b) enlarged photograph of the fixture associated with the photometric chart in Figure 8.4. Illustration (conference room): Prudential Lighting.

resemble the shape of a bat's wings. These curves result from a bat-wing lens.

On a polar candlepower distribution curve, zero, or the **nadir** (straight down), is the location of a light source. The concentric circles on the graph indicate the intensity expressed in candelas and the radiating lines are the angles of distribution (Figure 8.4, label b).

Figure 8.4 illustrates a photometric data chart of a direct luminaire with two fluorescent

T8s. Directly above the graph are summary data related to the luminaire (Figure 8.4, label b):

> D (direct) = 100% (indicates luminaire is a direct fixture with 100% of the light directed down)
>
> I (indirect) = 0% (indicates luminaire does not given any (0%) indirect light)
>
> Spacing criteria: Along 1.1; Across 1.3
>
> Lamp lumens are 2950
>
> Input watts are 59

The spacing criterion (SC) is a metric measurement that indicates luminaire locations for spaces requiring consistent illumination levels. The SC for the length of the luminaire is referred to as the "parallel" or "along" (1.1 in Figure 8.4, label b) and the short side of the luminaire is the "perpendicular" or "across" (1.3 in Figure 8.4, label b).

The height of direct luminaires is measured from the bottom of the fixture to a work surface that is 2 feet 6 inches above the floor (Figure 8.5). The measurement for indirect luminaires is from the ceiling to the work surface. Deviations from the recommended SC locations may result in illumination levels that are too high in some areas or too low in others.

Reflected light can be put to use. To maximize the amount of illumination derived from reflectance, luminaires should be installed close to walls, but not so close that they cause excessive brightness on the walls. Generally, the ideal distance from a wall to a fixture is half the center-to-center distance between fixtures.

## photometric data

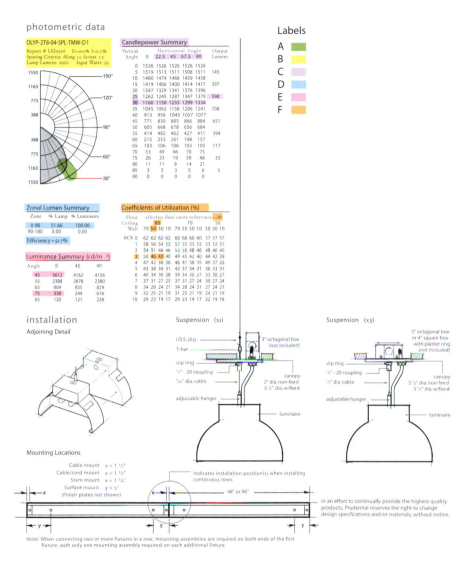

**OLYP-2T8-04-SPL-TMW-D1**

Report # LSI15526  D=100% I=0.0%
Spacing Criteria: Along 1.c Across 1.3
Lamp Lumens: 2950  Input Watts: 59

### Candlepower Summary

| Vertical Angle | Horizontal Angle 0 | 22.5 | 45 | 67.5 | 90 | Output Lumens |
|---|---|---|---|---|---|---|
| 0 | 1526 | 1526 | 1526 | 1526 | 1526 | |
| 5 | 1519 | 1513 | 1511 | 1508 | 1511 | 145 |
| 10 | 1480 | 1474 | 1466 | 1459 | 1458 | |
| 15 | 1419 | 1406 | 1400 | 1414 | 1417 | 397 |
| 20 | 1347 | 1329 | 1341 | 1376 | 1396 | |
| 25 | 1262 | 1245 | 1287 | 1347 | 1379 | 598 |
| 30 | 1160 | 1158 | 1233 | 1299 | 1334 | |
| 35 | 1045 | 1062 | 1156 | 1206 | 1241 | 708 |
| 40 | 913 | 956 | 1045 | 1057 | 1077 | |
| 45 | 771 | 830 | 885 | 866 | 884 | 651 |
| 50 | 605 | 668 | 678 | 656 | 684 | |
| 55 | 414 | 482 | 462 | 427 | 411 | 394 |
| 60 | 215 | 253 | 261 | 198 | 157 | |
| 65 | 103 | 106 | 106 | 103 | 105 | 117 |
| 70 | 53 | 49 | 46 | 70 | 75 | |
| 75 | 26 | 23 | 19 | 39 | 48 | 33 |
| 80 | 11 | 11 | 9 | 14 | 21 | |
| 85 | 3 | 3 | 3 | 5 | 6 | 5 |
| 90 | 0 | 0 | 0 | 0 | 0 | |

### Zonal Lumen Summary

| Zone | % Lamp | % Luminaire |
|---|---|---|
| 0-90 | 51.66 | 100.00 |
| 90-180 | 0.00 | 0.00 |

Efficiency = 51.7%

### Luminance Summary (cd/m $^2$)

| Angle | 0 | 45 | 90 |
|---|---|---|---|
| 45 | 3612 | 4162 | 4156 |
| 55 | 2388 | 2678 | 2380 |
| 65 | 804 | 835 | 829 |
| 75 | 338 | 244 | 616 |
| 85 | 120 | 121 | 228 |

### Coefficients of Utilization (%)

| Floor | effective floor cavity reflectance = .20 | | | | | | | | | |
|---|---|---|---|---|---|---|---|---|---|---|
| Ceiling | 80 | | | 70 | | | 50 | | | |
| Wall | 70 | 50 | 30 | 10 | 70 | 50 | 30 | 10 | 50 | 30 | 10 |
| RCR 0 | 62 | 62 | 62 | 62 | 60 | 60 | 60 | 60 | 57 | 57 | 57 |
| 1 | 58 | 56 | 54 | 53 | 57 | 55 | 53 | 52 | 53 | 52 | 51 |
| 2 | 54 | 51 | 48 | 46 | 53 | 50 | 48 | 46 | 48 | 46 | 45 |
| 3 | 50 | 46 | 43 | 40 | 49 | 45 | 42 | 40 | 44 | 42 | 39 |
| 4 | 47 | 42 | 38 | 36 | 46 | 41 | 38 | 35 | 40 | 37 | 35 |
| 5 | 43 | 38 | 34 | 31 | 42 | 37 | 34 | 31 | 36 | 33 | 31 |
| 6 | 40 | 34 | 30 | 28 | 39 | 34 | 30 | 27 | 33 | 30 | 27 |
| 7 | 37 | 31 | 27 | 25 | 37 | 31 | 27 | 24 | 30 | 27 | 24 |
| 8 | 34 | 28 | 24 | 21 | 34 | 28 | 24 | 21 | 27 | 24 | 21 |
| 9 | 32 | 25 | 21 | 19 | 31 | 25 | 21 | 19 | 24 | 21 | 19 |
| 10 | 29 | 23 | 19 | 17 | 29 | 23 | 19 | 17 | 22 | 19 | 16 |

### Labels

A
B
C
D
E
F

## installation

**Adjoining Detail**

**Mounting Locations**

Cable mount  x = 1 1/2"
Cable/cord mount  x = 1 1/2"
Stem mount  x = 1 1/2"
Surface mount  y = 5"
(Finish plates not shown)

x
y

Indicates installation position(s) when installing continuous rows.

48" or 96"

Note: When connecting two or more fixtures in a row, mounting assemblies are required on both ends of the first fixture, with only one mounting assembly required on each additional fixture.

**Suspension (x1)**

I.D.S. clip
T-bar
slip ring
1/2" 20 coupling
1/16" dia. cable
adjustable hanger
3" octagonal box (not included)
canopy
2" dia. non-feed
5 1/2" dia. w/feed
luminaire

**Suspension (x3)**

slip ring
1/2" - 20 coupling
1/2" dia. cable
adjustable hanger
3" octagonal box or 4" square box with plaster ring (not included)
canopy
5 1/2" dia. non-feed
5 1/2" dia. w/feed
luminaire

In an effort to continually provide the highest quality products, Prudential reserves the right to change design specifications and/or materials, without notice.

**FIGURE 8.4** The photometric chart of a linear direct luminaire with a parabolic louver. Photograph and illustration of the luminaire are in Figures 8.3a and b.

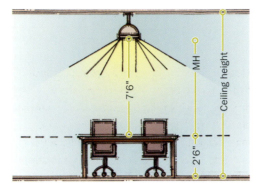

**FIGURE 8.5** In calculating lighting quantities, the height measurement for direct luminaires is determined from the bottom of the fixture to a work surface that is 2′ 6″ from the floor (Mounting Height = MH).

The formula for calculating the center-to-center distance between fixtures is:

SC ratio × mounting height (MH − distance from the bottom of the luminaire to the work surface) = spacing intervals (SI)

Example: The calculations below illustrate the spacing intervals for a luminaire that is 7 feet 6 inches (7.5 in calculation) from a work surface. (Remember 1.1 and 1.3 were provided by the manufacturer's photometric data sheet. See Figure 8.4.)

1.1 (along length of fixture) × 7.5 (MH) = 8.25 (SI)

or 8 feet on center along the length of the fixture

1.3 (along the short side of fixture) × 7.5 (MH) = 9.75 (SI)

or 10 feet on center along the short side of the fixture

To read the candlepower distribution graph on the photometric chart, identify a specific angle of view, and then read the associated candelas (Figure 8.4, label a). For example, for the direct linear luminaire, illustrated in Figure 8.3b, the emitted candelas at a vertical angle of 30° are approximately 1160 (Figure 8.4, label a).

This number is also available in the candlepower summary table (Figure 8.4, label c). Moving to the right in the same row will provide the emitted candelas at horizontal angles of 22.5 degrees, 45 degrees, 67.5 degrees, and 90 degrees. For example, at a vertical angle of 30 degrees, the emitted candelas at the 45 degrees horizontal angle are 1233 (Figure 8.4, label c). The last column in the candlepower summary chart indicates the output in lumens at various vertical angles. For example, at a vertical angle of 25 degrees, the output in lumens is 598 (Figure 8.4, label c).

The zonal lumens summary table (Figure 8.4d) provides a quick overview of lumens in two zones. Because the luminaire has a direct distribution of light, all the light is emitted in the zone between 0 and 90 degrees, that is, in the downward zone. The zonal lumens table also indicates the efficiency of the luminaire and lamp combination, which is 51.7 percent (Figure 8.4, label d).

In addition, the chart provides luminance summary (cd/m2) data (Figure 8.4, label e). For this luminaire, the luminance levels are higher at the lower vertical angles. For example, at a vertical angle of 45 degrees, the luminance is 3612, while at 75 degrees, it is 338. The remaining table in the chart, coefficients of utilization (%) (Figure 8.4, label f) is explained in the "Lumen Method" section under "Calculations" later in this chapter.

As illustrated in Figure 8.4, luminaires and reflector lamps with a symmetrical distribution are often illustrated on only one side of the graph because each half will be identical. It is important to note that indirect/direct luminaires have a candlepower distribution curve above and below nadir. If the luminaire distributes a high level of illumination toward the ceiling, to avoid annoying brightness or glare, it might be necessary to locate the fixture at a considerable distance from the ceiling. Luminaires that emit light from the top and sides of the fixture will have candlepower distribution graphs for vertical and horizontal light angles.

## Calculations

Calculations for determining illuminance can be done by hand or by using a lighting software package. This section reviews both methods. As mentioned at the beginning of this chapter understanding how the calculations are performed is critical to knowing the variables that affect the quantity of light on a work plane and in a space. To ensure a quality lighting environment, it is critical to recognize that the illuminance level identified through the calculations is only one of the variables to be considered in arriving at the final specifications. All the criteria discussed throughout this textbook and the uniqueness of a site and its users must be synthesized for the final lighting plan.

### LUMEN METHOD

This section focuses on the coefficients of utilization (%) data provided in the previous photometric chart (Figure 8.4, label f) as well as Tables 8.1 and 8.2, and Figures 8.4 and 8.6. The lumen method described in this section is an abbreviated method used to determine the average illuminance on horizontal surfaces in a room. These data can be useful in the initial stages of the lighting design process because they provide an estimate of the number of fixtures that should be used to achieve a uniform distribution of light in a space. To determine more accurate illuminance calculations, refer to IESNA (2000) or advanced lighting software programs.

To perform illuminance calculations, several elements must be identified:

○ **The proportions of a room**

○ **Luminaires and lamps**

○ **Location of work surfaces**

○ **Distance between work surfaces and luminaires**

○ **Reflectance values of ceilings, walls, and floors**

The calculations also require:

○ **Room-cavity ratios (RCR)**

○ **Coefficient of utilization (CU) for luminaires**

○ **Light loss factor (LLF)**

○ **Lamp lumen depreciation (LLD)**

○ **Luminaire dirt depreciation (LDD)**

The RCR is a formula designed to take into account the proportions of a space and the potential distance from the luminaires to the work surface:

$$\frac{5(H)\,(L + W)}{L \times W} = RCR$$

H—Height of room or distance from luminaire to work surface

L—Length of room

W—Width of room

**TABLE 8.1** Lamp Lumen Depreciation (LLD) Factors for Selected Lamps

| LAMPS | TYPICAL LLD FACTORS |
|---|---|
| Incandescent | .85 |
| Halogen | .92 |
| Fluorescent | |
| T8/730 | .90 |
| T8/830 | .93 |
| Compact Fluorescent | .85 |
| Metal Halide | .73 |
| Ceramic Metal Halide | .89 |
| High-Pressure Sodium | .80 |

**TABLE 8.2** Procedure for Determining Luminaire Maintenance Categories

| MAINTENANCE CATEGORY | TOP ENCLOSURE | BOTTOM ENCLOSURE |
|---|---|---|
| I. | 1. None | 1. None |
| II. | 1. None<br>2. Transparent with 15 percent or more uplight through apertures<br>3. Translucent with 15 percent or more uplight through apertures<br>4. Opaque with 15 percent or more uplight through apertures | 1. None<br>2. Louvers or baffles |
| III. | 1. Transparent with less than 15 percent upward light through apertures<br>2. Translucent with less than 15 percent upward light through apertures<br>3. Opaque with less than 15 percent uplight through apertures | 1. None<br><br>2. Louvers or baffles |
| IV. | 1. Transparent unapertured<br>2. Translucent unapertured<br>3. Opaque unapertured | 1. Transparent unapertured<br>2. Translucent unapertured |
| V. | 1. Transparent unapertured<br>2. Translucent unapertured<br>3. Opaque unapertured | 1. Transparent unapertured<br>2. Translucent unapertured |
| VI. | 1. None<br>2. Transparent unapertured<br>3. Translucent unapertured<br>4. Opaque unapertured | 1. Transparent unapertured<br>2. Translucent unapertured<br>3. Opaque unaperatured |

Source: Reprinted from the *IESNA Lighting Handbook* (9th ed.), pp. 9–20, with permission from the Illuminating Engineering Society of North America.

The **room-cavity ratio (RCR)** is used to determine the **coefficient of utilization (CU)** (Figure 8.4, label f). The CU depends on the space to be illuminated and the design of the luminaire. The CU indicates the ratio of initial lamp lumens to the lumens on a work surface for a particular luminaire, lamp, location of the task plane, and space.

CU percentages are available from luminaire manufacturers (Figure 8.4, label f). The CU table in Figure 8.4, label f, is based upon a floor cavity reflectance of .20. Ceiling reflectance percentages are 80, 70, and 50. Wall reflectance percentages are provided for 70, 50, 30, and 10.

LLF indicates the illuminance that is lost as a result of the type of lamp, the temperature of the space, time, input voltage, ballast, lamp position, interior conditions, and burnouts. There can be a 25 percent loss of lumens because of dirt, dust, and lamp depreciation.

IESNA (2000) has identified recoverable and nonrecoverable LLFs. The recoverable LLFs include room surface dirt depreciation, **lamp lumen depreciation**, lamp burnouts factor, and luminaire dirt depreciation. Nonrecoverable factors include ambient temperature, input voltage, ballast factor, and luminaire surface depreciation. For an abbreviated method of determining the average illuminance on horizontal surfaces in a room, LLF can be calculated by:

$$LLD \times LDD = LLF$$

LLD is a metric measurement of the loss of lumens due to the design of a lamp. Table 8.1 provides a list of LLD for selected lamps.

LDD accounts for the loss of light caused by dirt and dust accumulation. Important considerations for LDD are the design of the luminaire, the atmosphere of the space, and how often the lamps are cleaned. Table 8.2 and Figure 8.6 produced by IESNA (2000) illustrate maintenance categories for various luminaires, atmosphere considerations, and dirt conditions. This information serves as a reference for determining LDD. As defined by IESNA (2000), the categories include "very clean" (VC), "clean" (C), "medium" (M), "dirty" (D), and "very dirty" (VD). Lamps mounted in an exposed luminaire, in an environment that has a great deal of dust, such as a woodworking studio, would have to be cleaned very frequently to reduce significant light loss.

A simple method for determining average illuminance is the lumen method, also referred to as the **zonal cavity calculation**. This method provides only the average illuminance in a space and does not factor in variation in light levels. The basic formula for determining the average maintained illuminance on a work surface is:

$$Maintained\ fc = \frac{Number\ of\ lamps \times Initial\ lamp\ lumens \times LLF \times CU}{Area}$$

Example: A classroom with the following factors:

o  a space 30 feet × 30 feet with a 10-foot ceiling

o  work surface: 2 feet 6 inches (AFF)

o  distance from luminaires to the work surface: 5 feet 6 inches

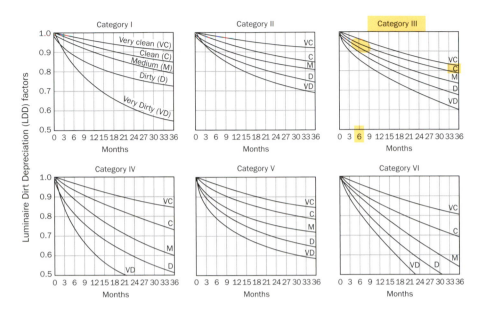

FIGURE 8.6 Luminaire Dirt Depreciation (LDD) factors for six luminaire categories (I through VI) and for five degrees of dirtiness.

- clean space

- lamp cleaning twice a year

- twelve surface-mount luminaires (Figure 8.4) with two F32T8 lamps in each luminaire (use the SC to determine an approximate number of luminaires)

- initial lamp lumens for an F32T8 is 2800 (information from a lamp manufacturer's catalog)

- LLD for an F32T8 lamp is .93 (Table 8.1—highlighted)

- LDD—maintenance category III (Table 8.2—highlighted)

- LDD is approximately .92 based upon category III, clean space, and lamps cleaned twice a year (Figure 8.6—highlighted)

- 80 percent ceiling reflectance, 50 percent wall reflectance, and

- 20 percent floor reflectance

The average maintained illuminance on a work surface in this space is 30 fc. This is determined by performing the following steps:

1. Determine the total number of lamps by multiplying the number of lamps per luminaire:

   2 (lamps in each luminaire) × 12 (number of luminaires) = 24

2. Calculate the LLF:

   .93 (LLD) × .92 (LDD) = .85 (LLF)

   .93 (Table 8.1—highlighted)

   .92 (Table 8.2 and Figure 8.6—highlighted)

3. Calculate the RCR:

$$\frac{5(7.5)\,(30 + 30) = 3\ (RCR)}{30 \times 30}$$

5—Given value in the formula

7.5—Distance from luminaires to work surface

30—Length of Room

30—Width of Room

4. Refer to manufacturer's photometric data chart to locate the CU (Figure 8.4, label f). The CU is approximately .46 given an RCR of 3 and a space with:

80 percent ceiling reflectance (pcc)

50 percent wall reflectance (pw)

20 percent floor reflectance

CU is approximately .46 (Figure 8.4, label f)

5. To determine the average maintained illuminance on the work surface, the values determined in the previous steps are then inserted into the formula:

$$\frac{\substack{24\ (\text{lamps}) \times \\ 2800\ (\text{Initial lamp lumens}) \times \\ .85\ (\text{LLF}) \times .46\ (\text{CU})}}{30 \times 30\ (\text{Room dimensions})} = 29.2\ \text{or}\ 30\ \text{fc}$$

Note that when the LLF and the CU are factored in, illuminance levels are decreased. This reflects characteristics of luminaires, interior architecture, and environmental factors in the space. Without these two considerations, the illumination level would be approximately 75 fc at the initial installation, and would not take into account what could occur in the space throughout the life of the installation. This notation helps to illustrate why it is important to consider all the systemic factors that affect illuminance.

## POINT-BY-POINT METHOD

The basic point-by-point method determines the fc level for a focal point. This method uses the inverse square law and cosine law, also referred to as Lambert's Law. The inverse square law is utilized only for point sources.

The inverse square law formula is:

$$E = I/d^2$$

E—illumination (fc)

I—luminous intensity (cd) of the source (Available from the lamp manufacturer. Refer to the lamp's candlepower distribution chart.) (Figure 8.7).

d—distance from the light source to a surface

The inverse square law is based on the principle that the illumination level on a surface decreases the farther the surface is from the light source. According to the formula,

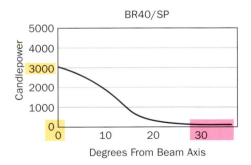

FIGURE 8.7 A candlepower distribution chart of a reflector BR40/SP. Note: highlighted figures on left are for the first point-by-point method (straight down) and the highlighted figures on the right are for the second example (30 degree angle).

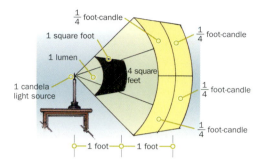

FIGURE 8.8 A demonstration of the inverse square law, whereby the level of illumination on a surface decreases the farther a surface is from the light source.

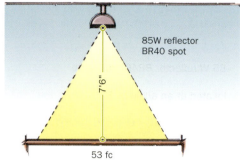

FIGURE 8.9 A light source located directly above a surface.

the factor by which the illumination on a surface is decreased is equal to the square of its distance from the source. Therefore, the illuminance on a surface 2 feet away from its source is one-fourth as much as the illumination 1 foot from the light source (Figure 8.8). The inverse square law formula can be utilized for determining the illuminance on a point from a light source that is located directly above the surface (Figure 8.9).

Example (Figure 8.9):

85 W reflector BR40 spot lamp

Located directly above a surface 7 feet 6 inches from the lamp

3000 (cd) /7.5$^2$ (distance from light source to surface) = 53.3 or 53 fc (E)

Note that 3000 refers to information in Figure 8.7.

The formula for the cosine law is E = I/d$^2$3 cos $\theta$, where $\theta$ (theta) is the angle between a ray from the luminaire falling on a point and a line perpendicular to the plane upon which that point is located.

The cosine law indicates that the illuminance on a surface will vary according to the cosine of the angle of incidence. Cosine and sine are used for horizontal and vertical surfaces, respectively; the corresponding formula for determining the illuminance on a vertical surface is: E = I/d$^2$ 3 sin $\theta$. Cosine and sine for angles can be found using a calculator.

Determining the illuminance for specific locations can be very complex because of the variety of areas within a space and the interdependence of the factors that affect lighting. For this reason, interior designers and engineers will generally use lighting software to perform the calculations. To facilitate a conceptual understanding of the process and the factors that are important to consider when determining illuminance for specific points, two representative examples follow.

The cosine law can be used to determine the illuminance on a horizontal surface when the luminaire, or the point to be lighted, is at an angle (Figure 8.10a).

Horizontal Surface Example (Figure 8.10a):

85 W reflector BR40 spot lamp

located at an angle of 30°

above a horizontal surface 7 feet 6 inches from the lamp

200 (cd) / $7.5^2$ (distance from light source to surface) $\times$ .866 (cos $\theta$) = 3.08 or 3 fc (E)

Note that 200 refers to information in Figure 8.7.

Vertical Surface Example (Figure 8.10b)

85 W reflector BR40 spot lamp

aimed at an angle of 30°

aimed at a vertical surface 7 feet 6 inches from the lamp

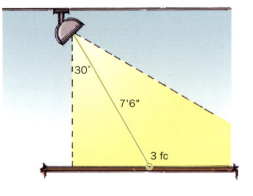

FIGURE 8.10B A light source located at an angle to a vertical surface.

200 (cd) / $7.5^2$ (distance from light source to surface) $\times$ .500 (sin $\theta$) = 1.77 or 2 fc (E)

Note that 200 is from information in Figure 8.7.

Interior designers conduct calculations for new construction as well as for the remodeling of existing spaces. Both applications utilize the calculation methods discussed in this section. For existing spaces, an interior designer will frequently want to obtain current fc levels by taking illuminance measurements in the field using a foot-candle meter (Figure 8.11a). This instrument indicates the fc levels for any area within the space, as well as the reflectance values of surfaces.

To determine a foot-candle level at a given location, an interior designer places the foot-candle meter in the specified location and reads the result. Usually, an interior designer will want the fc levels for both general and task lighting within a room. To obtain the general illuminance, an interior designer will establish

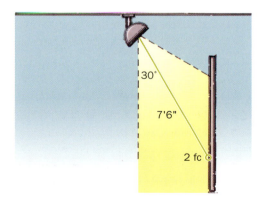

FIGURE 8.10A A light source located at an angle to a horizontal surface.

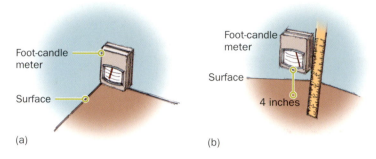

(a)

(b)

FIGURE 8.11A In the field, an interior designer can determine illumination levels by using a foot-candle meter.

FIGURE 8.11B An interior designer can determine the reflectance of a surface by placing a foot-candle meter approximately 4 inches away from the surface to record the fc level.

a grid, take readings at each cross-section of the grid, and then average the results.

Foot-candle readings for task lighting can be obtained by placing the foot-candle meter on each work surface. To determine an approximation of the reflectance of a surface, an interior designer will place the foot-candle meter approximately 4 inches from the surface and record the fc level (Figure 8.11b).

Lighting software packages are available for basic and advanced illuminance calculations using daylight and electrical light sources. Basic programs, including AutoCAD extensions, will predict the brightness of surfaces and patterns of light distribution on vertical and horizontal surfaces. Advanced programs are able to calculate illuminance in rooms with unique shapes, including sloped ceilings (Figure 8.12).

This chapter explores what is involved in determining the quantity of illumination in an interior. Many factors relating to the environment and the users of the space are covered, within the context of recommendations provided by IESNA and other international organizations. Quantity of lighting is only one of the factors that must be considered in designing a quality lighting environment.

## Quantity of Light and LEED Certification

For a checklist of how you can apply quantifying light in creating a LEED-certified building, see Box 8.1.

**FIGURE 8.12** Advanced lighting programs can calculate illuminance in rooms with a variety of configurations. (Graeme Watt [2000]g.watt@btconnect.com)

**BOX 8.1 Sustainable Considerations Related to Quantity of Light**

You can put the content of this chapter to work for you to create LEED-certified buildings by considering the following strategies:

o Reduce light pollution by employing luminaire placement strategies that help eliminate the spill of interior light to the outdoors.

o Minimize and optimize energy performance by selecting luminaires that have the most appropriate candlepower distribution for the task.

o Select luminaires with an efficient luminaire efficacy ratio (LER) to minimize and optimize energy performance.

o Minimize and optimize energy performance by using valuable information on luminaire manufacturers' photometric charts, such as candlepower distributions, luminance summaries, and coefficients of utilizations.

o Minimize and optimize energy performance by using information on luminaire manufacturers' photometric charts to determine the number of fixtures that should be used and their location. Using this information will help to avoid using too many or too few fixtures in a space as well as enhancing user satisfaction by having the optimum illumination for a task.

o Minimize and optimize energy performance by performing illuminance calculations, including the lumen and point-by-point methods. Using this information will help to avoid using too many or too few fixtures in a space as well as enhancing user satisfaction by having the optimum illumination for a task.

o Minimize and optimize energy performance by specifying the appropriate lamp, wattage, and optical qualities for a specific spot.

o Avoid construction waste in the future by specifying the correct number of luminaires for a space.

o Use a quality indoor-environment-specified low-emitting paint for any element of a lighting system to maximize illumination specify paint colors with a high reflectance (> 85%).

o In the fundamental/enhanced commissioning of the building energy systems monitor the installation, operation, and calibration of the lighting system, include illuminance levels at various locations in the spaces.

o Measure and verify the efficiency of illuminance levels.

o Monitor new sustainable developments in lighting systems to ensure the most efficient and cost effective lighting systems.

**TABLE BOX 8.1** LEED Categories Related to Quantity of Light

LEED CREDIT CATEGORY

SS (Sustainable Sites) Credit 1, Option 2, Path 6: Light Pollution Reduction

EA (Energy and Atmosphere) Prerequisite 1: Fundamental Commissioning of Building Energy Systems

EA Prerequisite 2: Minimum Energy Performance

EA Credit 1.1: Optimize Energy Performance—Lighting Power

EA Credit 1.2: Optimize Energy Performance—Lighting Controls

EA Credit 2: Enhanced Commissioning

EA Credit 3: Measurement and Verification

IEQ (Indoor Environmental Quality) Credit 4.2: Low-Emitting Materials—Paints and Coatings

IEQ Credit 6.1: Controllability of Systems—Lighting

IEQ Credit 6.2: Controllability of Systems—Thermal Comfort

ID (Innovation in Design) Credit 1: Innovation in Design

Source: USGBC. (2009). *LEED reference guide for green interior design and construction*. Washington, DC: U.S. Green Building Council.

# Fundamental Projects

**1. Research Design Project**

Search the Internet for three luminaire manufacturers. For each manufacturer, locate the photometric reports for three different luminaires. In a written report, provide the following information: (a) a summary of the photometric data for each luminaire; (b) comparison of photometric information of each manufacturer; and (c) an analysis of how an interior designer would utilize the photometric data in designing a quality lighting environment.

**2. Research Design Project**

Search the Internet for three luminaires for which data related to spacing criterion (SC) are provided. In a written report, summarize the SC for each luminaire and provide a rationale for differences between SC recommendations. Include how an interior designer would utilize the SC data for specifying luminaires.

### 3. Research Design Project

Search the Internet for three different lighting software packages. Write a report providing the following information for each program: (a) name of the program; (b) manufacturer; (c) computer power; (d) description of the program; (e) application suggestions; (f) price; and (g) advantages and disadvantages of the program.

# Application Projects

**1. Human Factors Research Project**

Visit three different spaces and record the following information about each space: (a) size of the room; (b) size and location of windows; (c) the types of luminaires and lamps and their locations; (d) the colors and textures of the ceiling, floor, and walls; and (e) how users are using the space. Use a foot-candle meter to record the fc level for general and task illuminance. Also record the fc levels for each wall. In a written report, summarize the data collected and analyze the adequacy of illumination. Provide suggestions for improving the space, including users' considerations and the quality of layered lighting.

**2. Research Design Project**

Identify a commercial and a residential space. Applying the lumen method, calculate a recommended illuminance level for each space. Also identify the recommended illuminance level for a task surface in each space by using the basic point-by-point method. In a written report, include the following items:

a. Floor plan of the spaces

b. Elevations of walls with windows

c. Summary of materials and colors in the spaces

d. Calculations resulting from the lumen method and the point-by-point method

e. Recommendations for luminaires and lamps

# Summary

o Measuring the quantity of lighting in an environment is based on the principles of radiometry and photometry. Radiometry is a science that focuses on measuring radiant energy. Photometry is a science derived from radiometry that includes the human response to the source of illumination.

o The basic categories for measuring lighting include luminous intensity, luminous flux, illuminance, luminance, and luminance exitance.

o To determine the direction, pattern, and intensity of light from reflector lamps and luminaires, interior designers refer to photometric data reports, such as those provided by lamp and luminaire manufacturers.

o A simple method for determining average illuminance is the lumen method, also referred to as the zonal cavity calculation. This method provides only the average illuminance in a space and does not consider variance in light levels. The basic formula for determining the average maintained illuminance on a work surface is:

$$\frac{\text{Number of lamps} \times \text{Initial lamp lumens} \times \text{LLF} \times \text{CU}}{\text{Area}} = \text{Maintained fc}$$

o The basic point-by-point method determines the fc level for a focal point. Determining the illuminance for specific locations can be very complex because of the variety of areas within a space and the interdependence of the factors that affect lighting.

o Interior designers conduct calculations for new construction as well as for the remodeling of existing spaces. Both applications utilize the calculation methods illustrated in this chapter. For existing spaces, an interior designer will frequently take illuminance measurements in the field by using a foot-candle meter.

# Resources

Banbury, S., Macken, W., Tremblay, S., & Jones, D. (2001). Noise distraction affects memory. *Human Factors, 43*(1), 12–29.

Benya, J., Heschong, L., McGowan, T., Miller, N., & Rubinstein, F. (2001). *Advanced lighting guidelines*. White Salmon, WA: New Buildings Institute.

Bierman, A., & Conway, K. (2000). Characterizing daylight photosensor systems performance to help overcome market barriers. *Journal of the Illuminating Engineering Society, 29*(1), 101–115.

## KEY TERMS

candlepower distribution curve
coefficient of utilization (CU)
illuminance (E)
lamp lumen depreciation (LLD)
light loss factor (LLF)
luminaire dirt depreciation (LDD)

luminaire efficacy ratio (LER)
luminance (L)
luminance exitance
luminous flux (F)
luminous intensity (I)
nadir

photometry
radiometry
room-cavity ratio (RCR)
steradian
zonal cavity calculation

Boyce, P. N., Eklund, N., & Simpson, S. (2000). Individual lighting control: Task performance, mood and illuminance. *Journal of the Illuminating Engineering Society, 29*(1), 131–142.

Boyce, P. R., Akashi, Y., Hunter, C. M., & Bullough, J. D. (2003). The impact of spectral power distribution on the performance of an achromatic visual task. *Lighting Research and Technology, 35*(2), 141–161.

Eklund, N., Boyce, P., & Simpson, S. (2000). Lighting and sustained performance. *Journal of the Illuminating Engineering Society, 29*(1), 116.

Erwine, B., & Heschong, L. (2000, March/April). Daylight: healthy, wealthy & wise. *Architectural Lighting Magazine.*

Figueiro, M. G., Eggleston, G., & Rea, M.S. (2002). Effects of light exposure on behavior of Alzheimer's patients: A pilot study. *Paper presented at the Fifth International LRO Lighting Research Symposium*, Orlando, FL.

Figueiro, M. G., & Stevens, R. (2002). Daylight and productivity: A possible link to circadian regulation. *Poster Session at the Fifth International LRO Lighting Research Symposium*, Orlando, FL.

Graham, R., & Michel, A. (2003). *Impact of dementia on circadian patterns. Lighting and circadian rhythms and sleep in older adults* (Technical Memorandum 1007708) Palo Alto, CA: Electric Power Research Institute (EPRI).

Graham, R., & Michel, A. (2003). *Sundowning: Lighting and circadian rhythms and sleep in older adults* (Technical Memorandum 1007708) Palo Alto, CA: Electric Power Research Institute (EPRI).

Knez, I. (2001). Effects of colour of light on nonvisual psychological processes. *Journal of Environmental Psychology, 21*(2), 201–208.

Knez, I., & Hygge, S. (in press). The circumplex structure of affect: A Swedish version. *Scandinavian Journal of Psychology.*

Knez, I., & Kers, C. (2000). Effects of indoor lighting, gender and age on mood and cognitive performance. *Environment and Behavior, 32*, 817–831.

Lockely, S. (2002). Light and human circadian regulation: Night work, day work, and jet lag. *Paper presented at the Fifth International LRO Lighting Research Symposium*, Orlando, FL.

Martin, L. E., Marler, M., Shochat, T., & Ancoli-Israel, S. (2000). Circadian rhythms of agitation in institutionalized patients with Alzheimer's disease. *Chronobiology International, 17*(3), 405–418.

Miller, N. (2002). Lighting for seniors: Obstacles in applying the research. *Paper presented at the Fifth International LRO Lighting Research Symposium*, Orlando, FL.

National Mental Health Association (2003). *Seasonal Affective Disorders*. http://www.nmha.org. Retrieved May 8, 2003.

Navvab, M. (2000). A comparison of visual performance under high and low color temperature fluorescent lamps. *Proceedings of the 2000 Annual Conference of the Illuminating Engineering Society of North America*. Washington, D.C.

Noelle-Waggoner, E. (2002). Let there be light, or face the consequences: A national concern for our aging population. *Paper presented at the Fifth International LRO Lighting Research Symposium*, Orlando, FL.

Passini, R., Pigot, H., Rainville, C., & Tetreault, M. H. (2000). Wayfinding in a nursing home for advanced dementia of the Alzheimer's type. *Environment and Behavior, 32*(5), 684–710.

Rea, M. S. (2002). Light—much more than vision. (Keynote). *Light and Human Health: EPRI/LRO5 International Lighting Research Symposium*. Palo Alto, CA: Lighting Research Office of the Electric Power Research Institute, 1–15.

Rea, M. S., Bullough, J. D., & Figueiro, M.G. (2002). Phototransduction for human melatonin suppression. *Journal of Pineal Research, 32*, 209–213.

Rea, M. S., Figueiro, M. G., & Bullough, J.D. (2002). Circadian photobiology: An emerging framework for lighting practice and research. *Lighting Research and Technology, 34*(3), 177–190.

Stevens, R. (2002). Epidemiological evidence indicating light exposure is linked to human cancer development. *Paper presented at the Fifth International LRO Lighting Research Symposium*, Orlando, FL.

Veitch, J. (2000, July). *Lighting guidelines from lighting quality research.* CIBSE/ILE Lighting 2000 Conference. New York, United Kingdom.

Veitch, J. A., & McColl, S. (2001). Evaluation of full-spectrum fluorescent lighting. *Ergonomics, 44*(3), 255–279.

Veitch, J., & Newsham, G. (2000). Exercised control, lighting choices, and energy use: An office simulation experiment. *Journal of Environmental Psychology 20*(3), 219–237.

Wapner, S., & Demick, J. (2002). The increasing contexts of context in the study of environment behavior relations. In R. Bechtel and A. Churchman (eds.), *Handbook of environmental psychology*. New York: Wiley.

Wu, W., & Ng, E. (2003). A review of the development of daylighting in schools. *Lighting Research and Technology, 35*(2), 111–125.

Zeisel, J. (2000). Environmental design effects on Alzheimer symptoms in long term care residences. *World Hospitals and Health Service, 36*(3), 27–31.

# PART TWO LIGHTING DESIGN APPLICATIONS AND THE DESIGN PROCESS

Part One provided the basics you need to design a quality lighting environment. Part Two examines how these lighting concepts and elements are integrated within the process required to design residential and commercial interiors. We also focus on how each step in the design process relates to creating LEED-certified building design. Chapters 11 and 12 conclude with examples of successful lighting design in top-rated LEED-certified residential and commercial buildings.

# 9 Lighting Design Process: Project Planning through Design Development

Basic concepts and elements of a quality lighting environment, including components of lighting systems, daylighting, directional effects of illumination, energy considerations, environmental factors related to lighting, and human factors, were explored in previous chapters. The primary purpose of Chapters 9 and 10 is to explain the lighting design process within the context of the content reviewed in Chapters 1 to 8. Lighting design is performed by architects, interior designers, and lighting designers. Frequently, a lighting designer develops the lighting design for an architect or interior designer.

This analysis of the lighting design process is broken down into two chapters. Chapter 9 covers details regarding the project planning process, as well as methods for conducting the comprehensive programming phase, schematic design, and design development. Chapter 10 deals with contractual documents, contract administration, and evaluation.

An important element in the success of the lighting design process is obtaining client approval at the conclusion of each phase and before proceeding to the next stage. This approval process is important to ensure that the client is in full agreement with the lighting design, costs, and schedule. If an interior/lighting designer proceeds to the next phase before

## OBJECTIVES

- Identify the activities involved in the initial phases of the lighting design process

- Identify the information that should be collected during the comprehensive programming phase and then be applied to developing the lighting criteria

- Understand relevant lighting-related information that should be collected by interviewing, surveying, and observing end users of an interior

- Understand how to analyze and synthesize the data collected in the comprehensive programming phase

- Describe the brainstorming process, including sketching techniques that can assist with the conceptualization of the lighting design

- Identify the purposes of the design development phase

- Apply an understanding of the design development phase to a lighting project

- Understand and describe the most salient factors in conducting oral presentations

receiving client approval, valuable time and resources may be wasted. A client may be reluctant to pay for services without having approved them, and a lack of communication can seriously affect the working relationship. An unhappy client will not use the designer's services again and may make negative comments to potential clients. This is a serious problem because a great deal of business in the field of interior design is generated by repeat business and word-of-mouth.

## The Lighting Design Process

The lighting design process may be divided into the following seven phases: (1) project planning; (2) comprehensive programming; (3) schematic design; (4) design development; (5) contract documentation; (6) contract administration; and (7) evaluation (Figure 9.1). Client involvement is essential at every phase of the lighting design process to ensure satisfaction with and approval of the elements of the program, including illumination plans, schedules, and budget.

As a result of gathering data through programming, the criteria of the lighting project are used as the foundation for developing schematic designs. This is a conceptual phase in which many schematics of the lighting environment are explored with the client and the team of professionals involved in the project. Some of the schematic drawings used include bubble diagrams, lighting distribution diagrams, and task-lighting relationship

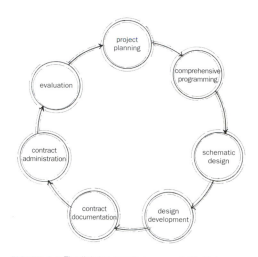

**FIGURE 9.1** The lighting design process divided into seven phases. As a cyclical process, the evaluation phase provides useful information to improve the existing and future projects.

sketches (Figure 9.2). A successful schematic design is then expounded and detailed in the design development phase. At this stage in the lighting design process, specific illumination methods, lighting systems, and layouts are presented to a client for discussion and evaluation. Upon approval by the client, registered professionals, such as architects and engineers, enter the contract documentation phase and begin developing working drawings, specifications, sections, cut sheets, and purchase orders. The contract administration phase is the implementation stage of the project.

The evaluation phase takes place after people are using the space or building. Often referred to as postoccupancy evaluation, this process is intended to determine user satisfaction with the lighting design. The data

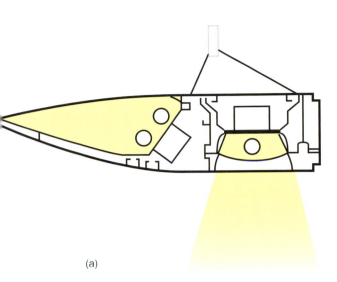

(a)

(b)

FIGURE 9.2 An example of (a) a schematic drawing of a (b) fixture depicting the direct and indirect distribution of light. (Courtesy of Selux.)

gathered during this phase should be used to improve any design problems. As illustrated by the directional arrows in Figure 9.1, information learned in the evaluation phase should also be used to benefit plans for future clients. A process focusing on continued improvement will result in the best possible quality lighting environments.

## Initial Phases

### PROJECT PLANNING

The primary purposes of planning are to develop a profile of the project and to determine the resources needed to achieve its objectives. An interior/lighting designer may be hired by a variety of people associated with residential and commercial interiors, including the owner(s), an architect, an engineer, or a contractor.

To develop the best possible lighting plan, an interior/lighting designer should be involved in the planning stage of the entire project. Within the context of the project's objectives and timeline, determined in consultation with the client and other professionals, an interior/lighting designer develops a plan for the lighting. Most lighting projects will have objectives related to users, tasks, sustainability, interior elements, spatial geometry, technology, illumination methods, codes, timelines, budgets, and maintenance. In addition, a client may be seeking LEED certification. Well-defined objectives outline the project and serve as the basis for the planning process.

The profile of the project, for planning purposes, should include a preliminary understanding of the needs of the owner, end users, and elements of the property. Understanding the scope of the work helps to determine the amount of time and resources needed to execute the project. This is critical information the interior/lighting designer should acquire during the planning stages because a client may have unreasonable expectations concerning the amount of time needed for construction, the feasibility of a design, or the cost of lighting systems.

For planning purposes, an interior/lighting designer must know the location of the property and whether the project involves an existing building, new construction, or speculative construction (Figure 9.3). Developing a lighting design for an existing structure might involve minor adjustments to an installation, retrofitting, or a completely new lighting scheme for an interior project with extensive renovation.

For new construction, the planning phase significantly affects the lighting plan. Ideally, the lighting plan should be developed in concert with the architectural concept. Planning at this stage gives the designer the opportunity to integrate daylight successfully and to create a design that enhances the appearance of the interior. The range of lighting possibilities diminishes as construction proceeds. When walls, ceilings, and floors are finished, it can be difficult to integrate structural and portable luminaires, and they can be costly to install. Speculative construction projects require a lighting plan that appeals to a variety of people.

## Early Site Visit

Early in the planning process, an interior/lighting designer should visit the site with the client. A walk-through with the client provides an excellent opportunity for discussing existing lighting problems and constraints and the initial ideas. In consultation with the owner, it should be determined whether luminaires should be replaced, eliminated, left in the space, retrofitted, or recycled. Initial visits should also include the recording of significant architectural details, preliminary measurements of rooms, existing luminaires, controls, and location of electrical outlets. The designer should take note of daylighting as well as reflectance characteristics of interior surfaces, and should take photographs of the interior.

In consultation with the client, the team members should develop a comprehensive plan, which includes the list of activities, responsible individuals, timeline, required resources, estimated costs, and billing dates. A project

FIGURE 9.3 For planning purposes the Berkeley Lab used Radiance software to create a building model of *The New York Times* new headquarters building in Manhattan (center of the photograph). Creating a model of the building within the context of its urban setting enabled the researchers to study how the path of the sun and other buildings would affect daylighting. (Courtesy of Lawrence Berkeley National Laboratory.)

**FIGURES 9.4** The programming phase for the planning of the new headquarters buildings for *The New York Times* included collecting data from daylighting mockups. Sensor networks were then used to collect data based upon these mockups. (Attila Uysal, SBLD Studio, Inc.)

schedule includes the timeline for activities, including important start and finish dates.

## PROGRAMMING

The programming phase includes interviews, observations, and an assessment of lighting systems, daylighting, and research initiatives (Figure 9.4). Preliminary information gleaned from the project planning phase provides the foundation for determining the type of data needed to design a quality lighting environment (Figure 9.5). It is during the comprehensive programming phase that data are collected about the end users, the physical characteristics of the space, and the applicable codes, ordinances, regulations, and LEED certification requirements.

Effective methods for obtaining information about end users and the interior include

**FIGURE 9.5** A computer simulation of how daylighting affects a space. Notice the changes in the light and shadow patterns on the wall and work surface that occurred as the sun moved through the day. This information is important for planning appropriate control of the sun and electrical sources. (Image rendered by Radiance, courtesy Saba Rofchaei and the Lawrence Berkeley National Laboratory.)

interviews, surveys, and field observation. In addition, a review of relevant literature and current research related to lighting should be conducted and documented. The results of such research can provide excellent insight and may be used to supplement project-specific data gathered in this phase. Interviews should be conducted with the client and, whenever possible, end users of the space, such as employees, customers, and perhaps visitors. The goal is to collect enough information to be able to make generalizations about the lighting environment.

Interviews and surveys provide good information regarding how the lighting design is perceived. However, it is difficult for people to describe in detail how they work or live in a space. Interviews and surveys cannot cover all the questions that might be relevant to understanding behavior in a space. That is where field observations come in. The use of multiple methodologies provides the greatest insight into human behavior and helps to validate results by checking data derived from one method against data from another. For example, in an interview a client might indicate that spotlights help to attract customers to a specific display. However, in observing customers in the store, it might be revealed that customers rarely look at the highlighted merchandise. Conflicting data need to be resolved through discussions with the client and perhaps further observation.

Effective interviews and surveys require research and preparation. Information learned from initial site visits and preliminary interviews with the client serve as the foundation for more specific questions. Questions can be written

in a structured or semistructured format. A structured arrangement is a list of questions without flexibility for asking follow-up questions. A semistructured format includes a list of questions that enables the interviewer to ask additional questions for clarification purposes or to obtain more information.

Interview and survey questions should always include an assessment of the present situation and anticipated future needs. Table 9.1 provides examples of questions that might be asked in interviews or surveys of residential or commercial clients. Questions may be divided into the following: (1) characteristics of the end users, including physiological and psychological attributes; (2) activity assessment; (3) perceptions of lighting; and (4) anticipated future changes.

The survey or interview questions should be modified to accommodate the unique needs and characteristics of each client. This is especially important when designing lighting for international clients because different culture and life experiences can affect expectations and perceptions of a lighting environment. Therefore, understanding the end users' perceptions of lighting is important in planning an environment that will meet their needs.

Understanding various perceptions of a lighting environment is important in commercial interiors as well as in residences. A demographic profile will help to identify characteristics of the end users. To determine perceptions of lighting, interview questions for commercial clients should be tailored to specific categories of end users. For example, in designing the lighting for a restaurant, different questions should be written for the

## TABLE 9.1 Residential/Commercial Client Questionnaire

Name: _____     Age: _____

Health Concerns (e.g., dementia, Alzheimer's disease, SAD, cognitive processing, hearing)

| VISUAL IMPAIRMENTS | YES | NO |
|---|---|---|
| Cataracts | | |
| Glaucoma | | |
| Diabetic retinopathy | | |
| Difficulty seeing contrasts | | |
| Difficulty with visual acuity | | |
| Difficulty detecting motion | | |
| Difficulty with depth perception | | |
| Reduced field of vision | | |
| Color blindness | | |
| Problems with glare | | |
| Problems with flickering lights | | |

**Anthropometric Data (provide measurements in a range)**

Distance from seat to eye level (inches or mm) _____

Distance from floor to eye level (inches or mm) _____

Reach distance (inches or mm) _____

**Activity Assessment**

| Room | Location in Room | Activity | Special Lighting Needs | User(s) | Day(s) of Week | Time of Day | Duration | Technology | Furniture | Luminaire(s) |
|---|---|---|---|---|---|---|---|---|---|---|
| | | | | | | | | | | |
| | | | | | | | | | | |
| | | | | | | | | | | |
| | | | | | | | | | | |
| | | | | | | | | | | |
| | | | | | | | | | | |
| | | | | | | | | | | |
| | | | | | | | | | | |
| | | | | | | | | | | |

(continued on next page)

TABLE 9.1 Residential/ Commercial Client Questionnaire (continued)

| PERCEPTIONS OF LIGHTING | YES | NO | DETAILS |
|---|---|---|---|
| Appropriate level of illumination | | | |
| Appropriate mood and atmosphere for activities | | | |
| Appropriate amount of daylight | | | |
| Appropriate energy conservation | | | |
| Appropriate environmental conservation | | | |
| Appropriate accent lighting for artwork or a special collection | | | |
| Problems with distribution of light on a task | | | |
| Problems with glare | | | Time of day: Time of year: |
| Problems with shadows | | | Time of day: Time of year: |
| Problems with reflections on task surfaces | | | |
| Problems with flickering | | | |
| Problems with color accuracy | | | |
| Problems with the apparent color of a room | | | |
| Problems with seeing objects | | | |
| Problems with seeing people | | | |
| Problems with reaching controls | | | |
| Problems with manipulating controls | | | |
| Problems with heat from lamps | | | |
| Problems with electrical outlets | | | |
| Problems with the apparent size of the room | | | |
| Problems with safety | | | |
| Problems with security | | | |
| Additional comments | | | |

**Anticipated Future Changes**

1. Changes in individuals living/working in the building:

2. Changes in number of rooms:

3. Changes in activities:

4. Anticipated renovation:

5. Furniture changes:

6. Changes in interior elements (floor coverings, wall coverings, ceilings, window treatments):

**TABLE 9.2 Commercial Client Questionnaire**

Project: _____     Location: _____

Name: _____     Role (owner, employee, customer): _____

| BUSINESS-RELATED DATA | |
|---|---|
| Purpose of the business/organization: | |
| Mission/goals/objectives of the business/organization: | |
| Image of the business/organization: | |
| Elements contributing to profits and ROI (return on investment): | |
| Energy and environmental conservation policies and practices: | |
| Current critical issues related to the industry: | |
| Current societal events affecting the business/organization: | |
| Anticipated changes in personnel: | |
| Anticipated changes in activities: | |
| Demographic profile of employees (sex, age, ethnic and cultural background): | |
| PROPERTY DATA | |
| Geographic location: | |
| Building owned or leased: | |
| Anticipated changes in space needs: | |
| Anticipated renovation: | |
| Anticipated furniture changes: | |
| Anticipated changes in interior elements (floor coverings, wall coverings, ceilings, window treatments): | |

owner(s), hostess, servers, maintenance crew, new customers, and returning patrons. Each group is engaged in different activities in the restaurant; hence, their satisfaction, expectations, and perceptions of the lighting environment may vary and should be taken into account in the new design. Table 9.2 provides examples of questions that may be used as a guide for developing a questionnaire for commercial interiors. The topics include business-related information, property data, end-user characteristics, activity assessment, and perceptions of lighting.

## Field Observations

As noted earlier, interviews and surveys should elicit basic information about perceptions of the lighting environment. However, the ideal situation is to combine the results of surveys and interviews with field observations. Observing in a residence may be rather awkward and is therefore rare. In addition,

**TABLE 9.3 Commercial Observations**

Project: _____     Location: _____

Observation Date: _____     Observation Start Time: _____     Observation Finish Time: _____

| | |
|---|---|
| Describe people in the space (number of people, employee, customer, approximate ages, special needs): | |
| Describe activities in the space: | |
| Describe the role of lighting in conducting activities: | |
| Describe unnatural movements that could be the result of poor lighting (e.g., shielding eyes, hesitations) | |
| Describe any modifications or adjustments to the environment conducted by end users that could be the result of poor lighting: | |
| Describe any problems associated with lighting and the principles of universal design: | |
| Identify preferred area(s): | |
| Identify any unoccupied area(s): | |

observations in a residence are generally not all that informative because the frequent personal contact with residential clients allows an interior/ lighting designer to acquire the necessary information more naturally and easily. The arrangement of commercial interiors, on the other hand, often enables an interior/ lighting designer to conduct field observations of human behavior. Therefore, whenever possible, observations should be conducted in an interior that will be renovated. With new construction, sites similar to the proposed project should be observed. Research related to the project may be reviewed and integrated into plans.

The primary purpose of field observations is to watch how people behave in a specific lighting environment. Table 9.3 provides a guide that can be used for conducting field observations. As with all the guides included in this chapter, this document should be modified to address the specifics of the site, the lighting system, and the end users.

Observations should occur at different times of the day, on different days of the week, and perhaps during different seasons of the year. For example, observation of behavior in a retail store would reveal different activity on Monday mornings, Saturday afternoons, and during the Christmas season. To gain the most insight into the interaction between lighting and behavior, a site should be visited at the times that are most germane to the project. The frequency of visits depends on the consistency of results; a site should be observed enough times for the observer to be able to conclude that specific behavior is fairly constant. For example, in observing behavior in a restaurant, it might be noted that someone trips on a step located at the entrance. On subsequent visits, if many people trip on the step, then it would be recorded as a significant problem and might be addressed by adding illumination to the edge of the tread. However, if over the course of several visits, only one person is observed to trip, and interviews with the employees reveal that they never noticed anyone having problems with the step, then perhaps additional illumination does not have to be installed at the entrance. By way of caution, note that a ramp must be provided to comply with the regulations found in the Americans with Disabilities Act (ADA) and International Building Code (IBC) regulations.

## Physical Assessment

Programming involves an assessment of the lighting system and the physical attributes of an interior that might affect the quality of illumination. This involves visiting the site and creating an inventory of luminaires, lamps, controls, electrical outlets, daylighting, architectural features, room configurations, furniture, colors, and material finishes. It is important to take photographs of the interior to assist with the schematic and design development phases of the lighting design process. In addition, sketches should be made of the floor plan, wall elevations, **reflected ceiling plan (RCP)**, and perhaps light distribution patterns. Sketches should

be drawn quickly; at this stage of the lighting design process, approximate dimensions are sufficient. For some projects, a floor plan and RCP might already exist. (Exact dimensions of interiors are recorded during the design development phase.)

As illustrated in Figure 9.6, each sketch of a room should include dimensions and the approximate location of interior elements such as luminaires, electrical outlets, controls, HVAC equipment, loudspeakers, sprinklers, smoke alarms, emergency fixtures, signage, windows, skylights, significant architectural details, structural members, cabinets, closets, and doors. For example, the floor plan in Figure 9.6 is the result of drawing a plan the approximate shape of the room. The overall room dimensions were recorded along with the approximate location of windows, electrical outlets, switching arrangements, wall-mounted luminaires, cabinets, and doors.

Elevations should include the vertical dimensions of the location of windows, architectural elements, luminaires, switches, and electrical outlets (Figure 9.7). The RCP illustrates the location of columns, HVAC equipment, luminaires, ceiling tiles, and any other elements located on the ceiling (Figure 9.8).

The programming phase is an excellent time to research current local, state, and federal codes and regulations. Codes and regulations must also be identified for projects involving historic buildings. In addition, the designer should survey current literature to determine the most effective lighting systems and practices, and review current information regarding a specific setting, such

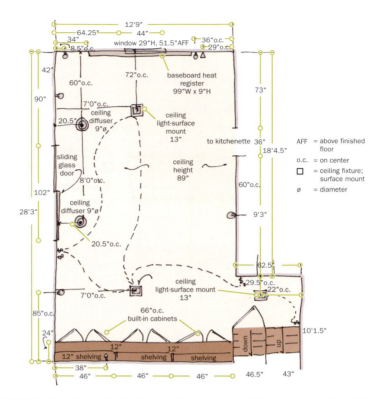

**FIGURE 9.6** A quick sketch of a plan view of a room. For preliminary purposes, the sketch should include dimensions and the approximate location of interior elements such as luminaires, electrical outlets, controls, columns, HVAC equipment, windows, and doors.

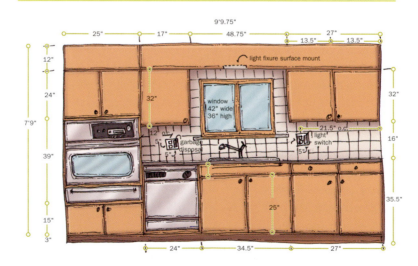

**FIGURE 9.7** A quick sketch of an elevation of a room. For preliminary purposes, the sketch should include vertical dimensions of the location of windows, architectural elements, luminaires, switches, and electrical outlets.

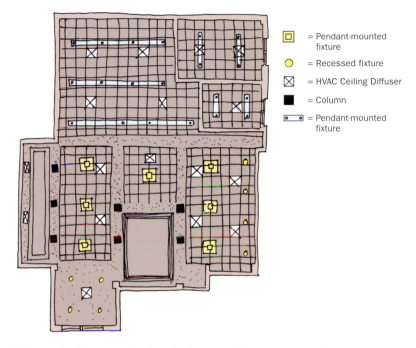

|   |   |
|---|---|
| ▣ | = Pendant-mounted fixture |
| ◯ | = Recessed fixture |
| ⊠ | = HVAC Ceiling Diffuser |
| ■ | = Column |
| •—•| = Pendant-mounted fixture |

**FIGURE 9.8** A quick sketch of a reflected ceiling plan (RCP) of a room. For preliminary purposes, the sketch should include the location of columns, HVAC equipment, luminaires, ceiling tiles, and any other elements located in the ceiling.

as an educational facility. To identify lighting products that use state-of-the-art technology, the designer should contact manufacturers' representatives and conduct a comprehensive review of product literature.

A thorough analysis of the data collected in the programming phase of the lighting design process provides the foundation for the project's lighting criteria. In general, lighting criteria should focus on the health, safety, and welfare of people and on protecting the environment. The needs and priorities of the client and end users and the characteristics of the environment determine specific lighting criteria. Considerations include accommodating the purpose of the space, lighting methods, structural constraints, budget, timeline, and psychological and physiological factors. Lighting criteria should be developed in consultation with other team members working on the project.

## Design Phases
### SCHEMATIC DESIGN
The schematic design phase consists of analyzing the results obtained during the comprehensive programming stage and then developing initial design concepts for the interior

illumination. Data gathered in the programming phase include information about the client, end users, physical characteristics of the space, and applicable codes, ordinances, and regulations. For each category, a synopsis should be written that reflects information most germane to the project. The identification of salient facts requires a thorough analysis, synthesis, and evaluation of the data.

A summary of the data collected through interviews, surveys, and field observations may be produced by: (1) thorough analysis of the data by reading the content numerous times, (2) creating a detailed description of the results, (3) developing a prioritized list of lighting requirements, and (4) determining potential problems. The results of the analysis should be in written and sketch form.

Responses from numerous interviews and surveys must be analyzed by identifying recurring themes or patterns. For example, in interviews of 50 people, only 2 might indicate the need for higher illumination in a corridor. This low response rate suggests that the existing illumination level might be appropriate and that perhaps the two people who mentioned the light in the corridor have different perceptions of brightness than most people do. Thus, new lighting for the corridor might not be included in the new lighting design. In contrast, if most of the people interviewed or surveyed identify a lighting problem in the corridor, then solutions should be developed.

The results of field observations should be a synthesis of all the visits. Multiple observations should be analyzed in the same way that responses from numerous interviews and surveys are analyzed, identifying only items that occur on a regular basis. The synopsis of people in the space should include a description of individuals, activities, unnatural movements, and modifications or adjustments to the environment that might be the result of poor lighting. A summary of how people are using the space should touch on the role of lighting in conducting activities, adherence to the principles of universal design, preferred areas, and unoccupied spaces. Many of the results related to specific locations within a building can be depicted in freehand sketches.

The various categories listed in the lighting assessment guide, including general lighting concerns, luminaires/lamps, lighting system controls, and safety/security/energy concerns, may all be summarized in written reports and sketches. These summaries are different from the results of an inventory of the lighting and interior. Inventory reports are objective listings of the lighting elements. In contrast, the assessment process is a means of subjectively reviewing the lighting plan. Thus, the analysis focuses on problems, constraints, positive attributes, and perceptions of the lighting environment.

The summary should include an analysis of the adequacy of power, complexities relating to access, and structural constraints. In addition to the written summaries, sketches can be developed using creative coding schemes that depict and reinforce the strengths and weaknesses of a lighting plan.

## Charrettes

The results of the analysis serve as the basis for the conceptualization process of the schematic design phase. In this stage, an interior/lighting designer and other professionals involved in the project engage in a comprehensive brainstorming process; a **charrette**. Sustainable design initiatives have popularized the use of charrettes because the process is an interdisciplinary and collaborative activity. The process involves combining brainstorming with immediate feedback loops. Charrettes are conducted in concentrated sessions that often involve several consecutive days.

There are a variety of brainstorming methods, and every team of professionals may have its own preferred method. Some of the most important factors in achieving effective results include allowing everyone to participate, expressing initial acceptance of all ideas, and exploring all possibilities to solve problems.

The effectiveness of charrettes also depends on the articulation of a topical inquiry that is clearly understood by all members of the team. The topical inquiry is essentially the issue that will be explored during a charrette. An example might be, "What are the concerns involved in providing task lighting for the staff working on the third floor of the ABC building?" The inquiry needs to be concise and understood by the participants because brainstorming ideas that are irrelevant to a project can waste a great deal of time. This can be discouraging to people, and they might be reluctant to take part in future sessions.

Charrettes can be intensely creative. They should include written comments and sketches and explore all possible solutions for a lighting problem. For example, when exploring the options available for an existing lighting system, the team might consider whether the luminaires should be retrofitted, replaced,

refurbished, renovated, rewired, reconfigured, or recycled. Options for improving lamps could include higher output, longer life, enhanced color, upgraded ballasts, relamping, or improved optics. Old lamps should be recycled.

Exploration of possible lighting methods might include daylighting, recessed, surface-mounted, track systems, or pendants. Discussions should also focus on options that address the lighting criteria. For example, one of the lighting criteria for a project might stipulate a romantic mood for a restaurant during dinner hours. Brainstorming around this criterion could explore which lighting method, luminaire, lamp, and level of illumination would create a romantic feeling given the specific attributes of the restaurant's environment.

A variety of sketching techniques can be used during charrettes (Figures 9.9a–d). During the sessions, it is common to review past drawings, so sketches should be saved, and a clean sheet should be used for each new concept under consideration. A preliminary drawing of a floor plan with furniture arrangements can serve as the basis for planning lighting.

In brainstorming for lighting options, suggestions may arise related to improving the relationship among daylighting, electrical illumination, controls, furniture arrangements, and architectural elements. By simultaneously considering all the elements that affect lighting, the team is likely to be able to produce a final plan for the interior that will result in a quality environment. One effective method for brainstorming lighting is to use tracing paper as an overlay for floor plans and elevations of the space. An overlay enables the team members to visualize the integration of

**FIGURE 9.9A** An example of a sketch of a luminaire. The design of the fixture and any changes could be discussed during a charrette. (Courtesy SPI Lighting.)

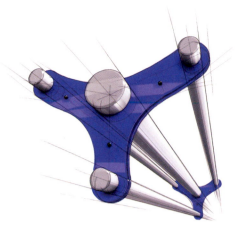

**FIGURE 9.9B** Another example of a sketch of a luminaire that could be explored during a charrette. (Courtesy SPI Lighting.)

**FIGURE 9.9C** A sketch of a suggested luminaire installed in the space helps the client to visualize the designer's concept. (Courtesy SPI Lighting.)

**FIGURE 9.9D** Sketching a suggested luminaire in alternative spaces provides a better understanding of the design of the fixture and its best application. (Courtesy SPI Lighting.)

lighting with the interior architecture, furniture, windows, doorways, and special features.

Sketches developed during charrettes should be compared to the schematics created during the analysis of the programming results. For example, Figure 9.10 demonstrates a sketch of a floor plan with a coding scheme that delineates safety, energy, glare, daylighting, and shadow concerns. In this example, it would be essential to make sure that the conceptual schematics address items related to safety, energy, glare, daylighting, and shadows. In

addition, whenever possible, sketches should be created of anticipated changes concerning end users and the interior. A drawing of anticipated growth areas should be a separate overlay (Figure 9.11). A series of overlays might be created to illustrate lighting changes with preset scene arrangements. Sketches of architectural details and schematics of custom-designed luminaires should also be developed during the conceptualization process.

During charrettes the team must often identify several lighting plans. One good

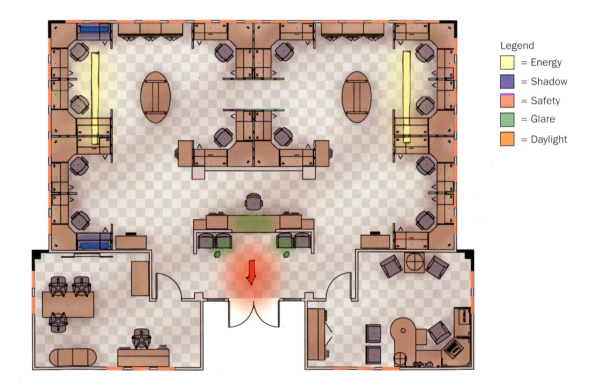

Legend

☐ = Energy
☐ = Shadow
☐ = Safety
☐ = Glare
☐ = Daylight

FIGURE 9.10 An overlay sketch of a floor plan illustrating use of a coding scheme to indicate safety, energy, glare, daylighting, and shadow concerns.

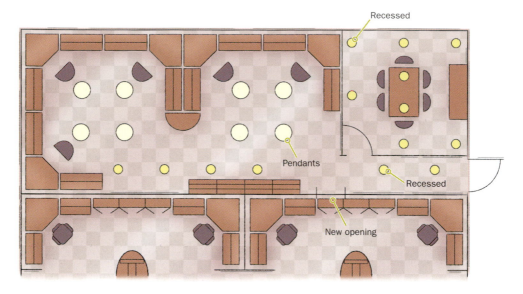

Recessed

Pendants

Recessed

New opening

**FIGURE 9.11** An overlay sketch of a floor plan illustrating anticipated growth areas and potential lighting needs.

reason for developing multiple designs is to have alternatives to present to a client. The schematic design phase is the best time to make sure the client is pleased with the lighting design, because at this stage everything can easily be changed. When a project proceeds beyond the schematic and design development phases, changes to the design can be expensive or even impossible. Alternatives presented to a client may take up a variety of themes, such as different lighting methods, styles of luminaires, price ranges, and approaches that require different timelines.

## DESIGN DEVELOPMENT

The design development phase provides an opportunity to formulate the creative ideas. The purposes of the design development phase are to work through the details of the conceptual lighting design and produce presentation media and specifications for the

client's approval. The design development phase begins after the client approves the concepts presented in the schematic design phase. The tasks involved in this phase are especially critical to the success of the project because the results are used to form the contractual agreements with the client, contractor, manufacturers, and suppliers. Therefore, it is important to think through and research all the details related to the lighting systems.

An interior/lighting designer should also make sure that the client fully understands and approves the lighting design, the intended effect of the lighting on the environment, and appropriate operation and maintenance practices. Working through the details of the project requires a thorough examination of the lighting system in every room. The variables to consider include lamps, luminaires, controls, daylighting, power sources, installation methods, and maintenance procedures.

A comprehensive approach to gathering information from manufacturers, suppliers, and tradespeople involves obtaining exact costs of lighting systems, including materials and labor for fabricating structural units or custom-designed luminaires. The exact lamps required for the parameters of the selected lighting methods should be the first items specified because the characteristics of the light source dictate the resulting lighting effects. For example, specific lamps must be selected to accommodate a project's lighting criterion that stipulates a particular beam spread or energy savings. After the lamps are selected, luminaires and controls appropriate to these lamps can be researched and specified in turn.

Specifications and updates of the total project serve as the foundation for developing presentation media and requirements for the lighting design. The design team should determine the most appropriate presentation drawings and specifications. Common drawings include a floor plan with a lighting overlay, a RCP, elevations, lighting detail drawings, perspectives, and axonometric views. These drawings may be hard-line (drafted), freehand, or created using computer-aided design (CAD) or computer-aided design and drafting (CADD) technology.

Lighting software programs can demonstrate virtual interiors and provide the flexibility to make quick changes to the lighting system or attributes of the interior (Figure 9.12). For example, the software allows an interior/lighting designer to produce a virtual room of the project, with exact dimensions, architectural details, surface colors, textures, and a proposed lighting system. The software illustrates how the lighting system affects the interior within the parameters determined by the characteristics of the space. When presenting the virtual lighting design to the client, various solutions may be explored by immediately changing the type of lighting method, lamp, luminaire, point of installation, or characteristics of the interior. This tool is a tremendous help in enabling a client to visualize a lighting design. Furthermore, the ability to view multiple options in fairly quick succession assists a client in determining which design is most appropriate for the project.

Drawings must be consistent with details provided in specifications. For example, luminaires on a lighting plan must be the same dimensions as those described in the specifications. The quantity and type of luminaires must also be identical. Notes on a drawing can be helpful in explaining complex specification details of a lighting system. Working out the details of the specifications includes researching expertise that might be needed to help specify and install special lighting systems. Experts might not be available at the location of the project, making it costly to hire professionals from communities far from the site. This problem is common when specifying new technologies.

Presenting technical information to a client requires a format, such as a job or project notebook, that enables materials to be compiled in a professional manner. The job notebook may include a variety of documents, such as the concept statement, drawings, lighting specifications, manufacturers' cut sheets, sketches of custom-designed luminaires, samples of finishes, detailed budget estimates, revised consultation fees, bidding recommendations, maintenance

**FIGURE 9.12** A simulation of an interior created by Radiance software. Notice how the software is able to display changes in intensity and the directional path of light, shade, and shadows. (Graeme Watt [1999] g.watt@btconnect.com.)

guidelines, commissioning recommendations, and projected timelines. It should be given to the client during the presentation.

Depending on the client's reactions, it may be necessary to make revisions to the lighting design. After a client is in complete agreement with the lighting design, the contract documentation phase can begin. Upon approval by the client, an interior/lighting designer develops recommendations for lighting specifications and submits the information to the registered professionals for review and final determination. Registered professionals, such as architects and engineers, begin the contract documentation phase by developing working drawings, specifications, sections, cut sheets, and purchase orders.

## LEED Certification and the Design Process

For a checklist of tasks related to LEED certification in each step of the design process, from project planning through design development, see Table 9.4.

**TABLE 9.4** LEED-Related Tasks—Project Planning through Design Development

| DESIGN PROCESS | LEED-RELATED TASKS |
|---|---|
| **Project Planning** | • Site selection should include examining daylighting opportunities and challenges as well as light pollution.<br>• Register project with GBCI (Green Building Certification Institute).<br>• @ www.gbci.org and pay registration costs.<br>• Determine which LEED certification the project team is pursuing (platinum, gold, silver, and certified).<br>• Manage LEED documentation process using LEED-Online. If necessary seek clarification and a ruling on credit interpretations.<br>• Begin collecting information and perform calculations that are required for documentation purposes.<br>• Identify a commissioning authority. |
| **Comprehensive Programming** | • Manage LEED documentation process using LEED-Online. If necessary seek clarification and a ruling on credit interpretations.<br>• Identify owner's project requirements.<br>• Collect information and perform calculations that are required for documentation purposes.<br>• Gather daylighting data, characteristics of the users, activities, and manufacturers of luminaires, lamps, controls, glass, windows, and products designed to control sunlight.<br>• Identify lighting products produced regionally, and made with recycled content and/or rapidly renewable materials. For wood-based products document certification with the Forest Stewardship Council.<br>• Acquire ASHRAE/IESNA Standard 90.1-2007 document and ENERGY STAR requirements. Identify means to determine lighting power density by using space-by-space method or whole building lighting power allowances.<br>• Identify areas for daylight and building reuse related to lighting systems (walls, ceiling systems, etc.).<br>• Identify means to redirect recyclable luminaires and other products associated with lighting systems (walls, ceiling systems, etc.).<br>• Identify luminaires and lighting systems that could be salvaged and determine the need for refurbishment.<br>• Identify low-emitting paints and coatings.<br>• Identify products that will enable people to have control of lighting and thermal comfort. |
| **Schematic Design** | • Manage LEED documentation process using LEED-Online. If necessary seek clarification and a ruling on credit interpretations.<br>• Collect information and perform calculations that are required for documentation purposes.<br>• Review the owner's project requirements and explore various options.<br>• Explore different approaches to maximizing daylighting and views from standing and seated positions.<br>• Explore ideas for innovation in design credits. |
| **Design Development** | • Manage LEED documentation process using LEED-Online. If necessary seek clarification and a ruling on credit interpretations.<br>• Collect information and perform calculations that are required for documentation purposes.<br>• Initial plans for daylighting and lighting systems.<br>• Projects may submit materials for a preliminary design phase review and a final design phase review.<br>• Develop and implement commissioning plan, including lighting and daylighting controls. |

Source: USGBC (2009). *LEED reference guide for green interior design and construction*. Washington, D.C.: U.S. Green Building Council.

# Fundamental Project

**1. Research Design Project**

Select five photographs of public interiors. For each space, identify the purpose of the space and provide a description of the lighting systems. Identify the information that should be gathered for detailed analysis of the space. Summarize your results in a written report and include the photographs.

## Application Projects

**1. Human Factors Research Project**

Identify three different public spaces. Use Table 9.3 as a model for creating an observation guide for each site. Visit each site as often as needed so that you will be able to present generalizations of how lighting affects behavior in the space. In a written report, include the following information: (a) a summary of the observations and the lighting system; (b) a summary of the strengths and weaknesses of the lighting in each space; (c) recommendations for improving the lighting environment; and (d) a list of questions that would be useful to ask the end users of the space.

**2. Human Factors Research Project**

Visit three buildings and conduct field observations. For each site, record how people are affected by the lighting design. Analyze and synthesize the observations. Make recommendations for improving the space. Summarize your results in a written report and include illustrations, photographs, or sketches.

# Summary

o The lighting design process may be divided into the following seven phases: (1) project planning; (2) comprehensive programming; (3) schematic design; (4) design development; (5) contract documentation; (6) contract administration; and (7) evaluation.

o The primary purposes of planning are to identify a profile of the project and to determine the resources required to achieve its objectives.

o In consultation with the client, the project's team members should develop a comprehensive plan that includes the list of activities, responsible individuals, timeline, required resources, estimated costs, and billing dates.

o The comprehensive programming phase involves collecting data regarding the end users, physical characteristics of the space, and applicable codes, ordinances, and regulations.

o Effective methods for obtaining information about end users and the interior include interviews, surveys, and field observations.

o Interview and survey questions should always ask about the present situation as well as anticipated future needs.

o The primary purpose of field observations is to watch how people behave in a specific lighting environment.

o Comprehensive programming involves visiting the site and creating an inventory of luminaires, lamps, controls, electrical outlets, daylighting, architectural features, room configurations, furniture, colors, and material finishes.

o Sketches of the floor plan, wall elevations, and reflected ceiling plan should be developed.

o The programming phase is an excellent time to research current local, state, and federal codes and regulations.

o Data collected in the programming phase of the lighting design process provide the foundation for the project's lighting criteria.

o The schematic design phase consists of analyzing the results obtained during the comprehensive programming stage and then developing initial design concepts for the interior illumination.

o A summary of the data collected through interviews, surveys, and field observations may be produced in the following ways: (1) thorough analysis of the data by reading

## KEY TERMS

charrette
reflected ceiling plan (RCP)

the content numerous times; (2) creating a detailed description of the results; (3) developing a prioritized list of lighting requirements; and (4) determining potential problems.

o The results of the analysis serve as the basis for the conceptualization process of the schematic design phase. In this stage, an interior/lighting designer and other professionals involved in the project engage in a comprehensive brainstorming process.

o Charrettes should include written comments and sketches, and they should explore all possible options for a lighting solution.

o At the conclusion of the schematic design phase, materials presented to the client may include a concept statement, freehand sketches, photographs of luminaires, a list of lighting equipment, preliminary costs, and projected timelines.

o The purposes of the design development phase are to work through the details of the conceptual lighting design and produce presentation media and specifications for the client's approval.

o Presenting technical information to a client requires a format, such as a job or project notebook, that makes it possible for materials to be compiled in a professional manner.

# Resources

American Institute of Architects (2000). *Architectural Graphics Standards*, 10th ed. New York: John Wiley & Sons.

Benya, J., Heschong, L., McGowan, T., Miller, N., & Rubinstein, F. (2001). *Advanced lighting guidelines*. White Salmon, WA: New Buildings Institute.

Clark, C. (2001). Computers are causing health problems. *Journal of End User Computing, 13*(1), 34–45.

Clodagh (2001). *Total design: Contemplate, cleanse, clarify, and create your personal space.* New York: Clarkson/Potter Publishers.

Illuminating Engineering Society of North America (IESNA) (2011). *IESNA lighting handbook* (10th ed.). New York: Illuminating Engineering Society of North America.

Mistrick, R., Chen, C., Bierman, B., & Felts, D. (2000). A comparison of photosensor-controlled electronic dimming systems. *Proceedings of the 2000 Annual Conference of the Illuminary Engineering Society, 29*(1), 66–80.

Whiton, S., & Abercrombie, S. (2002). *Interior design & decoration* (5th ed.). Upper Saddle River, NJ: Prentice-Hall.

# 10 Lighting Design Process: Contract Documents through Postoccupancy Evaluation

The final phases of the lighting design process include the development of contract documents, contract administration, and evaluation. These phases can be stressful, but they are also exciting because it's during these phases that the project is completed. The interior/lighting designer executes legally binding contracts with various entities involved with the project, including the client, suppliers, contractors, and tradespeople. Changes to the original **specifications** can be costly and create delays, and a variety of problems and conflicts may occur during construction and installation. Because these stages do not involve creative processes, frequently an interior/lighting designer is not as enthusiastic about fulfilling these responsibilities. Nevertheless, the final phases are absolutely critical to the success of a lighting design, and because these are the last experiences a client remembers, it is essential to conclude with a positive impression. Therefore, sufficient time must be allocated to developing accurate documents, consistent communication, careful supervision, and effective problem-solving.

In studying the content of this chapter, it is important to understand the material in terms of its generic application in the context of lighting. Specific architectural, engineering, and interior design firms develop a

**OBJECTIVES**

o Identify working drawings used to illustrate a lighting design

o Describe details that should be included in lighting working drawings and specifications

o Describe contracts that are frequently used for a lighting design

o Identify the tasks associated with contract administration of a lighting project

o Understand the purpose of the postoccupancy evaluation and how to apply the process to a lighting design

preferred format for drawings, specifications, and contracts. Standardized requirements are reviewed by an attorney and then serve as a template for developing contract documents. Moreover, each firm may have staff members who are responsible for developing particular documents, such as specifications or purchase orders. The information presented in this chapter is, therefore, intended to be a guide to the procedures and contractual requirements of engaging in the final phases of the lighting design process.

## Contract Documents

Contractual documents include working drawings and written specifications. **Working drawings** or **construction drawings** are graphical representations of a lighting system and serve to supplement the specifications, which consist of a written description of the parameters of the lighting system (Figure 10.1). Together, working drawings and written specifications are the basis for ordering products, installing wiring, and determining the location of luminaires, outlets, and controls. In contrast to presentation illustrations, which are produced in the design development phase, working drawings represent a legal contract. Therefore, they must be accurately scaled, contain detailed illustrations, and demonstrate that the plans comply with local codes.

Working drawings for a lighting design are developed in coordination with mechanical, plumbing, and structural systems. Laws mandate that registered professionals, such

as architects and engineers, stamp working drawings and specifications to certify that they meet the necessary standards. Therefore, the drawings developed by an interior/lighting designer must be submitted to registered professionals for review and further development. To ensure retention of the original intent of the lighting design, an interior/lighting designer should ask to review the working drawings prior to their being submitted to the local building department, contract closures, financial institutions, or a bidding process.

Commonly used working drawings consist of a **lighting plan**, **electrical plan**, **lighting/electrical plan**, and reflected ceiling plan (RCP). Drawings may also include elevations, sections, and details. **Lighting schedules** and general notes located on drawing sheets provide additional information regarding the lighting system. The production format, including dimensions, should be coordinated with other professionals working on the project. Drawings may be printed on sheets or presented in a job notebook.

Lighting plans generated by CAD software are typically developed in layers, enabling the designer to examine the relationships between lighting and other elements of a project. For example, a lighting plan can be viewed in conjunction with the HVAC system to make sure components do not overlap. An assessment of the electrical plan together with furniture arrangements can help to ensure access to power for portable luminaires. Any cross referencing of details on working drawings must also form part of the written specifications.

Symbol legends located on working drawings are essential for describing the

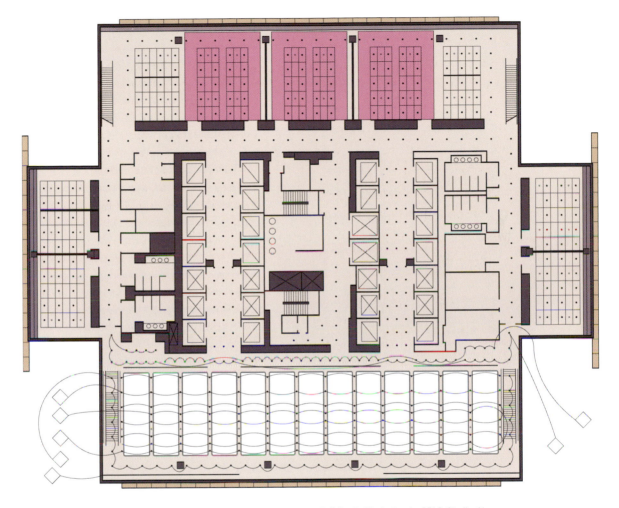

FIGURE 10.1 A lighting plan for the fifteenth floor of *The New York Times* Building in Manhattan by SBLD Studio, New York City.

type of luminaires, wiring configurations, switching systems, and outlets included in the design. Symbols and abbreviations are used to communicate complex details (Figures 10.2a and 10.2b). To promote standardization throughout the building industry, a task force of the American Institute of Architects (AIA) developed a set of universal symbols and abbreviations for architectural working drawings. Many of these symbols and conventions, such as door swings and mechanical systems, are also used on working

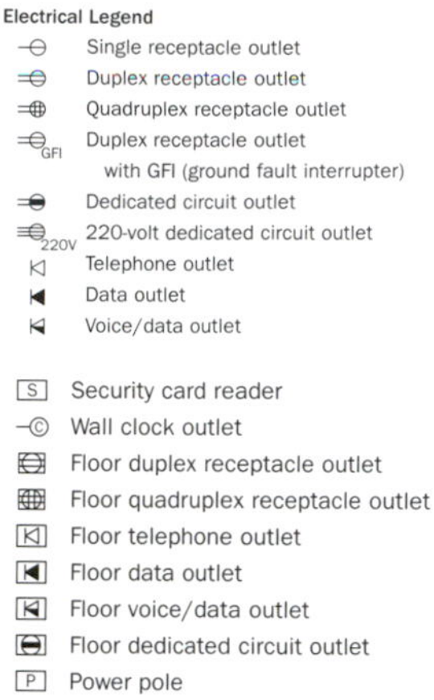

**Electrical Legend**

- ⊖ Single receptacle outlet
- ⊜ Duplex receptacle outlet
- ⊕ Quadruplex receptacle outlet
- ⊜$_{GFI}$ Duplex receptacle outlet
  with GFI (ground fault interrupter)
- ⊜ Dedicated circuit outlet
- ⊜$_{220V}$ 220-volt dedicated circuit outlet
- K⏺ Telephone outlet
- ◀ Data outlet
- ◀ Voice/data outlet

- S Security card reader
- ⊙ Wall clock outlet
- ⊜ Floor duplex receptacle outlet
- ⊞ Floor quadruplex receptacle outlet
- K Floor telephone outlet
- ◀ Floor data outlet
- ◀ Floor voice/data outlet
- ⊟ Floor dedicated circuit outlet
- P Power pole

**FIGURE 10.2A** Electrical legend. (NCIDQ.)

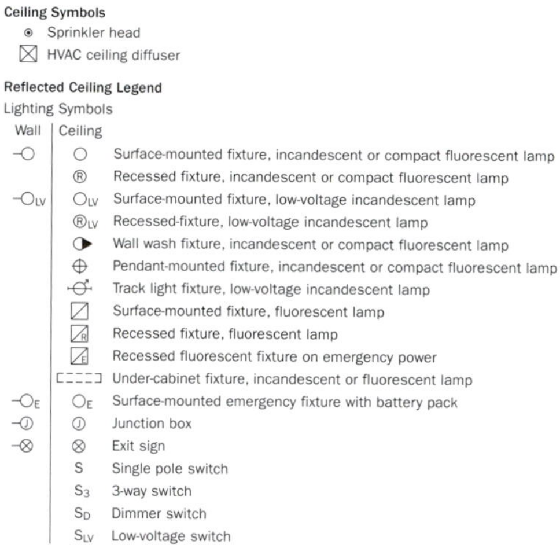

**Ceiling Symbols**
- ⊛ Sprinkler head
- ⊠ HVAC ceiling diffuser

**Reflected Ceiling Legend**

Lighting Symbols

| Wall | Ceiling | |
|---|---|---|
| ⊖ | ○ | Surface-mounted fixture, incandescent or compact fluorescent lamp |
| | Ⓡ | Recessed fixture, incandescent or compact fluorescent lamp |
| ⊖$_{LV}$ | ○$_{LV}$ | Surface-mounted fixture, low-voltage incandescent lamp |
| | Ⓡ$_{LV}$ | Recessed-fixture, low-voltage incandescent lamp |
| | ◗ | Wall wash fixture, incandescent or compact fluorescent lamp |
| | ⊕ | Pendant-mounted fixture, incandescent or compact fluorescent lamp |
| | -⊏- | Track light fixture, low-voltage incandescent lamp |
| | ▨ | Surface-mounted fixture, fluorescent lamp |
| | ▨ | Recessed fixture, fluorescent lamp |
| | ▨ | Recessed fluorescent fixture on emergency power |
| | ⊏----⊐ | Under-cabinet fixture, incandescent or fluorescent lamp |
| ⊖$_E$ | ○$_E$ | Surface-mounted emergency fixture with battery pack |
| ⊙ | ① | Junction box |
| ⊗ | ⊗ | Exit sign |
| | S | Single pole switch |
| | S$_3$ | 3-way switch |
| | S$_D$ | Dimmer switch |
| | S$_{LV}$ | Low-voltage switch |

**FIGURE 10.2B** Ceiling symbols and a reflected ceiling legend. (NCIDQ.)

drawings for a lighting design. In addition, there are specific symbols for electrical plans, including convenience outlets, switch outlets, auxiliary units, general outlets, data outlets, voice/data outlets, and switching arrangements.

Complex structures require separate lighting and electrical plans. Drawings for residential and small commercial buildings, on the other hand, often have only one plan that illustrates both lighting and electrical requirements. As illustrated in Figure 10.3, a lighting plan includes the location of luminaires, switches, and control loops. Luminaires should be scaled and represent a close approximation to the shape of the fixture. Complicated drawings might not have enough space to show scaled luminaires. In these situations, letters and subscripts may be used to identify specific luminaires, with either a circle or a hexagon surrounding the letters. The symbol and a brief description of the luminaire are then listed in the legends.

Dimension lines and notes may be used to identify the exact size and location of luminaires. Measurements are from the center (o.c.) of a luminaire to a fixed architectural element, such as the face of an exterior wall, window mullions, or the center of a partition. Spacing between multiple luminaires located in the same room is indicated by measurements from an architectural element to the center of each fixture.

A plan may also include mounting heights of fixtures that are located on vertical planes or suspended from the ceiling. The mounting height of luminaires located on a vertical plane, such as a wall or column, is from the above finished floor (AFF) to the center of the fixture (o.c.). The distance for suspended fixtures is from AFF to the bottom of the luminaire.

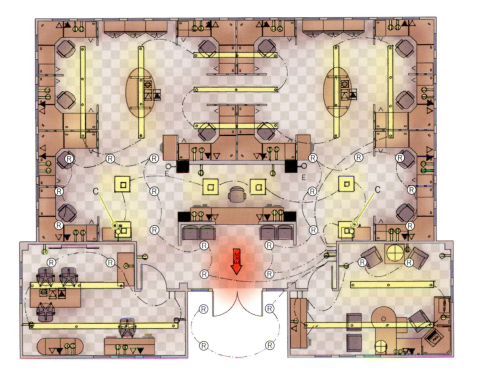

**FIGURE 10.3** A lighting plan that indicates the location of luminaires, switches, and control loops (see Figures 10.2a and 10.2b).

Switching arrangements are illustrated by the applicable switch symbol and control loops. As demonstrated in Figure 10.3, control loops are drawn from the switch(es) to the luminaire that is controlled by the switch(es). Control loops on a lighting plan are curved, whereas straight lines are used to represent wiring runs on an electrical plan.

Whenever possible, furniture arrangements should be included in a lighting plan. Drawing techniques for this purpose include overlays, layers, or the simple addition of furniture to the plan. Combining the placement of furniture

with the lighting plan can be helpful in ensuring that the luminaire is accurately positioned for a specific task or that it fulfills the intended purpose. Specifying the exact location of a luminaire must take into consideration differences in furniture dimensions, the number of items in a room, and how a space is arranged. For example, to ensure that a chandelier will be centered over a dining table, it is best to position all the furniture on the plan and then determine the location of the luminaire. The dimensions and placement of furniture also affect the location of luminaires intended for unique purposes, such as highlighting artwork.

Electrical plans can be extremely complicated and technical. As with all working drawings, registered professionals must officially approve the documents. Generally, an interior/lighting designer will be asked to describe only the lighting design, after which engineers determine power requirements. Detailed electrical plans illustrate the wiring runs from electrical panels to all equipment in a building, including lighting systems. Elements related to lighting systems in an electrical plan include luminaires, switches, outlets, junction boxes, and auxiliary units (Figure 10.4). As mentioned, small commercial buildings and residences

often have a single plan (a lighting/electrical plan) that combines electrical and lighting specifications. Such a plan includes the location of luminaires, switches, outlets, auxiliary units, junction boxes, and control loops (Figure 10.5).

In addition to recommending lighting systems, an interior/lighting designer should provide suggestions for the location of switches, sensors, and outlets. The location of these elements can significantly affect how well people function in a space. As discussed in Chapter 5, switches and outlets should be located in a position that reflects the principles of universal design and coincides with how people function in a space. Switches should be located on the lock side of a door and at

**FIGURE 10.4** An electrical plan including outlets, junction boxes, auxiliary units, furniture, and telephone/data outlets (see Figures 10.2a and 10.2b).

FIGURE 10.5 A lighting/electrical plan for a living room including the location of luminaires, switches, outlets, control loops, and furniture (see Figures 10.2a and 10.2b).

various other convenient locations within a room or space. Outlets should be convenient to reach from a variety of positions. Because outlets are inexpensive to install during the construction phase, their number should be determined by power needs, not a standardized layout. Sufficient outlets should be installed to provide electricity to all portable luminaires without the need for extension cords, outlet adapters, or running the fixture's cord over a long distance.

The location of outlets should also be dependent upon the configuration of vertical planes and furniture arrangements. For example, the location of outlets should be coordinated with a fireplace, built-in cabinets, or artwork. Generally, outlets should not be centered on a wall because electrical cords connected to the outlet may become a focal point. In addition, reaching an outlet can be very difficult when a large piece of furniture, such as a breakfront in a dining room, is placed in front of the outlet. The location of outlets should, therefore, take furniture arrangements into account. This can be especially challenging in rooms whose furniture is positioned away from the walls. A frequent solution to this problem is the use of floor outlets. On an electrical plan, dimension lines extending from the outlet to fixed architectural elements indicate the location of floor outlets.

Because outlets and switches are elements of the interior, they should also harmonize with the style, colors, and furnishings of the environment. Specifications for switches and outlets should include recommendations for products that enhance the design concept.

A reflected ceiling plan (RCP) is frequently included in working drawings. This plan is the image that one would see when looking in a mirror located on the floor; it illustrates the design of the ceiling, including the location of luminaires, architectural elements, sensors, and any HVAC equipment. An RCP is helpful for analyzing the functional and aesthetic components of the horizontal plane. Functionally, the plan is useful in determining whether the location of luminaires accommodates activities in the room and does not interfere with other structural elements on the ceiling plane. Aesthetically, the appearance of the ceiling affects the design of the interior space, especially in rooms with tall ceilings. In addition, an RCP helps the interior designer visualize how well the arrangement addresses the elements and principles of design.

A working drawing of an RCP includes the location of luminaires, switches, control loops, ceiling tiles, sensors, and any other element that intersects with the ceiling (Figure 10.6). These elements can include partitions,

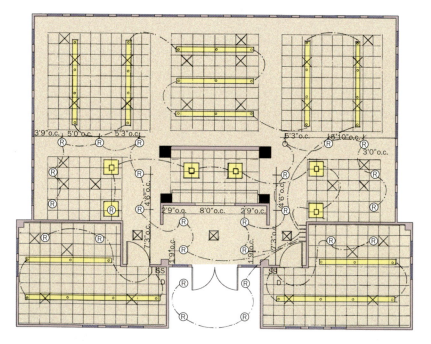

FIGURE 10.6 A reflected ceiling plan including the location of luminaires, switches, control loops, ceiling tiles, and other elements intersecting with the ceiling (see Figures 10.2a and 10.2b).

heating air ducts, diffusers, exposed beams, columns, speakers, skylights, cornices, coves, soffits, sprinkler heads, emergency lights, exit signs, and other signage. Ceiling materials and changes in ceiling heights should also be noted on the plan. Some plans include specific luminaire details such as lamp-aiming directions, occupancy control zones, and daylight dimming zones (Figures 10.7a and 10.7b).

The location of luminaires should be dimensioned following the same method used in a lighting plan. However, when a luminaire is located in the center of a ceiling tile, dimension lines do not have to be drawn. The arrangement of ceiling tiles should enhance the shape and size of the ceiling. When necessary, partial tiles are located along the perimeter of the room.

Elevation measurements provide a view of the arrangement of luminaires and other elements that can affect the visual composition of a wall, including furniture, objects, windows, or architectural features. Elevations are especially effective in demonstrating the location of wall-mounted luminaires, sensors, light shelves, valances, coves, or soffits.

Working drawings of integrated lighting systems, such as bookcases, soffits, or kitchen cabinets, require detailed illustrations. Detailed working drawings must communicate precise information to a fabricator and an installer. As scaled drawings, details indicate the exact size and location of all elements contained in an integrated system, including lamps, lamp holders, ballasts, transformers, structural elements, return air slots, baffles, reflectors,

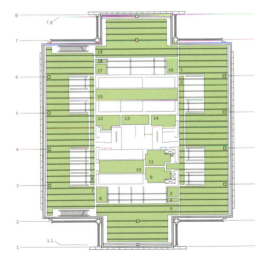

**FIGURE 10.7A** Occupancy control plan for the nineteenth floor of *The New York Times* Building in Manhattan by SBLD Studio, New York City. There are 19 zones in this plan.

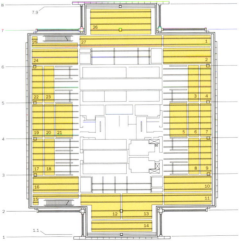

**FIGURE 10.7B** Daylight DALI dimming plan for the nineteenth floor of The New York Times Building in Manhattan by SBLD Studio, New York City. There are 27 zones in this plan.

glass, access grilles, cables, brackets, wiring, projectors, and mechanical support (Figure 10.8). Notes on detail drawings may include dimensions, material specifications, finishes, paint colors, and construction methods.

Supplementary to working drawings are written lighting specifications, which are important contract documents as well. Generally, information provided in specifications will override cross-referenced details illustrated in working drawings. Therefore, specifications must be accurate, comprehensive, and written in a clear and concise manner. Lighting specifications can be included in the furniture, furnishings, and equipment (FF&E) document. To assist in the development of accurate specification of details, the International Association of Lighting Designers (IALD) published a manual entitled Guidelines for Specification Integrity (2005). Topics include (1) building a foundation for specifying; (2) processes in the design, and construction document, bidding, and construction phases; and (3) specification approaches and languages (IALD, 2005). These guidelines should serve as a resource in writing lighting specifications.

## Contract Administration

Contracts are used to initiate the construction phase of a project. An interior/lighting designer prepares contracts with various individuals and businesses, including clients, manufacturers, suppliers, fabricators, vendors, independent contractors, and craftspeople. Contracts may be customized, or preprinted documents may be

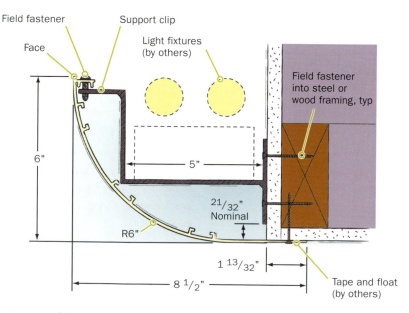

FIGURE 10.8 A detailed working drawing that communicates precise information to a fabricator and an installer.

provided by various professional organizations. Any contract used by an interior/lighting designer should be reviewed and approved by an attorney. A letter of agreement is frequently used as a contract between an interior/lighting designer and another party when the designer is bidding on a project, requesting services, or purchasing products. Letters of agreement may also specify design fees, unit pricing, delivery charges, shipping instructions, timelines, and any other terms or applicable conditions.

An interior/lighting designer may be involved in several activities associated with the construction phase, including reviewing documents, purchasing products, project management, monitoring costs, site supervision, and commissioning. The construction phase is a critical stage of the lighting design process, because the work performed affects the quality and integrity of the design. Therefore, it is important for an interior/lighting designer to be actively involved during this stage. The results of construction should reflect the design concept, working drawings, and specifications. Generally, monitoring a construction project requires a focus on service and management. Dedicating quality time to construction administration demonstrates to a client the designer's high level of professionalism and commitment. These positive impressions in turn foster loyalty on the part of clients.

Upon satisfactory completion of the lighting system, including commissioning, an interior/lighting designer may assist with scheduling the move-in and on-site supervision. Being present during the move-in can be very valuable in making sure furniture, artwork, and other objects do not interfere with sensors and are positioned correctly for specific tasks or a desired lighting effect.

After move-in is complete, a variety of documents should be given to the client, including product warranties, operational recommendations, maintenance manuals, commissioning reports, and recommendations for changes in the future. Operational recommendations should include any information relevant to using a lighting system, such as programming controls, adjusting luminaires to accommodate different users, automated window coverings, maximum wattages, and instructions for aiming and focusing.

The maintenance manual should include relamping recommendations, replacement instructions, recommissioning policies, and materials and methods for cleaning lenses, finishes, and lamps. Many of the instructions provided in the maintenance manual should be directly from manufacturers' product documentation. It is advisable to create a system for labeling the lamp(s) that correspond to specific fixtures so that the wrong lamp is not installed in a luminaire during relamping. Recommendations for future changes should include suggestions for modifying a lighting system to accommodate changes in tasks or in the interior environment, such as modifications to partitions, an increase in the number of employees, or changes in a display in a retail environment.

## Postoccupancy Evaluation

The purposes of **postoccupancy evaluation (POE)** are to assess the effectiveness of the lighting design, make modifications whenever possible, and acquire information that may be used to improve future projects. Evaluations should be conducted at various intervals after move-in. A good approach is to visit the site within the first three months after move-in, then six months later, and then at least one year later. A follow-up after two years demonstrates a commitment to the integrity of the design and can lead to new work because discussions can revolve around the possibility of upgrades or new lighting systems. Visits after move-in are also a good opportunity to make sure new end users are acquainted with the proper operation of the lighting system and luminaires, and controls are accurately adjusted.

The primary focus of the evaluation should be to determine how well the lighting design achieves the goals of the project. A useful starting point is to reexamine data collected during the programming phase of the lighting design process. Questions used in surveys and interviews can serve as the foundation for determining the level of satisfaction with the lighting design. POE may consist of informal discussions with the client and end users, or it can be a formalized process involving considerable analysis of the data.

Field observations may also be helpful in evaluating how well people interact with the lighting system. Special attention should be devoted to ensuring that daylight harvesting systems are working properly, and people are satisfied with lighting levels, ambient temperatures, and their ability to control task lighting.

Many factors will determine the appropriate method, including the number of end users, the complexity of the project, and the uniqueness of the lighting design. In determining the appropriate methodology, input should be derived from the client and other professionals involved with the project. A client can provide valuable insight into what evaluation methods are appropriate for the end users and the working conditions of the environment. Where the interior/lighting design is one component of an entire project, another professional, such as the architect or a contractor, could initiate POE.

To determine the level of satisfaction with an entire project, a survey often uses general questions, such as "How satisfied are you with the quality of lighting?" A response to this question will provide information regarding the level of overall satisfaction, but it does not reveal which elements of the lighting design are the most satisfactory or whether there are any illumination problems. Whenever possible, items on a survey or an interview guide should be written in a manner that elicits specific information and details regarding various parts or aspects of the lighting design.

The lighting design process is cyclical in the sense that the results obtained during the POE phase will inform subsequent projects. Combining this information with technological advances in lighting systems is invaluable to the success of designing a quality lighting environment in the future.

## LEED Certification and the Design Process

For a checklist of tasks related to LEED certification in each step of the design process, from contract documentation through evaluation, see Table 10.1

**TABLE 10.1** LEED-Related Tasks: Contract Documentation through Evaluation

| DESIGN PROCESS | LEED-RELATED TASKS |
|---|---|
| **Contract Documentation** | • Manage LEED documentation process using LEED-Online. If necessary seek clarification and a ruling on credit interpretations.<br>• Collect information and perform calculations that are required for documentation purposes.<br>• Construction documents related to lighting, electrical systems, and controls.<br>• Commissioning requirements, including lighting and daylighting controls, combined with construction documents.<br>• Commissioning design review prior to mid-construction documents. |
| **Contract Administration** | • Manage LEED documentation process using LEED-Online. If necessary seek clarification and a ruling on credit interpretations.<br>• Collect information and perform calculations that are required for documentation purposes.<br>• Review contractor submittals for commissioned energy systems, including lighting and daylighting controls.<br>• Install metering equipment for lighting systems and controls.<br>• Verify installation and performance of commissioned systems, including lighting and daylighting controls.<br>• Develop manual of commissioned systems, including lighting and daylighting controls.<br>• Verify completion of training and develop commissioning report, including lighting and daylighting controls.<br>• At the completion of construction submit all attempted credits for review. |
| **Evaluation** | • Manage LEED documentation process using LEED-Online. If necessary seek clarification and a ruling on credit interpretations.<br>• Collect information and perform calculations that are required for documentation purposes.<br>• Review operations and monitor commissioned systems, including lighting and daylighting controls, within eight to ten months after occupancy and substantial completion. |

Source: USGBC (2009). *LEED reference guide for green interior design and construction*. Washington, D.C.: U.S. Green Building Council.

# Fundamental Project

**1. Research Design Project**

Review a set of working drawings and specifications prepared by an architectural firm. Analyze the lighting and electrical specifications. In a written report, address the following items: (a) a lighting inventory; (b) an electrical inventory; and (c) symbols and descriptions provided in the legends.

## Application Projects

**1. Research Design Project**

Identify a floor plan for a residential or commercial building. Develop a set of lighting working drawings for the structure, including a plan view of the lighting, electrical, and reflected ceiling. Follow IESNA (2011) guidelines for the lighting symbols.

## 2. Human Factors Research Project

Identify a commercial client and the end users of the space. Develop a list of interview and survey questions for the purpose of conducting a POE. Questions should be specific to the end users of the space. In a written report, include the following information: (a) a list of the questions; (b) an outline of the plan for interviewing and surveying the end users; (c) the rationale for different questions; (d) the rationale for who will be interviewed and surveyed; and (e) how the results will be used for future projects.

# Summary

o Working or construction drawings are a graphic representation of a lighting system. Together with written specifications, they are used to order products, install wiring, and determine the location of luminaires, outlets, and controls.

o Commonly used working drawings include a plan view of the lighting, electrical, lighting/electrical, and reflected ceiling. Drawings may also include elevations, sections, and details. Lighting schedules and general notes located on drawing sheets provide additional information regarding the lighting system.

o A lighting plan indicates the location of luminaires, switches, and control loops.

o An RCP includes the location of luminaires, architectural elements, and any HVAC equipment, seen as they would appear in a mirror on the floor.

o As a supplement to working drawings, lighting specifications are extremely important contract documents.

o Contracts are used to initiate the construction phase of a project. An interior/lighting designer prepares contracts with various individuals and businesses, including clients, manufacturers, suppliers, fabricators, vendors, independent contractors, and craftspeople.

o Site supervision during construction and installations must be conducted in accordance with local laws and regulations.

o The purposes of a postoccupancy evaluation are to assess the effectiveness of the lighting design, conduct modifications whenever possible, and acquire information that can be used to improve future projects.

# Resources

American Hotel & Lodging Association (2003). *2003 Lodging Industry Profile*. Washington, D.C.: American Hotel & Lodging Association.

Baraban, R. S., & Durocher, J. F. (2001). *Successful restaurant design* (2nd ed.), New York: John Wiley & Sons.

Benya, J. R. (December 1–6, 2001). *Lighting for schools*. Washington, DC: National Clearinghouse for Educational Facilities.

Benya, J., Heschong, L., McGowan, T., Miller, N., & Rubinstein, F. (2001). *Advanced lighting guidelines*. White Salmon, WA: New Buildings Institute.

## KEY TERMS

construction drawing (working drawing)
electrical plan

lighting plan
lighting schedule
lighting/electrical plan

postoccupancy evaluation (POE)
specifications

working drawing (construction drawing)

Bernstien, A., & Conway, K. (March 2000). *The public benefits of California's investments in energy efficiency*. Prepared for the California Energy Commission by the RAND Corporation. MR-1212.0-CEC.

Bornholdt, D. (2001). *Green Suites International & GE Lighting Team to bring solid energy savings to light*. http://www.hospitalitynet.org

Boyce, P. N., Eklund, N., & Simpson, S. (2000). Individual lighting control: Task performance, mood and illuminance. *Journal of the Illuminating Engineering Society, 29*(1), 131–142.

Clark, C. (2001). Computers are causing health problems. *Journal of End User Computing, 13*(1), 34–45.

Duro-Test Lighting (2003). *Importance of lighting in schools*. http://www.full-spectrum-lighting.com, 1–3.

Fannin, J. (2003). Hotel safety: Consumer demand presents a marketing opportunity. *HSMAI Marketing Review*, Spring, 27–33.

Illuminating Engineering Society of North America (IESNA) (2011). *IESNA lighting handbook* (10th ed.). New York: Illuminating Engineering Society of North America.

Institute of Store Planners (2002). *Stores and retail spaces*. Cincinnati, OH: ST Publications.

Institute of Store Planners (2001). *Stores and retail spaces*. Cincinnati, OH: ST Publications.

Lang, S. (2003). *Good lighting for healthcare buildings. Business briefing: Hospital engineering & facilities management*. Berkeley, CA: Lawrence Berkeley National Laboratory.

Lawrence Berkeley National Laboratory (2003). *Lighting energy savings opportunities in hotel guest rooms: Results from a scoping study at the Redondo Beach Crown Plaza*. http://www.lbl.gov

Leibrock, C. A. (2000). *Design details for health: Making the most of interior design's healing potential*. New York: John Wiley & Sons.

Lerum, V., & Buvik, K. (2000). *Sun, light, and air: Monitoring the energy performance of the new Grong school building*. ASES Solar 2000 Conference, Madison, WI. 493–497.

Lodging Magazine. (March, 1–4, 2003). Lodging trends. *Lodging Magazine*, http://www.lodgingmagazine.com, 1-4.

Malkin, J. (2002). *Medical & dental space planning: A comprehensive guide to design, equipment, & clinical procedures*. New York: John Wiley & Sons.

Maniccia, D., Von Neida, B., & Tweed, A. (2000). Analysis of the energy and cost savings potential of occupancy sensors for commercial lighting systems. *Proceedings of the 2000 Annual Conference of the Illuminating Engineering Society of North America*.

Mattila, A. S. (2001). Creating customer loyalty in restaurants. *Cornell Hotel and Restaurant Administration Quarterly, 42*(6), 73–79.

McGowan, J. (June, 2002). Buildings online. *Energy User News*. http://www.energyusernews.com

Northeast Energy Efficiency Partnership (2002). *Combining quality design and energy efficiency for private offices, open-plan offices, office corridors*. www.neep.org

Northeast Energy Efficiency Partnership (2002). *"Energy effective" lighting for classrooms: Combining quality design and energy efficiency*. www.neep.org

Northeast Energy Efficiency Partnership (2000). Combining quality design and energy efficiency for retail and grocery daylighting. www.neep.org

Northeast Energy Efficiency Partnership (2000). Combining quality design and energy efficiency for small retail lighting. www.neep.org

Passini, R., Pigot, H., Rainville, C., & Tetreault, M.H. (2000). Wayfinding in a nursing home for advanced dementia of the Alzheimer's type. *Environment and Behavior, 32*(5), 684–710.

Pegler, M. M. (2001). *Stores of the Year, No.13*. New York: Visual Reference Publications.

Plympton, P., Conway, S., & Epstein, K. (2000). *Daylighting in schools: Improving student performance and health at a price schools can afford*. ASES Solar 2000 Passive Conference, Madison, WI., 487–492.

Simeonova, M. (2003). *Healthy lighting. The Center for Health Design*. http://www.healthdesign.org, 1–3.

Sleep Foundation (2003). The impact of sleep problems. http://www.sleepfoundation.org, 1–12.

United States Environmental Protection Agency (EPA) (2001). *Design for the environment*. http://www.epa. gov/

Veitch, J., & Newsham, G. (2000). Exercised control, lighting choices, and energy use: An office simulation experiment. *Journal of Environmental Psychology 20*(3), 219–237.

Whitehead, R. (2002). *Lighting design sourcebook*. Gloucester, MA: Rockport Publishers.

# 11 Residential Applications

Residential design encompasses an enormous variety of structures throughout the world in cities, suburbs, small towns, and even on water. Residences have been constructed in every conceivable style, in an extremely broad range of sizes, and in an amazing array of configurations. The complexity increases when one factors in the diversity of furniture, floor coverings, wall coverings, colors, materials, equipment, and accessories, which are unique to every residence. This tremendous diversity creates an exciting challenge for interior designers, particularly for lighting systems tailored to each particular client and the characteristics of his or her residence (Figure 11.1).

Quality lighting requires an approach that integrates the users of a space with their activities and the specific elements of the environment, including orientation, colors, textures, materials, furniture, accessories, and the geometry of the space. Lighting must also be designed to accommodate the client's budget, preferred taste, and lifestyle, as well as the installation limitations of the residence.

**OBJECTIVES**

o Apply an understanding of the content covered in previous chapters to the practice of designing lighting for residences

o Identify and apply important criteria for illuminating transitional spaces

o Identify and apply important criteria for illuminating activities that occur in multifunctional and dedicated spaces

o Integrate energy conservation, sustainable practice, safety, security, and human factors related to physiology and psychology into residential lighting design

FIGURE 11.1 Residences provide the opportunity to specify innovative luminaires. An inspirational design is evident in *Neon* (2003) by the lighting designer, Paul Cocksedge. (P. Cocksedge_NeON_03_photo © Richard Brine.)

(Figure 11.2). Layered lighting does not have to be expensive and can be accomplished with portable luminaires; the challenge is remembering to plan layered lighting in every room. Moreover, layered lighting can conserve energy by restricting higher light levels specifically where they are needed and using lower illumination levels for most areas in a space. In determining lighting techniques and the lighting system, all options should be considered for every room. It is frequently taken for granted that a certain type of luminaire is always appropriate for a specific room or task in a residence. For example, a popular approach for a kitchen is a surface-

## Transitional Spaces

Quality residential lighting environments are complex to design, but their integration with other interior elements should appear seamless. The holistic approach involves content covered in the previous chapters, including sustainability, daylighting, layered lighting, illumination zones, color, directional effects of illumination, and lighting systems. Designers of residential lighting should also consider energy conservation, sustainable practice, safety, security, and human factors related to physiology and psychology.

Layered lighting is important for all rooms in a residence, including bathrooms. Residential rooms often have only one layer of lighting, such as a task light over a bathroom mirror

FIGURE 11.2 Too often bathrooms have only one light source, which is not adequate for the space. (© Bea Cooper/Alamy.)

mounted fluorescent fixture in the center of the ceiling. An entryway will often have a glass and brass pendant suspended on a chain. Of course, there may be rooms where these luminaires would be perfect, but assuming that they are always appropriate in prescribed places is a mistake. A quality residential lighting environment is designed expressly for the unique needs of clients, their style of living, and all the elements of each room.

## ENTRYWAYS AND FOYERS

The transitional spaces in residences include entryways, foyers, hallways, and staircases. Often the terms *entryway* and *foyer* are used interchangeably. For the purposes of this section, entryway or entry is the term referring to the space located immediately outside the front entrance of a residence, and foyer is the interior area. Often, entry lighting includes one or two luminaires located next to the front door. This may be adequate for safety and security purposes; however, the lighting in this location should also set the tone for the overall design concept of the residence because this is the first impression people have when approaching the residence (Figure 11.3). Some clients may want a very dignified, formal feeling for the entrance, and others may want a casual, informal atmosphere. Lighting can reinforce the desired impression by the design of the luminaires, illumination levels, and highlighted elements.

Luminaires for the entryway should reflect the architectural style of the home, and the size of the fixture should be on an appropriate scale for the size of the door and entryway as well as the home as a whole (Figure 11.4). A designer

FIGURE 11.3 Entry lighting that sets the tone for the overall design concept of the residence and provides light for safety purposes. (Greg Hursley.)

selecting exterior luminaires must analyze the entire elevation of the residence. Sometimes a luminaire next to a door is too small for the surrounding elements; one common practice is to use the same entry light on a residence regardless of whether the entrance has a single door or a set of double doors. To achieve good proportion, the residence with double doors needs larger entry luminaires.

The entry and foyer are major transition areas from the outside to the interior. As a result, the illumination level of the entry and foyer must accommodate daylight and evening light. To have a smooth adaptation transition during the day, the foyer should have natural

FIGURE 11.4 The luminaires for the entryway reflect the West Indies architectural style of the residence and are an appropriate scale for the size of the door and the gate. (© Richard Sexton 2004.)

FIGURE 11.5 Transitional light levels should exist for entering and exiting a residence.Someone entering this residence would experience gradual changes in illumination as they move from the front door to the adjoining rooms. (Shelley Metcalf.)

light, supplemented by electrical lighting for cloudy days or if the windows are too small to provide adequate levels of daylight. For the evening hours, lighting in the landscape can help to ease the illumination level differences between the outdoors and the interior as people arriving move from a dark environment to a lighter one. In addition, appropriate levels should be planned for guests' departure from the residence, moving from a bright setting to a darker one. The eye takes longer to adapt when going from a bright to a dark setting. A transitional lighting plan should accommodate the variability of both situations (Figure 11.5).

## HALLWAYS AND STAIRCASES

Hallways and staircases are also transitional areas in a residence; therefore, little time is typically spent analyzing elements in these areas, such as architectural details or artwork on the walls. Moreover, because people moving through a hallway or staircase are interested primarily in whatever room it is they are heading toward, their concentration is often diverted from the interior elements on the way. Most people are in a standing position as they walk through a hallway or progress up and down stairs. The combination of minimal time, movement, and a standing position creates unique lighting challenges that must be addressed in order to achieve a quality lighting environment (Figure 11.6).

FIGURE 11.6 The glass floor is a creative approach to creating an interesting hallway, and daylight from the skylight is distributed to the floor below. (Timothy Hursley.)

## Hallway Lighting

Hallway challenges include layered lighting techniques, attracting attention to interesting elements that might exist on vertical planes, reducing the apparent length of long hallways, avoiding dark areas, creating safe passage during sleeping hours, and providing convenient switching arrangements. Layered lighting is often absent from hallways because people feel the only illumination necessary is task lighting. Illumination should be planned so that people can safely walk through hallways, but ambient and accent lighting are also important considerations. Variations in lighting,

including accent lighting, can help to reduce the apparent length of a hallway and can help to avoid dark areas. For layered lighting, all vertical and horizontal planes should be considered, including structural luminaires in the ceiling, transoms above doors, and interior windows (Figure 11.7). Hallways rarely have natural light, so transoms and those openings known as interior windows on walls adjoining hallways can provide excellent illumination during the day.

A hallway that provides passage from bedrooms to bathrooms needs illumination that creates a safe environment during the sleeping

Glass panel

**FIGURE 11.7** The fixed glass panels in the partition distribute daylight to adjacent spaces. (Chuck Choi.)

hours. To assist the eye with adaptation, lighting during this time period should be low. The illumination level and location of the fixtures should be determined by the visual abilities of the users of the residence. Controls play an important role in safety and convenience. Switches for luminaires should be accessible at various locations in the hallway, including at the end of the space and next to bedroom and bathroom doors. To ensure adequate illumination at the appropriate locations, hallways can be equipped with occupancy sensors or photosensors.

## Staircase Lighting

The combination of movement and changes in elevation can pose safety issues for vertical circulation. Staircases should be illuminated in a manner that provides a clear distinction between the risers and treads. The projecting edges of the treads should be visible. This can be accomplished in a variety of ways, including locating luminaires at the top and bottom of staircases and lighting each step. Generally, to help avoid the safety hazards of seeing a bright light source as one walks down the stairs lighting at the bottom of a staircase should be dimmer than the luminaire located at the top. Recessed light sources along the wall or in the treads, low-voltage strip systems along the edges of the treads, or integrated light in the railing can illuminate each step (Figure 11.8). Accent lighting should highlight interesting elements, such as architectural moldings or artwork, on walls adjoining a staircase. Often, a staircase is a beautiful focal point in a residence, in which case accent lighting should highlight the most intriguing elements of the design. Silhouette lighting can be an effective technique for emphasizing an elegant staircase.

**FIGURE 11.8** Recessed light sources along the wall of a stairway are one approach to lighting steps. (Greg Hursley.)

# Task-Specific Illumination

Quality lighting environments enhance the way people live and work in their residences. This requires lighting that is client- and site-specific. As described in Chapter 9, a thorough assessment needs to be conducted to determine who performs which activities where in the residence. In determining lighting approaches, a distinction should be made between guests and people living in the residence. People who are not familiar with an interior, especially overnight guests, might require special lighting techniques.

## TASKS PERFORMED IN MULTIPLE SPACES

To design a task lighting plan that is client- and site-specific requires an assessment of all the variables associated with performing a particular task. This includes an analysis of the task, characteristics of the user(s), reflectance, illumination source, luminaire performance data, and dimensions of furniture. The needs of special populations must always be addressed as well.

Tasks that are visually demanding or require special accuracy require very precise illumination. Information must be collected regarding the visual abilities and anthropometric data of the users of the residence. **Anthropometric data**, or detailed measurements of the human body, are valuable for determining the proper location of luminaires, switches, and outlets; for example, the proper location for reading depends partly on the vertical distance from the seat to the eyes. Torso and head dimensions can be determined by measuring the user or referring to anthropometric charts. Sections that follow in this chapter identify criteria that are important for specific tasks, including appropriate dimensional factors. This information can be applied to the specific needs of users within the context of their environment.

People read in numerous locations in a residence; however, effective lighting should be planned for areas where frequent and prolonged reading occurs (Figure 11.9).

Effective illumination for reading requires proper integration of the individual and the layers of lighting, the task light source, and the parameters of the furniture. The layers of lighting should have appropriately balanced illumination levels given the intensity of the light needed for reading. Because lighting for reading is typically at a high illumination level, appropriate levels for other lighting throughout the room will help to avoid extreme contrasts and the resulting eye fatigue.

The task light source should be directed at the reading material and should distribute the appropriate illumination level (Figure 11.10).

FIGURE 11.9 People read in numerous locations in a residence. Effective lighting includes not only illumination in areas where frequent and prolonged reading occurs but also layered lighting around these areas to prevent eyestrain caused by extreme contrasts. (© UpperCut Images/Alamy.)

FIGURE 11.10 A task light source next to a bed should be directed at the reading material. Notice the CFL in the pendant luminaire. (Ed Reeve/Getty Images.)

The lamp should be concealed from the eyes of the reader. Luminaires with translucent shades in white or off-white can be effective because they provide direct and indirect illumination on the task. Opaque or dark-colored shades, on the other hand, restrict the quantity and distribution of illumination on a task.

Certain measurements are needed to provide effective light for reading with a portable luminaire on a table next to a chair. These include the vertical distance from the user's eye level to the floor, the size of the fixture, and the dimensions of the furniture (Figure 11.11). The ideal condition is for the bottom of the shade to be level with the reader's eyes. Thus, the total distance from the floor to the reader's eye level must equal the distance from the floor to the bottom of the shade. A change in any of the elements can affect the effectiveness of the lighting. For example, the situation shown in Figure 11.11 was created for a female adult with a seat-to-eye measurement of 32 inches (80 cm). If a child sits in the chair, the lighting is no longer effective because his or her eyes

FIGURE 11.12 Effective task lighting should be planned for writing as well as reading. A user should be able to adjust the position of the fixture and the level of illumination. (© Red Cover/Alamy.)

FIGURE 11.11 Determining the appropriate location of a luminaire for reading requires multiple measurements of people, furniture, and the fixture. Ideally, for reading, the total distance from the floor to the reader's eye level must equal the distance from the floor to the bottom of the shade.

would be lower and, therefore, exposed to a bare lamp. An adult using a chair with a lower seat, or a higher table, would have the same result.

Effective task lighting should also be planned for writing (Figure 11.12). People write in a variety of rooms in a residence, but most writing occurs on a horizontal surface. A luminaire mounted on the surface should be approximately 12 inches (30 cm) from the individual and 15 inches (38 cm) to the right or left of the paper or keyboard (Figure 11.13). To avoid shadows on the task, the luminaire should be located to the left of a right-handed person and to the right of a left-handed person. The bottom of a shade should be level with the eyes of the writer. The other criteria described

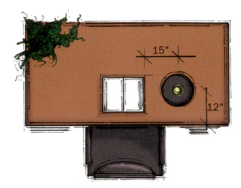

FIGURE 11.13 Plan view of the placement of a luminaire on a desk or table for the purpose of reading and writing. To avoid shadows on the task the luminaire should be located to the left side of a right-handed person and to the right side of a left-handed person. The bottom of the shade should be level with the eyes of the user.

FIGURE 11.14 Plan view of the suggested placement of luminaries for working at a computer.

in the discussion related to reading can also be applied to the writing task.

Frequently, a surface used for writing is also used for operating a computer. Unfortunately, the two tasks have different illumination requirements because writing is performed on a horizontal surface while computer work is conducted on a vertical plane. The solution is to employ multiple luminaires, techniques, and controls. An effective method for illuminating a work surface with a computer is to locate diffused luminaires above the user, either in front of the individual or at the side (Figure 11.14).

People should not watch a television screen in the dark. A television screen can emit a high level of illumination, which contrasts significantly with dark surroundings. Illumination should exist in all areas of a room, including behind the television, next to the screen, and surrounding the viewer (Figures 11.15a and b). As more residences

are creating media rooms or home theaters, effective layered lighting techniques must be used to accommodate these unique illumination requirements.

Task lighting in residences must also be planned for hobbies or other activities perhaps related to an individual's profession. These tasks can include painting, sewing, playing the piano, playing cards or games, and other activities. For all of these activities, the lighting must be planned to avoid glare in the eyes of the users and prevent shadows of heads or hands from being cast on the tasks. The surrounding areas should always have lighting that creates smooth transitions between illumination levels.

Formal and informal conversation occurs throughout a residence; however, in rooms where conversations often occur, lighting should be designed to encourage and enhance the activity (Figure 11.16). Based on the lifestyle of the client, prime conversational areas could be the living

FIGURE 11.15A To view a television illumination should exist in all areas of a room, including the area next to the screen. (Arcaid/Marc Gerritsen.)

FIGURE 11.15B Scene controls were used to change the environment from television viewing (Figure 11.15a) to a casual setting filled with daylight. (Arcaid/Marc Gerritsen.)

FIGURE 11.16 A pleasing lighting plan for conversation. To enjoy the city skyline in the evening requires eliminating glare on the glass from the fixtures. To reduce glare these recessed fixtures have full optic cutoffs.

room, kitchen, dining room, or bedrooms. Generally, lighting that is conducive to conversation is relaxing and enhances the facial features of people. This typically involves soft, indirect lighting at low to moderate illumination levels. Illumination on people can be reflected from surfaces, diffused through a soft fabric, or derived from a combination of the two. Avoid direct illumination that grazes the front of people's faces or is aimed at their eyes. Bright light sources behind people should also be avoided, because the silhouette effect can make it impossible for people to see the faces of those seated across from them.

FIGURE 11.17 A wall of clear and diffused daylight is an excellent approach to providing effective task lighting in a kitchen. (© Iconpix/Alamy.)

## TASKS PERFORMED IN DEDICATED SPACES
### Kitchens

Food preparation and cleanup require special lighting considerations because of the danger of burns and cuts. Areas to consider include counters, ranges, and the sink. A variety of lighting techniques can be employed for the specific tasks done in kitchens (Figures 11.17 and 11.18a and b). The horizontal nature of these tasks requires illumination from directly above the work area. Luminaires and their locations must be carefully planned to eliminate glare and shadows on tasks. Lamps should be selected with high color rendering index (CRI) ratings so that the colors of food can be seen accurately.

Layered lighting becomes very important in kitchens because direct illumination of a fairly high intensity is needed for critical tasks, whereas ambient lighting helps to moderate the contrasts between brighter and darker areas.

Accent lighting provides a work environment with visual interest, especially in a kitchen that is also used as a primary gathering place. Controls with a range of variability are useful for accommodating the multiple activities and tasks conducted in kitchens.

Illumination on counters, including islands, can be derived from luminaires mounted under wall cabinets or fixtures installed in soffits or the ceiling (Figure 11.19). Luminaires under wall cabinets can be located at the front or back edge of the cabinetry. Glare can pose a problem with this technique when the counter or backsplash has a shiny or glossy finish. Luminaires installed in soffits or the ceiling can be recessed or surface-mounted. The point of installation must be carefully planned to avoid casting an individual's shadow on the task and to allow adequate clearance space for cabinet doors.

FIGURE 11.18A There is a variety of ways to creatively incorporate daylight into a kitchen. Sidelighting can provide uniform illumination and help to eliminate glare and shadows on tasks. (Julia Heine/McInturff Architects.)

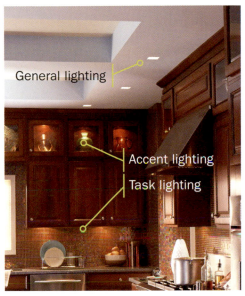

FIGURE 11.19 Luminaires mounted under the wall cabinets provide task lighting for the counters. Fixtures in the cabinets are used for accent lighting and the recessed square-shaped fixtures in the ceiling provide general lighting. (www.element-lighting.com.)

FIGURE 11.18B Sidelighting is enhanced by the angled surfaces that are painted white. Electrical light sources provide illumination during the evening. (Julia Heine/McInturff Architects.)

Luminaires located above a cooktop or sink can be an effective method of illumination (Figure 11.20). As always, the light source should be positioned so as to eliminate glare and avoid having people work in their own shadow. Glare can be especially problematic for work conducted at the cooktop because frequently those surfaces are made up of highly reflective materials. Light directed from the right and left of the worker can help to eliminate shadows on a task. This cross-lighting technique can be effective because each light source serves as direct and fill lighting simultaneously. To facilitate cleaning associated with the grease from cooking,

FIGURE 11.20 An innovative solution to providing task lighting for an island in a kitchen. Notice the accent lighting on the plates and dividers on the back wall. (Getty Images/ Douglas Gibb.)

approach, other methods should always be considered. Furthermore, one fixture is never the answer for an entire room (Figure 11.21). In a dining room, luminaires should be expressly selected for the task of eating, but need not be located above the center of the table. For example, illuminating the four corners of a table can provide excellent task lighting and soft illumination on the faces of people seated at the table, especially if the table is relocated or expanded with table leaves.

The size and location of luminaires should be carefully planned in a dining room. In the case of a pendant fixture, the size must be appropriate for the dimensions of the table and room; frequently, a dining room fixture is too small or too large for the table and the size of

luminaires surrounding the cooktop should have sealed covers and surfaces that are easy to wash.

There are many methods for illuminating kitchen cabinetry, and many techniques involve hiding sources within the structural elements of the cabinets. Whenever possible, the interior of cabinets in food-preparation areas should be illuminated; this is especially important for corner and base cabinets. The light source should be positioned to illuminate most of the items in the cabinet, including those in the back.

### Dining Rooms

A variety of techniques and types of luminaires can be used to illuminate the eating area. Frequently, a pendant fixture is located over a table. Although this can be an effective

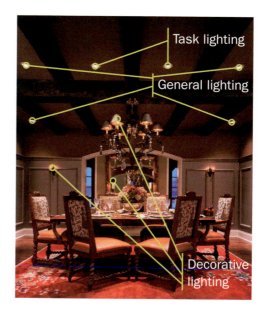

FIGURE 11.21 A dining room that was planned for layered lighting. (Courtesy Juno Lighting Group.)

FIGURE 11.23A Daylighting should be planned for bedrooms. (© Adrian Sherratt/Alamy.)

FIGURE 11.22 The pendant fixture in this dining room is too small for the size of the room, table, and is too high from the table. (© Red Cover/Alamy.)

the room (Figure 11.22). An appropriate size is determined by following the principles of the golden section. To avoid having people hit their head on a pendant fixture when they stand up, the luminaire should be approximately 6 inches (15 cm) from the edges of the table. A pendant should not interfere with artwork on a wall or a beautiful view from a window; for these situations, the space between a table and the ceiling should be unobstructed. This might be accomplished by using concealed light sources.

## Bedrooms and Carpets

Rooms for sleeping and playing have some unique lighting considerations (Figures 11.23a and b). The ages of the occupants are an

FIGURE 11.23B Another creative approach to daylighting in a bedroom. The clerestory windows provide daylight and privacy. (Douglas Hill/Corbis.)

important issue. Lighting and electrical outlets must be safe for children of all ages and the elderly. Cords on portable luminaires should not be accessible from any location in a room to avoid tripping, and designers should also avoid luminaires that fall over easily. All outlets should be covered with protective seals. To promote eye development, infants should have some level of illumination at all times of the day. The lighting in rooms for children should be planned to accommodate the changing activities that occur in the space as the children become older. Playing with blocks on the floor requires different illumination from studying at a desk or working at a computer. Whenever possible, projection of future lighting needs for children's spaces should occur during the earliest phases of a project.

People of all ages need adequate illumination to move through rooms during the evening hours. Illumination that is kept on at a low level throughout the night or triggered by occupancy sensors or photosensors can provide sufficient evening illumination. People who share a room often awaken in the morning at different times. Separate lighting systems can provide illumination for the person who must get up, whereas maintaining a fairly dark environment for the person still sleeping.

Residences built during the past several years often have no lighting in closets. Illumination in closets is essential not only to enable people to see the items they are handling or retrieving, but also to prevent accidents when belongings fall (Figure 11.24). The bare incandescent lamp, formerly a common approach for closets, should be

avoided because the brightness can cause disability glare and the lamp poses a fire hazard. In a confined space, adequate clearance around a light source should always be provided. To illuminate items on shelves and hanging on rods, an effective approach is to locate a light source at a high position on the wall across from the objects. Low, supplementary lighting should be provided to illuminate objects on the closet floor.

FIGURE 11.24 An illuminated clothes pole is an excellent way to light clothes in a closet. Light should also be provided close to the floor of the closet. (Lumenpulse Lighting Inc.)

FIGURE 11.25A A recessed light in the ceiling provides good illumination in the shower. (Douglas Hill/Corbis.)

FIGURE 11.25B The floor next to a shower is often a slick area. Light fixtures directed to this area could help to alert someone to a slippery surface. (Max Spencer-Morris.)

## Bathrooms

Effective illumination is critical in grooming areas. Many accidents occur in bathrooms, so illumination should be designed to promote a safe environment. The combination of water and slick surfaces creates a treacherous situation requiring good illumination of all areas in a bathroom, including steps, bathtubs, showers, and any locations likely to have standing water (Figures 11.25a and b). Illumination on handrails and grab bars can be very helpful. Luminaires in the shower must be rated for wet locations and should be positioned so as to minimize shadows and eliminate glare not only in the shower but throughout the bathroom. Glare should be determined based on both sitting and standing positions of residents.

Illumination for applying makeup and for shaving has special requirements (Figures 11.26a and b). Some of the most important criteria include accurate color rendering properties, clarity in seeing details, and a uniform distribution of illumination. Lamps for facial grooming should have a CRI rating of 100. The desired color temperature of the lamp can vary with the ethnicity of the user; generally, Western and Eastern cultures prefer warm and cool light sources, respectively.

For accurate vision of facial details, illumination should be diffused and located next to the face, and all shadows on the face must be eliminated. The quality of illumination is affected by the interaction of lamp characteristics with the type of diffuser used on a luminaire. For example, an effective combination for facial grooming is an opal diffuser with fluorescent lamps. To determine the best lighting effect, various lamps and

**FIGURE 11.26A** Daylighting on each side of the mirror provides excellent illumination for applying makeup and for shaving.

**FIGURE 11.26B** The light fixtures with diffused shades provide a uniform distribution of light, which is important for applying makeup and for shaving. The location of the windows provides excellent lighting for grooming.

diffusers should be tested. Ideally, luminaires should surround a face on the top and sides (Figure 11.27), but at the very least they should be located next to both sides of the face. Lamps or the center of shades should be located at cheek level. A full-length mirror should have a fixture mounted above it.

Quality residential lighting should be unique to every combination of user, activity, and environment. Too often, prescribed lighting solutions have been applied to residences without regard for the specific characteristics of the situation. An interior designer should specify a lighting plan that incorporates relevant issues presented in previous chapters of this textbook within the context of the client's needs.

## Quality Lighting in Top-Rated LEED-Certified Residential Buildings

"Case Study: Living Homes" provides an example of a residential project that uses energy-efficient lighting as well as other sustainable characteristics. This LEED-certified Platinum residence is a sustainable modular home designed by the renowned California architect Ray Kappe.

**FIGURE 11.27** Another approach to providing lighting for grooming. Mounting the fixtures on the mirrors intensifies the light source. (Douglas Hill/Corbis.)

Skylight

Flourescent
fixture

# Case Study: Living Homes

### Design Problem Statement

Design a contemporary residence that is not only attractive and easy to live in and maintain, but also provides a zero negative environmental impact.

### Project Background

BUILDER: LivingHomes (www.livinghomes.net)

ARCHITECT: Ray Kappe

LOCATION: California

ROOMS: 4 bedrooms, 3 baths, "LivingRoof"

SIZE: 2,480 square feet (230 square meters)

Trellis

Deck

Outdoor luminaire reclaimed from yard sale

## Lighting Design Strategy

- Design orientation that maximizes daylighting.

- Photovoltaic system on the LivingRoof that provides 75 percent of the residence's energy needs and shade.

- Open two story floor plan.

- One-inch floor-to-ceiling Low-E insulated glass that provides high R-values.

- LEDs rather than incandescent lamps for downlights and portable desk fixtures.

- Skylights in master and secondary baths with florescent lighting above the mirrors.

- Exterior trellises and decks to help control sunlight.

- Interior ultraviolet resistant shading system in the bedroom.

- Woven roll-down shades that provide privacy as well as views of the outdoors.

- Hewlett Packard computer runs the residence's lighting, climate, security, and entertainment systems.

LEDs

Open floor plan

## Platinum LEED Certification

Out of a possible 108 LEED Certification points, the LivingHome's residence received 91, including points for Homeowner Awareness (1) and Innovation and Design Process (1.5). The residence is expected to save approximately 7,471 KWh of electricity each year.

# Fundamental Projects

**1. Research Design Project**

Select photographs of entries, foyers, hallways, and staircases. Identify the electrical luminaires in the spaces and determine the lighting category (general, task, accent) of each. If a luminaire does not exist for a category of lighting, suggest one that would be effective. The identification and analysis should be submitted in written form. Photographs must be included.

**2. Human Factors Research Project**

Select photographs of areas for reading, conversation, writing, working at a computer, and watching television. Identify the lighting for the task involved, and determine its effectiveness. Where necessary, provide suggestions to improve the effectiveness of the lighting for the specific activity. The identification and analysis should be submitted in written form. Photographs must be included.

**3. Human Factors Research Project**

Select photographs of kitchens, dining rooms, bedrooms, and bathrooms. Identify the ambient, task, and accent lighting, and determine the effectiveness of illumination. Where necessary, provide suggestions to improve the effectiveness of the lighting for a specific purpose. The identification and analysis should be submitted in written form. Photographs must be included.

# Application Project

**1. Human Factors Research Project**

Select a residential project from one of your studio classes. Research energy codes and standards applicable to the client, and LEED certification requirements for homes. If possible, interview and/or ask the client to complete a survey similar to the document provided in Chapter 9 (Table 9.1). For the project complete the following items:

a. A lighting/electrical plan of the residence

b. Suggested luminaires and controls for two major areas

c. A written summary of a daylighting strategy for the residence that emphasizes benefits to the users of the residence

d. A written report summarizing the results of the interviews/ survey, if applicable

e. A written report that includes a list of suggestions for achieving LEED certification

# Summary

○ Layered lighting is important for all rooms in a residence, including bathrooms.

○ Luminaires in an entryway should reflect the architectural style of the home, and the size of the fixture should be on an appropriate scale for the size of the door and entryway, as well as of the home as a whole.

○ The entryway and foyer are major transition areas from the outside to the interior. As a result, the illumination level of the entry and foyer must accommodate daylight and evening hours.

○ Hallway lighting considerations include layering, attracting attention to interesting elements on vertical planes, reducing the apparent length of long hallways, avoiding dark areas, creating safe passage during sleeping hours, and providing convenient switching arrangements.

○ Staircases should be illuminated in a manner that allows clear distinction between risers and treads.

○ Quality lighting environments enhance the way people live and work in their residences. This requires lighting that is client- and site-specific. A thorough analysis needs to be conducted to determine who performs which activities where in the residence.

○ Anthropometric data, or detailed measurements of the human body, are valuable for determining the proper location of luminaires, switches, and outlets.

○ Food preparation and cleanup require special lighting considerations because of the dangers of burns and cuts.

○ Rooms for sleeping and playing represent some unique lighting considerations. The ages of the occupants are an important issue.

○ Effective illumination is critical in grooming areas. In view of the high number of accidents that occur in bathrooms, illumination should be designed to help promote a safe environment.

# Resources

Allen, P. S., Jones, L. M., & Stimpson, M. F. (2004). *Beginnings of interior environments* (9th ed.). Upper Saddle River, NJ: Pearson/Prentice Hall.

American Institute of Architects (2000). *Architectural graphics standards* (10th ed.). New York: John Wiley & Sons.

**KEY TERM**

anthropometric data

Benya, J., Heschong, L., McGowan, T., Miller, N., &
Rubinstein, F. (2001). *Advanced lighting guidelines*.
White Salmon, WA: New Buildings Institute.

Burde, E. (1992). *Design presentation techniques*.
New York: McGraw-Hill.

Ching, F. D. K. (2003). *Architectural graphics*
(4th ed.). New York: John Wiley & Sons.

Coleman, C. (ed.) (2001). *Interior design handbook of
professional practice*. New York: McGraw-Hill.

Illuminating Engineering Society of North America
(IESNA) (2000). *Document DG-3-00: Application
of luminaire symbols on lighting design drawings*.
New York: Illuminating Engineering Society of
North America.

International Association of Lighting Designers
(IALD) (2002). *Guidelines for specification
integrity*. Chicago: International Association
of Lighting Designers.

Knackstedt, M. V. (2002). *The interior design business
handbook*. New York: John Wiley & Sons.

Koenig, P. A. (2000). *Design graphics: Drawing
techniques for design professionals*. Upper Saddle
River, NJ: Pearson Education/Prentice Hall.

Koomen-Harmon, S., and Kennon, K. (2001). *The
codes guidebook for interiors* (2nd ed.). New York:
John Wiley & Sons.

Pile, J. F. (2003). *Interior design* (3rd ed.). New York:
Harry N. Abrams.

Ramsey, C. G., & Sleeper, H.R. (2000). *Architectural
graphic standards* (10th ed.). New York: John
Wiley & Sons.

Smith, W. D., & Smith, L.H. (2001). *McGraw-Hill on-
site guide to building codes 2000: Commercial and
residential interiors*. New York: McGraw-Hill.

Steffy, G. R. (2002). *Architectural lighting design*
(2nd ed.) New York: Van Nostrand Reinhold.

Wakita, O. A., & Linde, R.M. (2003). *The professional
practice of architectural working drawings*
(3rd ed.). New York: John Wiley & Sons.

# 12 Commercial Applications

Important considerations in lighting residential interiors were discussed in Chapter 11. This chapter explores the most frequent commercial interiors that designers are commissioned to work on. Some of the most important issues affecting all commercial structures include designing for diverse populations, safety concerns, protecting the environment, and energy conservation. People with a wide range of abilities, communication skills, and perceptions work in or visit commercial buildings; therefore, the principles of universal design are a critical component in designing a quality lighting environment for these spaces that is as safe as possible for all users. Also, because commercial interiors consume tremendous amounts of resources and electricity, energy codes are becoming more stringent every year. By implementing effective conservation practices, an interior designer can comply with the codes and help make a positive impact on our planet.

The principles of a quality lighting environment must be applied to all types of commercial structures and to every space within a building. This chapter focuses on how lighting affects the end users in offices, schools, healthcare institutions, hospitality interiors, and retail establishments. Designing the lighting for commercial interiors requires a thorough understanding of the goals of the organization and the characteristics of the end users (Figure 12.1). The environment must be responsive to the needs of

**OBJECTIVES**

o  Describe common lighting considerations in commercial facilities, including structural elements, needs of the end users, principles of universal design, and public areas

o  Identify and apply important lighting considerations in offices, educational facilities, and healthcare institutions

o  Identify and apply important lighting considerations in the hospitality industry and retail stores

the client, the people who work in the building, and people who visit for a limited amount of time. As reviewed in Chapter 9, creating functional and aesthetic designs requires interaction with users of the environment and the application of observational skills.

Designers must collaborate with multiple professionals engaged in the planning and construction process, including architects, engineers, contractors, electricians, building inspectors, acoustical experts, and fire-prevention specialists.

FIGURE 12.1 A creative approach to medical facilities was accomplished after understanding the needs of the users. To avoid the monotony of analyzing radiological images in the space the lighting plan included LEDs mounted in tubes. (© 2008 Boris Feldblyum.)

# Task-Oriented Commercial Interiors

The most common task-oriented commercial interiors are offices, educational facilities, and healthcare institutions. Designers need to plan, install, and evaluate lighting for commercial interiors within the parameters of the project, including the budget and schedule. This requires an extensive collaborative effort with the client, end users, and professionals who work on the project.

In designing lighting for a variety of users, it is critical to incorporate the principles of universal design. As discussed in Chapter 11, illumination must specifically address the needs of users, their activities, the site, interior architecture, furniture, equipment, and characteristics of the elements of the space. Even within the context of commercial spaces used for the same purpose, such as restaurants, every commercial building has unique requirements that must be addressed in the lighting.

**FIGURE 12.2A** To create a "fresh new design" for the research company, U.S. Data designers developed a nontraditional approach to the lighting as well as the interior. (Assassi.)

## OFFICES

Lighting for offices is affected by management philosophies and the technology that employees use. Management is always interested in operating a profitable business by producing quality work and retaining good employees. Throughout the history of office interiors, managers have attempted to identify the specific conditions that would ensure success and reflect the corporate culture (Figures 12.2a and b). This includes the design of office space, furniture, equipment, and lighting.

A common management philosophy is to create an environment that is flexible to the

**FIGURE 12.2B** The nontraditional approach to the new design for US Data included an innovative approach to the lighting in the conference room. (Assassi.)

changing needs of a business and the global economy. This frequently involves downsizing, reducing excess, eliminating categories of workers, instituting shared spaces, and pursuing international opportunities. To reduce absenteeism and retain quality employees, management has focused on the personal needs of employees. For example, to create a homelike environment, "living rooms" in an office serve as locations for meetings or casual conversation.

Many employees have flexible schedules, work in a variety of locations, and engage in telecommuting. These individuals often need work space when they come to the office. Customized lighting in these spaces helps to individualize an office that is shared by many people.

Because collaboration remains important in the eyes of managers, the office needs space for interaction, such as "touchdown" areas. To encourage spontaneous collaborative activities, touchdown spaces are distributed throughout a building. To reduce travel expenses,

many managers have elected to invest in videoconferencing facilities. All these changes in management philosophies require unique approaches to illuminating the office.

It is important to review how the technology that people use in an office helps to determine appropriate lighting environments. In the earliest offices, employees performed most of their work on the horizontal plane of a desk. The work involved writing, using a typewriter, and reading a variety of documents, including carbon copies. The lack of strong contrast and the importance of speed and accuracy prompted management to install lighting fixtures that emitted high quantities of illumination. In addition, to ensure bright illumination on a task, direct light sources were used without adequate shielding.

The next major development in office technology was the portable computer. Researchers focused on developing the optimum lighting system that can provide effective illumination for people working at a computer and writing at a desk (Figure 12.3).

(a)

(b)

**FIGURE 12.3** Studies have been conducted to examine optimum lighting in offices. Compared to the uniform distribution of fixtures on the (a) left side the clustered arrangement on the (b) right side provides more direct illumination on task surfaces. (Courtesy of Zumtobel.)

Because computer manufacturers are constantly improving the surfaces of VDT screens, problems associated with glare and veiling reflections could eventually become obsolete.

The use of videoconferencing technology poses unique lighting challenges because the interaction between the camera, transmission, and lighting are extremely complex. (The variables to consider when designing lighting for videoconferencing are discussed later in this chapter). The progression to wireless technology has enabled employees to work in various locations throughout a building. Designers will have to plan effective task lighting in a variety of locations in order to accommodate these new ways of working.

### Ergonomics and Lighting Solutions

Critical to quality illumination in an office environment is the relationship between ergonomics and lighting. Tasks performed in an office can cause vision problems and repetitive stress injuries, such as carpal tunnel syndrome (CTS). Office workers report problems such as eyestrain, visual fatigue, and blurred vision. In addition, they indicate that problems associated with vision have indirectly caused other physical ailments, such as headaches. Musculoskeletal injuries can occur when people work in unnatural positions or engage in repetitive motions. For example, one cause of CTS is the repetitive wrist motion that occurs when people work at a keyboard for long periods of time.

Lighting has a role in helping to reduce vision problems and musculoskeletal injuries. Task lighting in offices should be designed to accommodate the specific needs of each end

FIGURE 12.4 The *Leaf* task fixture by Yves Béhar (next to the computer) is designed to accommodate the specific needs of each end user. To adjust the intensity of the light or the color from warm to cool the user slides their hand along the grooves in the base of the fixture. The arm is also adjustable. *Leaf* is also 98 percent recyclable. (Herman Miller.)

user (Figure 12.4). Even though employees might be engaged in the same tasks, each individual has different vision requirements; therefore, an employee should be able to control the type of lighting he or she needs in order to perform tasks. This can be accomplished by specifying luminaires and controls that the end user is able to operate. **Localized lighting** techniques allow an employee to position light sources where they are needed and at the appropriate illumination level. Vision problems should decline when people can create the optimum lighting for their tasks and work environment.

Ineffective lighting can contribute to musculoskeletal injuries. For example, an end user may move to an unnatural or awkward position to avoid glare and veiling reflections, and develop back or neck problems as a result of working in such a position for a long period of time. To prevent CTS, individuals are encouraged to vary their working positions. This might involve alternating between standing and sitting. For multiple positions to be successful, however, lighting must be designed to accommodate various locations. Localized lighting, controlled by the end user, can provide the flexibility required for changing lines of sight.

Allowing the end users to determine their lighting needs should also help resolve the problems associated with too much light in an office environment. Currently, many offices have excessively high illumination levels because of the historical belief that bright lights improve productivity and provide stimulation in the work environment. Effective lighting for computer tasks should take into account the light provided by luminous VDT screens, and ensure appropriate illumination levels between the screen, the immediate work area, and surrounding areas. Glare and veiling reflections can be avoided by eliminating a direct angle of light distribution from luminaires and windows.

Office environments have a variety of users, daylight conditions, configurations, furniture styles, and interior materials (Figure 12.5). Lighting should be customized to the unique requirements and needs of each client and should include layered lighting in every space. Many of the same tasks are performed in private offices and open-plan areas. For tasks performed in offices, lighting should be

**FIGURE 12.5** Lighting plans for the Fornari headquarters in Milan, Italy accommodated unique furniture designs, architectural details, and maximized daylighting. As a reflection of sustainability the headquarters is located in an abandoned ceramic factory. (Courtesy of Giorgio Borruso Design/Photo: Alberto Ferrero.)

designed to eliminate glare on work surfaces, avoid severe contrasts in the distribution of lighting, illuminate vertical surfaces, diminish shadows, and provide effective localized lighting for end users. Open-plan offices can be complicated to illuminate because the potential for glare and veiling reflections is significant due to numerous ceiling fixtures and perhaps glass exterior walls. To determine visual problems associated with multiple luminaires located throughout a large area, designers must analyze work areas for every station in the space.

## Conference Rooms

Technology has significantly influenced the design of conference rooms. In addition to being the traditional place in which to hold meetings, conference rooms have become the location for viewing audiovisual presentations, working at computers, and conducting teleconferences. Lighting for such multifunctional spaces must accommodate the full range of activities, which occur at varying times of day, as well as the specific needs of each end user (Figures 12.6a and b). Lighting for discussion purposes should be designed to enhance facial features, enable participants to view a whiteboard, and provide

task lighting for note taking on paper or on a computer. When the purpose of the room changes to viewing an audiovisual presentation, perimeter lighting should be soft throughout the room and in the area surrounding a screen or television monitor. In addition, task lighting for taking notes should be available for every person in the room.

## EDUCATIONAL FACILITIES

Lighting for educational facilities should be efficient and support philosophies of learning. Many research studies and reports have

(b)

(a)

**FIGURE 12.6A** An innovative approach to integrating daylighting and electrical sources into a dramatic design for a conference room in Liechtenstein's Federal State Parliament. Designers developed an effective solution for providing task lighting in a space with a pitched ceiling. (Lukas Roth, Cologne.)

**FIGURE 12.6B** An exterior view of the building that includes the conference room in Figure 12.6a. Notice the conference room skylights at the peak of the pitched roof. (Lukas Roth, Cologne.)

demonstrated the importance of daylight to learning (Heschong, 2003; Heschong, 2001; Benya, 2001; Heschong, 1999; Lane, 1996; Plympton, Conway, & Epstein, 2000; Ravetto, 1994; Thayer, 1995) (see Figure 12.7). As discussed in Chapter 3, daylight enhances visual acuity, which provides better light for reading and writing. Daylight also has positive psychological and physiological effects on people by reducing stress, satisfying circadian rhythms, and encouraging positive attitudes.

The Heschong Group (1999) found that students in classrooms that had significant daylight had higher test scores than students working in classrooms with little or no daylight. The Alberta Department of Education in Canada and schools in Raleigh, North Carolina, reported health and educational benefits for children who were exposed to daylight. Research also found that absenteeism was lower in educational facilities illuminated by daylight.

A variety of activities occur in classrooms. Many educators believe that the best learning occurs when students are exposed to different approaches to teaching (Figure 12.8). These include lectures, discussion, deskwork, interactive media, or groupwork. Many classrooms are designed to accommodate a lecture format and collaborative small-group activities. Classroom activities can occur at desks, at tables, or on the floor. Technology has had a tremendous impact on education by presenting students with a variety of ways to learn. Educators can present information to students by means of computers, television monitors, screens, flipcharts, chalkboards, or whiteboards.

As demonstrated in research studies, daylight is important in the classroom. Every effort should be made to incorporate daylight into every space, including corridors. For existing structures, this could include adding skylights, light wells, clerestories, roof monitors, light shelves, and tubular skylights. To accommodate times when a classroom needs to be dark, effective shading devices must be installed at every window in a room, including any glazing on partition walls. To supplement daylight, electrical lighting systems

**FIGURE 12.7** The Chartwell School is an excellent example of maximizing daylight in classrooms. Photocells are used to coordinate daylight with electrical sources. Chartwell School is LEED platinum. (Michael David Rose.)

FIGURE 12.8 Daylighting for the Chartwell School included nontraditional learning spaces. (Michael David Rose.)

preferable to limit accent lighting and specify energy-efficient lamps. When a lecture is occurring in a classroom, lighting should be directed on the speaker, task luminaires should be aimed at desks to enable students to write notes, and uniform, perimeter illumination should exist throughout the room. Perimeter lighting in a classroom is very important because students must often read material that is on vertical surfaces, such as whiteboards, chalkboards, flipcharts, or bulletin boards (Figure 12.9). Specific lighting might have to be included to illuminate the walls surrounding windows, where teaching materials are frequently located. During the day, these vertical surfaces will be dark unless light is directed at the area.

must be energy-efficient and easy to maintain, and must have a long life.

Pendant luminaires, whether direct or indirect, provide an excellent diffused quality of illumination. When properly spaced, they also ensure a uniform distribution pattern, which can help to eliminate dark areas in a classroom. Efficient ballasts should work in tandem with controls, such as daylight or motion sensors. Multilevel switching, with user override for automatic controls, can be coordinated to respond to daylight contours. The quantity of light in classrooms should follow the recommendations in the *IESNA Lighting Handbook*. The ninth edition recommends 40 fc to 50 fc (400 lux to 500 lux) in classrooms, and 20 fc to 40 fc (200 lux to 400 lux) for computer classrooms.

Layered lighting should be used throughout the school building. To conserve energy, it is

FIGURE 12.9 To enable students to see learning materials mounted on walls requires perimeter lighting. This should be accomplished with daylighting and electrical sources. Walls next to windows should be illuminated to avoid disability or discomfort glare. (© Paúl Rivera/ archphoto.com.)

FIGURE 12.10 Controls are critical in rooms that require a variety of lighting scenes, such a large lecture halls. (© David Sailors/Corbis.)

Educators often combine lectures with audiovisual presentations (Figure 12.10). Many classrooms are not planned to accommodate the variable lighting needed to take notes in a dark environment. For these conditions, low levels of illumination should exist in the area around the speaker, on the surface used to hold the speaker's notes, at desks for note-taking, and at the perimeter of the room. Illumination that is close to a monitor or screen must be strategically planned to avoid washing out images. A dark setting can be problematic because of the bright and dark contrasts.

Computers are located in different settings throughout a school building. For example, some whole classrooms are dedicated to computer work. Many students use laptop computers in lecture halls while the teacher also uses a computer to access relevant materials and personal files. Every setting involving the use of computers must have

lighting that supports the task. Illumination considerations for computers, discussed earlier in this chapter and textbook, apply to classrooms. Rooms should be glare-free and have a diffused, uniform distribution of illumination.

For situations in which students work in groups in a classroom, a different lighting effect should be planned (Figure 12.11). To encourage discussion and stimulate creative thinking, illumination for group discussions could be similar to the lighting conditions used for casual conversation in a living room. Changing the lighting environment is important in a classroom; the variance in illumination can be a psychological stimulus and can reinforce the transition to a different subject or activity.

FIGURE 12.11 To encourage discussion and stimulate creative thinking, illumination for group discussions could be similar to the lighting conditions used for casual conversation in a living room. (Tim Griffith Photography.)

One of the reasons for having windows in the classroom is that the variability associated with climatic conditions and outdoor views stimulates the brain.

## HEALTHCARE INSTITUTIONS

Healthcare institutions encompass a variety of facilities, such as hospitals, medical offices, clinics, and residential long-term care units. As with other commercial structures, the practices and policies of users affect lighting. Early healthcare facilities primarily focused on the needs of doctors rather than on patients and their families. Thus, rooms in medical buildings were designed primarily for medical purposes, and support facilities for family members did not exist.

As the medical profession gained a better understanding of the importance of family and the environment for the recovery of patients, healthcare facilities improved the design of patient rooms and provided for the needs of family and friends. New facilities, such as birthing rooms, hospice centers, healing gardens, and age-in-place residential units, focus on empowering patients. In addition to providing effective lighting for medical procedures, and technologies, interiors need lighting that improves the psychological well-being of patients and meets the needs of family members.

To assist people in locating rooms, especially in a crisis, it is desirable to design illumination that enhances wayfinding (Figure 12.12). Such lighting must be effectively integrated with signage. For safety, security, and aesthetic purposes, dark areas should not exist. Visitors often use reception areas

**FIGURE 12.12** A brightly lit map titled "Our World" serves as wayfinding in the Cincinnati Children's Hospital & Medical Center. The map's mural panels display rain forest, coastal regions, plains, deserts, mountains, and tropics. Note how the lit murals simultaneously work to provide a pleasant distraction for patient and family while guiding them precisely from one location to another. (Jon Miller © Hedrich Blessing.)

and waiting rooms when they are waiting to hear about the results of surgery or a medical procedure; a serene lighting environment can help to reduce stress and anxiety associated with those situations. Lighting should also help to create some level of privacy for people who may have emotional responses to hearing results. Some ways of providing privacy include avoiding direct illumination on people's faces and using small pools of light to give the impression that a large room is divided into smaller, private areas.

Quality lighting is important in these settings because many of the tasks being performed demand accuracy. Appropriate lighting will eliminate glare and shadows while promoting a professional and positive impression. Daylight can also help significantly in creating a healthy and pleasing environment (Figure 12.13). Research indicates positive effects of daylight on patients in healthcare facilities. As noted in Chapter 3, Littlefair (1996) reported on the positive effects of reflected daylight in hospital rooms. The variability of daylight can serve as a stimulus for people who must stay in one location for a long period of time, and natural light can assist with the body's circadian rhythm. Coordinating the body's circadian rhythm is especially important for people who are disoriented after a long surgery or recovery period. Natural light can also be helpful in making skin tones more visible.

Electrical lighting in healthcare facilities must enable medical personnel to see accurately during tasks such as carrying out medical procedures, reading reports, recording health

information, and performing tests (Figures 12.14a and b). In addition, lighting should help to promote a healthy, professional, and clean impression of the facilities. Layered lighting should be included in most spaces, especially in public areas and patient rooms. Some medical procedures and technologies require specialist lighting fixtures. For example, in magnetic resonance imaging (MRI) due to the magnetic components used in the equipment light fixtures should be made of non-ferrous materials. Fixtures in surgical areas must be rated for damp locations as well as other requirements

FIGURE 12.14A Electrical lighting in healthcare facilities must enable medical personnel to see accurately during tasks such as carrying out medical procedures, reading reports, recording health information, and performing tests. (Brad Feinknopf Photography.)

FIGURE 12.13 Daylighting is critical to a healthy and pleasing environment. Research indicates positive effects of daylight on patients in healthcare facilities. (Courtesy of ZGF Architects LLP; © Eckert & Eckert.)

FIGURE 12.14B A workstation for the neurological specialists discussed in Figure 12.1. The watts per sq ft. is 1.1 and illuminance level is 30 fc (Barr, 2009). (© 2008 Boris Feldblyum.)

that involve electromagnetic interference and radio frequencies. Specification of these fixtures must be done in consultation with medical personnel.

The most energy-efficient electrical sources should be specified for each task. Highly specialized lighting and illumination in critical areas might require less efficient lighting systems. However, most spaces in healthcare facilities should have efficient lighting systems because they require illumination 24 hours a day seven days a week. Ensuring illumination at the appropriate level requires strict enforcement of cleaning and maintenance guidelines for lighting systems. Medical

personnel must be able to detect skin tones accurately and examine someone without shadows obstructing details. Lamps with color rendering index (CRI) ratings of 100 should be used for spaces involving activities that require color rendition accuracy, such as examination rooms, recovery rooms, and laboratories.

Lighting must accommodate the needs of patients and medical personnel and must be flexible enough to accommodate a variety of positions, activities, and locations in a room (Figure 12.15). Controls should be accessible from different positions, including by someone

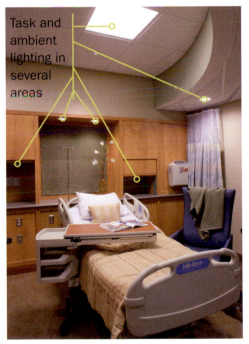

Task and ambient lighting in several areas

FIGURE 12.15 Lighting must accommodate the needs of patients and medical personnel, and must be flexible enough to accommodate a variety of positions, activities, and locations in a room. (Brad Feinknopf Photography.)

lying or sitting up in bed or seated in a chair. Illumination must also be planned for tasks performed in a chair, for walking through the room, for bathroom activities, and to accommodate circadian rhythms. Lighting above a bed should be flexible. Light levels should be low when patients are sleeping (refer to Figures 5.5a–c, which refer to amber lighting in senior center bedroom and bathrooms) and sufficiently bright when required for medical purposes. The medical profession has become very specialized, and many different members of the medical staff work with patients in their room. For example, physical and occupational therapists often work with patients soon after surgery. Illumination must accommodate the tasks involved with their procedures and equipment.

## Customer-Oriented Commercial Interiors

Interior designers are hired to design a variety of customer-oriented commercial interiors. The most common projects are hotels, restaurants, and retail spaces.

### HOTELS

The hotel industry is one of the largest retail businesses in the world. Hotels have a variety of amenities, prices, and room sizes, and they exist in a variety of locations, including on highways, in suburban and urban settings, and in resort areas. Hotels are operated as chains, franchises, or independents. Frequently, the design of chains and franchises is dictated by corporate standards. To reflect a sense of the community and reinforce a theme, some hotel designs are influenced by location.

Some hotels feature sustainable designs and practices. These variable traits of the hotel industry are important criteria for specifying a quality lighting environment.

People want a hotel to have a comfortable sleeping environment, clean bathrooms, and effective security (Figures 12.16a and b). To exceed minimum expectations, many hotels are implementing a variety of personalized services that require special lighting.

Guests must have a good night's sleep or they will not consider future visits. According to the National Sleep Foundation (NSF), sleep deprivation can have a negative effect on the physical and psychological health of people. The elderly, especially those with dementia, experience disruptions in their sleep. Sleep deprivation can become more pronounced when people travel because circadian rhythms are altered.

Bright lights in guest rooms can disturb sleep and make it difficult for someone to adjust to a new time zone. Variable illumination levels and room-darkening window treatments in guest rooms can help to normalize biological clocks. Furthermore, the growing use of personal devices that require electricity to recharge batteries has necessitated the need for more electrical outlets in guest rooms.

To create a calm and relaxing environment, some hotels are adding spas in guest rooms. These can include oversized bathtubs, multiple pulsating showerheads, mood music, aromatherapy scents, and candles. Electrical lighting in guest bathrooms can contribute to the ambience by reinforcing the mood and enhancing the appearance of people (Figure 12.17). This requires a bathroom lighting

FIGURE 12.16A The illuminated glass partition with the rotating television is an innovative approach to separating the sleeping area from the office area in this hotel guest room in São Paulo, Brazil. The other side of the room is shown in Figure 12.16b. (Image courtesy of Design Hotels™.)

FIGURE 12.16B The office area in the hotel guest room described in Figure 12.16a. (Image courtesy of Design Hotels™.)

FIGURE 12.17 A bathroom designed for a spa experience should have a lighting system with the flexibility to have low levels of illumination for the bathing area and bright sources around mirrors for grooming. (© J Marshall - Tribaleye Images/Alamy.)

system with the flexibility to have low levels of illumination for the bathing area and bright sources around mirrors for facial grooming.

In the commercial sector, lodging is the fourth most intensive consumer of energy in the United States. Bornholdt (2001) indicates that lighting can consume 40 percent of the property's overall electrical costs. To reduce energy consumption and conserve resources, lighting systems in hotels must be efficient and maintained on a regular basis. Daylight should supplement and replace electrical sources as often as possible (Figures 12.18a and b). Among all the rooms in a hotel, guest rooms, and meeting spaces consume the greatest amount of energy; therefore, these spaces should have energy-efficient lighting systems and should be considered first in a retrofit operation.

FIGURE 12.18A Daylighting enhances the interior of this hotel in Zermatt, Switzerland as well as providing spectacular views of the Swiss Alps. (Image courtesy of Design Hotels™.)

FIGURE 12.18B Daylighting is especially important for task lighting at the tables in the hotel in Zermatt, Switzerland. (Image courtesy of Design Hotels™.)

## Energy Conservation Possibilities for Hotel Lighting

Research on end-user practices and energy-consumption patterns has determined that lights remaining on in unoccupied spaces waste a great deal of energy in hotels. For example, at the Lawrence Berkeley National Laboratory, research focused on identifying which luminaires were used, how often, and the amount of time they were on in guest rooms and guest bathrooms. The findings indicate that luminaires are primarily used in the morning from six to ten o'clock, and after five o'clock in the evening. Bathroom fixtures and table luminaires in the guest room were on the most, an average of eight and five hours, respectively. The study recommends that occupancy sensors be used in guest bathrooms to conserve energy. Hotel staff should be told to turn off lights in unoccupied guest rooms and bathrooms. The hotel card-key switches described in Chapter 7 are an effective approach to conserving energy in guest rooms.

Controls can play an important role in conserving energy in hotels. In addition to installing occupancy sensors in guest rooms, it is advisable to equip stairways and corridors with motion detector controls or timers. Controls can be calibrated to change lighting automatically in areas whose activities and illumination needs fluctuate. For example, a reception desk is typically busy with people checking in and out during the early part of the day. During the rest of the day, the reception area does not need high quantities of illumination at every station (Figure 12.19). Corridors surrounding meeting rooms can also vary in usage patterns. Controls should reduce the level of illumination in corridors when meetings are in session because the corridors are typically unoccupied at such times.

## Lighting Creative Environments in Hotels

Most hotels have a theme or an image that is projected in the design of the facilities. Lighting can reinforce the theme in various ways. The most obvious method is to select luminaires that reflect the theme and are integrated with the environment. Illumination levels and special lighting effects should support the desired mood of the hotel at various times of the day while taking into account any specific design element that functions as an overall theme. For example, a hotel in the mountains might have rough textures as the dominating concept. For this situation, lighting techniques that specifically enhance rough textures should be selected. Fabulous views of a city skyline or a sunset over the ocean are often focal points of a hotel. To maximize guests' ability to see the views, sunlight must be shielded from end users, and, in the evening, light sources must be carefully planned to avoid reflections of fixtures on the glass.

## First Impressions: Lighting Hotel Entrances and Reception Areas

Lighting at the entrance of a hotel should give guests an impression of safety and security. As people enter the hotel, lighting

FIGURE 12.19 To accommodate a 24-hour schedule a variety of lighting scenes should be programmed for a hotel reception desk. Notice how lighting creates an interesting silhouette of the "floating" staircase. (Photography © Paul Warchol.)

should immediately help with wayfinding. Many people are first-time users of the facilities, so lighting can help direct people to the reception desk, public areas, and guest rooms. Lighting for the reception desk area should provide excellent illumination for people reading hotel statements and signing bills. To meet the needs of the hotel staff and guests, task illumination must be well planned on both sides of the desk. People use the lobby area for a variety of activities, including reading maps and brochures with fine print, meeting people, and having conversations (Figure 12.20). Lighting in lobbies must be

FIGURE 12.20 Lighting in this hotel in Tokyo is ideal for conversations and for enhancing facial features. (Image courtesy of Design Hotels™.)

FIGURE 12.21A This hotel guest room in Stockholm, Sweden accommodates the needs of guests who want to relax, work, and as shown in Figure 12.22b enjoy a lighting experience. (Image courtesy of Design Hotels™.)

FIGURE 12.21B A creative lighting experience for guests at a hotel in Stockholm, Sweden. (Image courtesy of Design Hotels™.)

flexible enough to accommodate this range of activities, making the faces of people easy to see from a variety of angles, and providing task lighting to serve the needs of reading. To respond to diverse moods and activities, lighting in the lobby should create a different atmosphere during the day from that in evening hours.

A primary goal of hotel operators is to create a homelike environment in guest rooms. This includes providing lighting to accommodate the diverse tasks performed in various locations in guest rooms. Technology has enabled people to use guest rooms for a variety of purposes, including working at a computer, playing video games, and watching movies (Figures 12.21a and b).

A focus on work-related amenities has given rise to 24-hour business centers and executive technology suites and floors. Lighting for work-related activities in these spaces must be appropriate for laptops, reading, and meetings. Illumination should also provide the appropriate atmosphere for relaxation, including creative applications involving the interplay of light with water in bathrooms.

Large public areas in hotels are used for a variety of activities, including conferences, meetings, receptions, and weddings. These spaces are often designed so they can be arranged into various configurations with the use of soundproof partitions. Lighting must accommodate the various tasks, including working at computers, viewing audiovisual presentations, taking notes, delivering and listening to speeches, dining, dancing, and conversation. Every possible room configuration should have lighting that will accommodate the various activities. In addition, corridor areas surrounding meeting rooms are often used to conduct business; therefore, to ensure illumination that meets the needs of work-related tasks, these areas should have luminaires that can be controlled by end users.

## RESTAURANTS

All restaurants share the common goal of earning profits through customer satisfaction. People who are happy with the quality of food, service, and ambience become repeat customers and can further increase profits by communicating the positive attributes of the business to friends and family members. Consistency is a valued commodity for a successful restaurant. After this is attained, any changes to the restaurant, including the lighting, may be perceived as altering the quality of the food. Because lighting is often considered the most important element in the design of a restaurant, it is important to be sure that the lighting is ideal from the start (Figure 12.22).

The perfect lighting approach provides appropriate illumination for tasks and creates an atmosphere. Lighting plays an important

FIGURE 12.22 Lighting is an important element in the design of this New York City restaurant. One of the rooms has daylighting. (© Michael Moran.)

role in attracting people to a restaurant and helping them to feel comfortable while dining. Lighting on the outside of the restaurant must highlight characteristics outside that would entice people to come in. Lighting can also help to inform the customer about the degree of formality and price range: generally, understated lighting techniques are used for more formal and expensive restaurants, whereas bright, theatrical lighting schemes often reflect a more casual and moderate price range. Lighting that helps to communicate proper dress expectations and prices is especially useful for potential customers who are unfamiliar with the restaurant.

Lighting in the reception area should be exceptional because this is the first impression customers have of the interior of the restaurant. As a transitional area from the outside, the reception area should have appropriate illumination levels that assist with the adaptive function of the eyes. A positive reaction will encourage people to stay and may reduce anxieties associated with waiting for a table. Lighting should also help to create the desired emotional response to the thematic concept of the restaurant. A fine restaurant often has soft, warm illumination. Restaurants catering to people who are looking for an adventurous evening have lighting that is bright, colorful, and perhaps synchronized with music (Figure 12.23).

Lighting for walking through the restaurant should serve several purposes. For safety reasons, effective illumination must be provided in the pathway, especially transitional areas involving steps. However, lighting should not emphasize pathways. As people walk through the restaurant, illumination levels should change to emphasize the focal points in the space.

Lighting at the tables should include adequate illumination for people to read menus (Figure 12.24). This is especially important for the elderly, who are likely to have vision

FIGURE 12.24 Lighting at the tables in this restaurant in Kolkata, India has appropriate illumination for people to read menus. (Image courtesy of Design Hotels™.)

problems. Table lighting should also enhance the appearance of food and of the people seated at the table. It is critical that lighting render the colors of food accurately. Deviations from true colors may be interpreted as spoiled food.

To accommodate all the purposes of lighting in restaurants, various sources should be coordinated through the use of layered lighting techniques. Whenever possible, daylight is a wonderful source of illumination for restaurants serving breakfast, lunch, and brunch (Figure 12.25). Electrical sources should have a warm color temperature and, whenever possible, should be energy-efficient. To enhance the appearance of food and skin tones, incandescent lamps are frequently used in restaurant lighting systems. Compact fluorescent lamps (CFLs) are an excellent energy-efficient source, and fluorescent lamps help to reduce

FIGURE 12.23 Restaurants catering to people who are looking for an adventurous evening have lighting that is bright, colorful, and perhaps synchronized with music. Guests can select the color for their evening in the "party pods." (Photo: Jeff Meyer, shop12 design/lighting design: Jon Cambell, shop12 design.)

**FIGURE 12.25** Daylight is a dramatic source of illumination for this restaurant in Paris. (© VIEW Pictures Ltd/Alamy.)

the heat generated by incandescent lamps. To help servers do their jobs efficiently, illumination at service stations should provide adequate lighting on beverages, utensils, and dishes while not creating an annoying source of brightness to patrons in the dining room.

## RETAIL STORES

The earliest retail stores were located at street level in residential buildings. Later designs included bazaars and arcades. These structures were dependent upon daylight for their operations. A decorative approach to integrating daylight was to install skylights covered with beautiful stained glass (Figure 12.26). As electricity and electrical sources advanced, many retailers opted for eliminating the penetration of daylight, preferring the ability to control the environment by manipulating electrical lights.

Lighting must reinforce the store's image. There is a wide spectrum of retail stores

FIGURE 12.26 The earliest retail stores had daylighting. Some retailers, such as the Galeries Lafayette department store in Paris, enhanced the shopping experience by using stained glass. (© Ferruccio/Alamy.)

12.27a and b); a window display environment with a back is more controlled, so lighting can be planned specifically for the merchandise within the confined space. This setting is ideal for using spotlights to direct eyes to a product. Window displays without backs can be confusing to viewers because merchandise and lighting in the background create a diversion. However, many retailers prefer a window display with an open back because it enables people to see a lot of merchandise while walking by the store. To emphasize products in window displays without backs, illumination contrasts between the various areas should be carefully monitored, and other methods of attraction may be considered, such as using colored lights in the window or lighting with movement.

After a customer has entered a store, lighting has a significant role in the overall plan of the space, circulation, and visual merchandising (Figure 12.28). As always,

representing every price range and a variety of products and services. Generally, lighting for a discount retail store provides uniform, bright illumination from industrial luminaires. Typically, higher-end stores have lower ambient light levels and spotlights that create the contrast required to highlight products. Each of these lighting techniques reflects an image and promotes a value statement.

Lighting for store windows depends on the layout of the area. Window displays are designed with and without backs (Figures

**FIGURE 12.27A** Lighting for store windows depends on the layout of the area. Window displays with a back is more controlled, so lighting can be planned specifically for the merchandise within the confined space. This setting is ideal for using spotlights to direct eyes to a product. (Courtesy of Adam Hayes, Illumination by Hayes.)

**FIGURE 12.27B** Lighting for window displays without backs are challenging because of competing merchandise and light sources inside the store. This problem was resolved in this retail by integrating the merchandise displayed in the windows with the interior of the store in Tokyo, Japan. (© Iain Masterton/Alamy.)

**FIGURE 12.28** Lighting in this retail store guides the eye through the merchandise and the store by highlighting displays. Pools of light help to guide the eye to each display case in the foreground and the illuminated cabinet at the top of the staircase draws the eye to the next level. (© Armourcoat Surface Finishes.)

lighting should accommodate people with visual disabilities and assist in other aspects of the principles of universal design. Layered lighting techniques must support the plan of the space and the objectives of merchandising. Frequently, lighting is used to designate various areas within a store. For example, in a department store, the cosmetics, shoe, and women's departments might have different levels of illumination and luminaires. Retailers often use different ceiling heights, surfaces, and colors to designate different areas or products.

Lighting can assist in wayfinding by illuminating the path to departments and merchandise. Frequently, light from ambient and accent sources can help to provide illumination for aisles. Illumination should assist customers in finding merchandise and contribute to their safety by highlighting changes in elevation, surface materials, and sharp corners of displays. Because customers walk through aisles from a variety of directions, lighting must be carefully analyzed from multiple points to ensure a glare-free setting. This includes monitoring reflections from shiny finishes on walls and floors. For example, a highly polished marble floor can cause annoying glare from ceiling fixtures.

In addition to illumination in aisles, perimeter lighting can help customers to understand the size and shape of the store and locate merchandise (Figure 12.29). Quick apprehension of the store's configuration encourages customers to explore the entire store. Perimeter lighting can easily be integrated into vertical planes and must effectively illuminate signage and products

**FIGURE 12.29** Illumination in aisles and perimeter lighting help customers to understand the size and shape of the store and locate merchandise. (Laszlo Regos Photography, Berkley, MI.)

found in areas of the store that are farthest from the entrance. Because people are drawn to light, perimeter wall illumination also encourages customers to walk to all areas within a store, including those at the edges. Customers will avoid dark spaces, on the other hand, so it is important to analyze a store plan carefully to determine the location of these areas. In addition, for security purposes and to help curtail theft, the sales staff must be able to see all areas within a store.

Quality lighting is critical to visual merchandising. Effective lighting must start with the product and an understanding of how to illuminate the most appealing characteristics of the merchandise. In stores with a lot of products in various colors, textures, and sizes, this is a significant challenge. Lighting must put the focus on one product, or on one detail of a product, within a setting that has many items in close proximity. This requires an understanding of the characteristics of

the product because obviously products are made from a wide variety of materials and in different colors, textures, shapes, and sizes. A visualization prioritization scheme can also be very helpful.

Another important consideration to visual merchandising is the necessary flexibility to accommodate the variables and changes in displays throughout the year. For example, a retailer may elect to highlight a specific area or characteristic of a product, such as the texture of a woolen sweater. Lighting flexibility can include a variety of factors, such as aiming angles, illumination intensities, color temperatures, and degree of focus. To enhance the appearance of products and provide excellent visibility for evaluating merchandise, light sources should be as close to the merchandise as possible (Figure 12.30). Spotlighting merchandise on tables or gondolas, for example, is easier to accomplish with tiered units that expose merchandise on every shelf.

**FIGURE 12.30** Light sources close to the merchandise enhance the products and provide excellent visibility for evaluating the luggage. (Photo courtesy of Amerlux Global Lighting Solutions.)

Serious consideration should be given to the areas within a store that are typically point-of-purchase locations. Important areas are dressing rooms and the sales transaction counter. Frequently, illumination in dressing rooms is derived from industrial types of luminaires, with light sources that have low color rendering ratings. Instead, lighting in dressing rooms should enhance the appearance of the merchandise and the customers because this is one of the most critical decision points for a consumer. Lighting should surround mirrors and provide excellent color rendition. Lighting should also be excellent at the point where people are purchasing merchandise because customers can easily change their mind and not buy the product.

Quality lighting for retail stores must balance the goals of the retailer, energy codes, and environmental concerns. To enhance merchandising and increase sales, retailers frequently use high-energy-consuming lamps, such as incandescent and halogen lamps. However, to comply with energy codes and maximum watts-per-square-foot requirements, designers have to consider energy-efficient lighting systems with the lowest life-cycle costs. The watts-per-square-foot maximums prescribed by energy codes are based upon the type of retail space. For example, mass merchandising buildings have more stringent requirements than boutiques. Daylighting can help to satisfy energy code requirements.

Ensuring energy-efficient lighting systems for retail stores also requires care in selecting the appropriate luminaire and electrical source. For example, in a retail environment calling for

multiple highlighted areas, low-voltage track systems are more energy-efficient than line-voltage tracks. Highlights should use narrow beam spots rather than flood lamps. Lamps in a retail environment should have long life, excellent color rendition, and high light output. Currently, halogen, fluorescent (linear and compact), metal halide lamps, and LEDs are the most energy-efficient sources. Tremendous technological improvements in metal-halide lamps have precipitated great interest in using this source for multiple retail applications. Continuing improvements in LEDs OLEDs, and fiber optics will provide even more energy-efficient solutions in the future (Figure 12.31).

Color rendition will always be critical in retail stores. Ideal sources have CRI ratings of 100 and warm color temperatures between 3,000K and 3,200K. Returns frequently occur because customers are not happy with a color after they

**FIGURE 12.31** LEDs embedded in glass suggest a futuristic image to the shopping mall. (Schott.)

leave the store. Thus, lighting should render colors as faithfully as possible, and daylight is an excellent source for this.

As with all commercial environments, controls have a significant role in conserving energy and creating various settings for different moods (Figure 12.32). Retail stores should have automatic controls calibrated with the store's operating hours. For limited applications, occupancy sensors could be set to dim lights when departments are unoccupied and to increase illumination levels when someone enters a space. Generally, occupancy sensors are effective only in retail establishments with low traffic. Controls can be programmed for various scenes in different departments at various times of the day. This should include a special arrangement for evening maintenance. Efficient lamp maintenance is critical in a retail environment

**FIGURE 12.32** Lighting is used to create an intriguing impression of shoes displayed in the Prada store Beverly Hills. (© Kenneth Johansson/Corbis.)

because products in the dark do not sell. Lamps should be quickly replaceable, accessible, and easy to change. Such lamps help the maintenance staff and sales associates who must often replace lamps during store hours. The number of different types of lamps should be kept to a minimum because relamping can be very confusing when multiple sources are used in various locations in the store.

Creating a quality lighting environment for commercial structures is a complex process that cannot rely on one-size-fits-all prescriptive solutions. All clients should receive a lighting plan that is unique to the needs of their users, the interior elements of each space, and the site. Illumination must accommodate a variety of people performing numerous tasks in very diverse settings. In addition, interior designers must be cognizant of how world events can affect corporate and institutional philosophies because these philosophies will, in turn, affect interiors and lighting. Continuous changes in technology also have a significant influence on lighting systems; therefore, designers should constantly monitor improvements in the lighting field so as to be able to specify the most energy-efficient technologies. This is especially critical for commercial buildings because of the enormous consumption of electricity.

## Quality Lighting in a LEED-Certified Commercial Building

"Case Study: Innovative Commercial Lighting" provides an example of energy-efficient lighting in a commercial building. The commercial real estate firm, Cushman & Wakefield, in Atlanta was rated gold in the USGBC's LEED for Commercial Interiors building rating system. The building was also in compliance with ASHRAE/IESNA 90.1; the watts per sq ft was .82. Fortunately, as energy-efficient technologies continue to progress, there will be many more commercial buildings that comply and exceed standards established by LEED as well as government regulations.

MR16 37 IR for accent lights

Cold cathode cove lighting

Infrared halogen sources for artwork and signage

Gabriel Benzur/Gabriel Benzur Photography

# Case Study: Innovative Commercial Lighting

### Design Problem Statement

Design a contemporary office space that not only projects an innovative image, meets the needs of its employees, and creates an environment that encourages collaboration, but is also energy efficient enough to earn LEED certification.

### Project Background

CLIENT: Cushman & Wakefield, a commercial real estate firm

DESIGNERS: Morgan Gabler & Jim Youngston of Gabler-Youngston Architectural Lighting Design

LOCATION: Atlanta, Georgia

SPACE: Lobby, private offices, conference rooms, and workspaces

SIZE: 32,600 square feet (3,029 square meters)

### Lighting Design Strategy

Gabler performed a life cycle analysis to determine the most cost-effective lighting system for the long term. The design strategy focused on conserving energy while customizing the type of lighting that was appropriate to the needs of employees as well as special features of the office.

Most of the resulting lighting solutions use energy-efficient sources, including T5 fluorescents and CFLs. Less energy-efficient sources were used (sparingly) for special purposes such as accenting artwork and decorative fixtures. Shared workspaces, the break room, mother's room, and hallways use residential-influenced fixtures to make these spaces more employee friendly.

Pendants with flourescent lamps

26-W triple tube CFLs

28-W T5 flourescent lamps

Transluscent wall panels

Gabriel Benzur/Gabriel Benzur Photography

### LEED Certification—Gold

The office was rated gold in the USGBC's LEED for Commercial Interiors building rating system. In compliance with ASHRAE/IESNA 90.1 the watts per sq ft was .82.

Source: Hall, E. (April 2009). Going green, getting gold. *LD + D* pp. 55–58.

Pendants and sconces with halogen lamps

Gabriel Benzur/Gabriel Benzur Photography

## Application Projects

**1. Human Factors Research Project**

Identify an office, school classroom, and public area in a healthcare facility to observe during various times of the day and week. In a written report that may include sketches and photographs, address the following items:

a. Determine whether the space meets all the criteria for a quality lighting environment. How can the lighting be improved?

b. Given the users and elements of the space, identify special vision needs.

c. Determine the human response elicited from the space and identify the lighting techniques that contribute to the response.

d. Evaluate the energy efficiency of the lighting system, including daylighting. How can the space be improved to conserve energy and natural resources?

**2. Human Factors Research Project**

Identify a restaurant, retail store, and public area in a hotel and observe them during various times of the day and week. In a written report that may include sketches and photographs, address the following:

a. Determine whether the space meets all the criteria for a quality lighting environment. How can the lighting be improved?

b. Given the users and elements of the space, identify special vision needs.

c. Determine the human response elicited from the space, and identify the lighting techniques that contribute to the response.

d. Evaluate the energy efficiency of the lighting system, including daylighting. How can the space be improved to conserve energy and natural resources?

# Summary

o Lighting systems for commercial interiors should enhance visual comfort while accommodating functional and aesthetic requirements. A lighting plan should always aim for minimal impact on the local and global environment.

o Tasks performed in an office can cause problems with vision and musculoskeletal injuries, such as carpal tunnel syndrome (CTS). Poor task lighting can encourage users to assume positions that contribute to such problems.

o Lighting for educational facilities should be efficient and support philosophies of learning.

o Healthcare facilities include hospitals, medical offices, clinics, and residential long-term care units. In addition to providing effective lighting for medical procedures, interiors need lighting that improves the psychological well-being of patients and meets the needs of family members.

o In designing hotel lighting, it is important to understand the concerns of the hotel industry and the client's corporate philosophy. Hotels are part of the service industry; thus, customer satisfaction is the primary focus.

o Lighting plays an important role in attracting people to a restaurant and making them feel comfortable while dining. To accommodate all the purposes of lighting in restaurants, various sources should be coordinated in layered lighting techniques.

o Quality lighting is critical in retail stores and should be determined by the quality and type of merchandise. The goals of retailers are to project an image to consumers, attract customers to the store, focus attention on merchandise, reduce or eliminate returns, and create a memorable experience, all of which translates into future visits. Lighting has a major role in accomplishing these goals.

# References

Barr, V. (March 2009). Collegial not clinical. *LD+A, 39*(3), 38–43.

Heschong Mahone Group (HMG) (2003). *Daylight and retail sales*. For the California Energy Commission's Public Interest Energy Research (PIER) program.

Heschong Mahone Group (HMG) (2001). *Re-analysis report: daylighting in schools, additional*

## KEY TERM

localized lighting

*analysis—CEC PIER*. For the California Energy Commission's Public Interest Energy Research (PIER) program.

# Resources

Allen, P. S., Jones, L. M., & Stimpson, M.F. (2004). *Beginnings of interior environments* (9th ed.). Upper Saddle River, NJ: Pearson/Prentice Hall.

American Institute of Architects. (2000). *Architectural graphics standards* (10th ed.). New York: John Wiley & Sons.

Benya, J., Heschong, L., McGowan, T., Miller, N., & Rubinstein, F. (2001). *Advanced lighting guidelines*. White Salmon, WA: New Buildings Institute.

Binggeli, C. (2002). *Building systems for interior designers*. New York: John Wiley & Sons.

Ching, F. D. K. (2003). *Architectural graphics* (4th ed.). New York: John Wiley & Sons.

Ching, F. D. K. (2002). *Building construction illustrated* (3rd ed.). New York: John Wiley & Sons.

Coleman, C. (ed.) (2001). *Interior design handbook of professional practice*. New York: McGraw-Hill.

Crawford, T., & Bruck, E. D. (2001). *Business and legal forms for interior designers*. New York: Allworth Press.

Fielder, W. J., & Frederick, H. J. (2001). *The lit interior*. Boston: Architectural Press.

Illuminating Engineering Society of North America (IESNA) (2000). *Document DG-3-00: Application of luminaire symbols on lighting design drawings*. New York: Illuminating Engineering Society of North America.

International Association of Lighting Designers (IALD) (2002). *Guidelines for specification integrity*. Chicago: International Association of Lighting Designers.

Knackstedt, M. V. (2002). *The interior design business handbook*. New York: John Wiley & Sons.

Koenig, P. A. (2000). *Design graphics: Drawing techniques for design professionals*. Upper Saddle River, NJ: Pearson Education/ Prentice Hall.

Koomen-Harmon, S., & Kennon, K. (2001). *The codes guidebook for interiors* (2nd ed.). New York: John Wiley & Sons.

Laseau, P. (2001). *Graphic thinking for architects & designers* (3rd ed.). New York: John Wiley & Sons.

McGowan, M., & Kruse, K. (2003). *Interior graphic standards*. New York: John Wiley & Sons.

Pile, J. F. (2003). *Interior design* (3rd ed.). New York: Harry N. Abrams Inc.

Piotrowski, C. M. (2002). *Professional practice for interior designers* (3rd ed.). New York: John Wiley & Sons.

Ramsey, C. G., & Sleeper, H. R. (2000). *Architectural graphic standards* (10th ed.). New York: John Wiley & Sons.

Smith, W. D., & Smith, L. H. (2001). *McGraw-Hill on-site guide to building codes 2000: Commercial and residential interiors*. New York: McGraw-Hill.

Steffy, G. R. (2002). *Architectural lighting design* (2nd ed.). New York: Van Nostrand Reinhold.

Wakita, O. A., & Linde, R. M. (2003). *The professional practice of architectural working drawings* (3rd ed.). New York: John Wiley & Sons.

# Lighting Manufacturers, Distributors, and Suppliers

## CONTROL AND EQUIPMENT MANUFACTURERS

**Advance Transformer**
www.advance.philips.com

**BRK Electronics**
www.brkelectronics.com

**Bryant Electric**
www.bryant-electric.com

**Douglas Lighting Controls**
www.douglaslightingcontrol.com

**Fulham Company**
www.fulham.com

**Honeywell**
www.honeywell.com

**Intelligent Lighting Controls**
www.ilc-usa.com

**Labsphere**
www.labsphere.com

**Leviton Manufacturing**
www.leviton.com

**Litecontrol**
www.litecontrol.com

**LiteTouch**
www.litetouch.com

**Magnetek**
www.magnetek.com

**Novitas**
www.novitascapital.com

**Pace Technologies**
www.pacepower.com

**Pass & Seymour Legrand**
www.legrand.us

**RAB Electric Manufacturing Lighting**
www.rabweb.com

**Sensor Switch**
www.sensorswitch.com

**TORK**
www.tork.com

**The Watt Stopper**
www.wattstopper.com

## LAMP MANUFACTURERS

**Broada**
www.broadalighting.com

**Bulbtronics**
www.bulbtronics.com

**DuraLamp USA**
www.duralamp.com

**Eiko**
www.eiko-ltd.com

**GE Lighting**
www.gelighting.com

**Halco Lighting Corporation**
www.halcolighting.com

**LEDtronics**
www.ledtronics.com

**Lights of America**
www.lightsofamerica.com

**Lumenyte International Corporation**
www.lumenyte.com

**Osram Sylvania**
www.sylvania.com

**Panasonic Lighting Corporation**
www.panasonic.com

Philips Lighting

www.lighting.philips.com

Satco Products

www.satco.com

Schott-Fostec, LLC (Fiber Optics)

www.schott-fostec.com

Westinghouse Lighting
Corporation Bulbs

www.westinghouse lightbulbs.com

## LUMINAIRES

AAMSCO Manufacturing Lighting

www.aamsco.com

Access Lighting

www.accesslighting.com

Alera Lighting

www.aleralighting.com

Alkco Lighting

www.alkco.com

The American Glass Light
Company

www.americanglasslight.com

American Lighting

www.americanlighting.net

Andromeda

www.andromedamurano.it

Arroyo Craftsman Lighting

www.arroyo-craftsman.com

Artemide

www.artemide.us

ATYS

www.atysdesign.com

Banci

www.banci.it

Bayworld Industries

www.bayworld.com

Bega/US

www.bega-us.com

Belfer Lighting Group

www.belfergroup.com

Bergworks GBM

www.cyberg.com

Beta-Calco

www.betacalco.com

B-K Lighting

www.bklighting.com

Boyd Lighting Company

www.boydlighting.com

Bruck Lighting Systems

www.brucklighting.com

Capri Lighting

www.caprilighting.com/capri

Casella

www.casellalighting.com/

Chimera

www.chimeralighting.com

Christopher Moulder

www.christophermoulder.com/

City Lights Antique Lighting

www.citylights.nu

**Citybarn Antiques**
www.citybarnantiques.com

**Color Kinetics**
www.colorkinetics.com

**Columbia Lighting**
www.columbia-ltg.com

**Cooper Lighting**
www.cooperlighting.com

**Cree LED Lighting**
www.creelighting.com/

**Dabmar Lighting**
www.dabmar.com

**Design Centro Italia**
www.italydesign.com

**Designplan Lighting**
www.designplan.com

**Dyna-Lite Selection**
www.dynalite.com

**ELA Lighting**
www.ela-lighting.com

**ELCO Lighting**
www.elcolighting.com

**Elite Lighting Company**
www.elitelighting.com

**Engineered Lighting Products**
www.elplighting.com

**EYE Lighting International**
www.eyelighting.com

**Fiberstars**
www.fiberstars.com

**Flos**
www.flos.com/int-en-home

**Fontana Arte**
www.fontanaarte.it

**Foscarini**
www.foscarini.com/

**Frandsen**
www.frandsen-lyskilde.dk

**Giorgetti**
www.giorgetti-spa.it

**Halo**
www.haloltg.com

**Hampstead Lighting & Accessories**
www.hampsteadlighting.com

**Hans Duus Blacksmith, Inc**
www.hansduusblacksmith
.com/hansduus

**H. E. Williams**
www.hewilliams.com

**Historical Arts & Casting**
www.historicalarts.com

**House of Troy**
www.houseoftroy.com

**Hubbardton Forge & Wood**
www.vtforge.com

**Ingo Maurer**
www.ingo-maurer.com

**Inlighten Studios**
inlightenstudios.com

**Ivalo Lighting**
www.ivalolighting.com

**Johnson Art Studio**
www.johnsonartstudio.com

**Juno Lighting**
www.junolighting.com

**Justice Design Group**
www.jdg.com

**Kartell**
www.kartell.com

**Kim Lighting**
www.kimlighting.com
www.kreon.com

**Kundalini**
www.kundalini.it

**LaMar Lighting**
www.lamarlighting.com

Lampa
www.lampa.com

Latigo Lights
www.latigolights.com

LBL Lighting
www.lbllighting.com

LED Effects
www.ledeffects.com

Ledalite
www.ledalite.com/

Lee's Studio
www.leesstudio.com

Leucos Lighting
www.leucos.com

Lighting by Gregory
www.lightingbygregory.com

The Lighting Quotient
www.thelightingquotient.com

Lightolier
www.lightolier.com

Lightway Industries
www.lightwayind.com

Lightworks
www.lightworkslighting.com

Limn Company
www.limn.com

Lite Energy/Horizon
www.liteenergy.com

Lithonia Lighting
www.lithonia.com/

Los Angeles Lighting
www.lalighting.com

Louis Poulsen Lighting
www.louispoulsen.com

LSI Lightron
www.lsilightron.com

Luceplan
www.luceplan.com

Lucifer Lighting Company
www.luciferlighting.com

Lumaxam Lubrication
www.lumax.com

Lumileds
www.philipslumileds.com

Luminaire
www.luminaire.com

Lumux Lighting
www.lumux.net

Lutron Electronics
www.lutron.com

Luxo Corporation
www.luxous.com

Lyn Hovey Studio
www.lynhoveystudio.com

Mark Architectural Lighting
www.marklighting.com

Martin Professional
www.martin.com

MaxLite
www.maxlite.com

Molo
www.molodesign.com/

MP Lighting
www.mplighting.com

Murano Due
www.muranodue.com

Museum of Modern Art Store
www.momastore.org

National Specialty Lighting
www.nslusa.com

Natural Lighting
www.daylighting.com

Nessen Lighting
www.nessenlighting.com

Newstamp Lighting
www.newstamplighting.com

Nora Lighting
www.noralighting.com

**Norbert Belfer Lighting**
www.belfergroup.com

**Norlux Corporation**
www.norluxcorp.com

**Oluce**
www.oluce.com

**Pathway Lighting Products**
www.pathwaylighting.com

**Peerless Lighting**
www.peerless-lighting.com

**Precision Architectural Lighting**
pal-lighting.com/

**Prescolite**
www.prescolite.com

**Prisma Lighting**
www.pil-usa.com

**Progress Lighting**
www.progresslightingoutlet.com

**Promolux Lighting International**
www.promolux.com

**RSA Lighting**
www.rsalighting.com

**se'lux**
www.selux.com

**Sistemalux**
www.sistemalux.com/en/

**SLD Lighting**
www.sldlighting.com

**So-Luminaire Daylighting Systems**
soluminaire.com

**Spectrum Lighting**
www.spectrum-lighting.com

**SPI Lighting**
www.spilighting.com/

**SPJ Lighting**
www.spjlighting.com

**Steel Partners Inc.**
www.steelpartnersinc.com

**Sternberg Vintage Lighting**
www.sternberglighting.com

**Studio Italia Design**
sid-usa.com

**SunLED Corporation**
www.sunled.com

**Sunrise Lighting**
www.sunriselighting.com

**Tech Lighting**
www.techlighting.com

**Times Square Lighting**
www.tslight.com

**Translite Sonoma**
www.translite.com

**Turn of the Century Lighting**
www.turnofthecenturylighting.com

**W.A.C. Lighting**
www.waclighting.com

**Xenon Architectural Lighting**
www.xenonlight.com

**Yankee Craftsman**
www.yankeecraftsman.com

**Zaneen Lighting**
www.zaneen.com

**Zelco**
www.zelco.com

## RECYCLING CORPORATION

**American Ecology Corporations (U.S. Ecology)**

www.americanecology.com

**Bethlehem Apparatus Company**

www.bethlehemapparatus.com

**Chemical Waste Management Program**

www.stanford.edu/dept/EHS/prod/enviro/waste/guide/refguide.pdf

**Earth Protection Services**

www.earthpro.com

**Full Circle Recycling**

www.fullcirclerecycling.com

**Lamp Environmental Industries**

www.lei-inc.net

**Lighting Resources**

www.lightingresourcesinc.com

**Mercury Recovery Services**

www.hgremoval.com

**U.S. Ecology**

www.americanecology.com

**USA Lights & Electric**

www.usalight.com

**Zumtobel Staff**

www.zumtobel.us

# Professional Organizations, Government Agencies, and Trade Associations

**ADA Guide**
www.access-board.gov/adaag/
html/adaag.htm

**Adaptive Environments**
www.adaptiveenvironments.org

**American Council for an Energy-Efficient Economy**
www.aceee.org

**American Hospital Association**
www.aha.org

**American Hotel & Lodging Association**
www.ahla.com/

**American Institute of Architects**
www.aia.org

**American Institute of Graphic Arts**
www.aiga.org

**American Lighting Association**
www.americanlightingassoc.com

**American National Standards Institute**
www.ansi.org

**American Optometric Association**
www.aoanet.org

**American Society of Civil Engineers**
www.asce.org

**American Society of Furniture Designers**
www.asfd.com

**American Society of Heating, Refrigerating, and Air-Conditioning Engineers**
www.ashrae.org/

**American Society of Interior Designers**
www.asid.org

**American Society of Landscape Architects**
asla.org

**American Solar Energy Society**
www.ases.org

**Architectural Lighting**
www.archlighting.com

**Architectural Record**
www.archrecord.construction.com

**ARCOM Master Systems**
www.arcomnet.com

**Arthritis Foundation**
www.arthritis.org

**Association of Energy Engineers**
www.aeecenter.org

**Association of Energy Services Professionals**
www.aesp.org

**Association of General Contractors of America**
www.agc.org

**Association of Registered Interior Designers of Ontario**
www.arido.ca

**British Contract Furnishing Association**
www.thebcfa.com

**Building Operating Management**
www.facilitiesnet.com/

**Building Owners & Managers Association**
www.boma.org

**Buildings Magazine**
www.buildings.com

**Business and Institutional Furniture Manufacturer's Association**
www.bifma.com

**Center for Health Design**
www.healthdesign.org

**Chartered Institution of Building Services Engineers**
www.cibse.org

**Color Association of the United States**
www.colorassociation.com

**Color Marketing Group**
www.colormarketing.org

**Construction Specifications Institute**
www.csinet.org

**Consulting-Specifying Engineer Magazine**
www.csemag.com

**Contract Lighting Magazine**
www.contractlighting.net

**Contract Magazine**
www.contractmagazine.com

**Cost Estimating Resources**
cost.jsc.nasa.gov/resources.html

**Council for Interior Design Accreditation**
www.accredit-id.org

**EC & M (Electrical Construction & Maintenance) Publications**
www.ecmweb.com

**Electric Power Research Institute (EPRI)**
www.my.epri.com

**Electrical News**
www.electricalnews.com

**Energy & Environmental Building Association**
www.eeba.org

**Energy & Power Management**
www.sustainablefacility.com

**Eyetronics**
www.eyetronics.com

**FabricLink: Educational Resources for Fabrics, Apparel, Home Furnishings, and Care**
www.fabriclink.com

**Florida Solar Energy Center**
www.fsec.ucf.edu

**Foundations for Design Integrity**
www.ffdi.org

**Frame Magazine**
www.framemag.com

**Green Building Guide Primer**
www.energybuilder.com/greenbld.htm

**Green Lights Program**
www.epa.gov

**Home Furnishings International Association**
www.hfia.com

**Human Systems Integration Information Analysis Center**
www.hsiiac.org

**Illuminating Engineering Society of North America**
iesna.org

**Industrial Designers Society of America**
www.idsa.org

**Institute of Store Planners**
www.ispo.org/

**Interior Design Society**
www.interiordesignsociety.org

**Interior Designers of Canada**
www.interiordesigncanada.org

**International Association of Lighting Designers**
iald.org

**International Code Council**
www.iccsafe.org

**International Colour Authority**
www.internationalcolour authority.org

**International Commission on Illumination**
www.cie-usnc.org

**International Council of Graphic Designers Associations**
www.icograda.org/web/home/index.html

**International Dark-Sky Association**
www.darksky.org

**International Facility Management Association**
www.ifma.org

**International Furnishings and Design Association**
www.ifda.com

**International Interior Design Association**
www.iida.org

**Intertek Testing Services – ETL SEMKO (Commercial and Electrical)**
www.interteketlsemko.com

**Lambda Research Corporation**
www.lambdares.com

**LD+A Magazine**
www.iesna.org/LDA/iesnalda.cfm
www.iesna.org

**Lighting Analysts**
www.lightinganalysts.com

**Lighting Research Center– Rensselaer Polytechnic Institute**
www.lrc.rpi.edu

**Lighting.com (Online Resources for Everything Lighting)**
www.lighting.com

**Lightsearch.com (Lighting Manufacturer and Product Directory)**
www.lightsearch.com

**Live Design Magazine**
livedesignonline.com

**Maintenance Solutions Magazine**
www.facilitiesnet.com/ms

**Metropolis Magazine**
www.metropolismag.com

**Mondo*Arc Magazine**
www.mondiale.co.uk/

**National Association of Homebuilders Research Center**
www.nahbrc.org

**National Association of Women in Construction**
www.nawic.org/

**National Council for Interior Design Qualification**
www.ncidq.org

**National Council on Qualifications for the Lighting Professions**
ncqlp.org

**National Fire Protection Association**
www.nfpa.org

**National Institute for Occupational Safety and Health**
www.cdc.gov/niosh

**National Institute of Standards and Technology–Child Anthropometric Data**
www.itl.nist.gov/iaui/ovrt/projects/anthrokids/ncontent.htm

**National Kitchen & Bath Association**
www.nkba.org

**National Lighting Bureau**
www.nlb.org

**National Research Council**
www.nationalacademies.org/nrc

**National Technical Information Service**
www.ntis.gov

**National Trust for Historic Preservation**
www.preservationnation.org

**Neocon Trade Shows**
mmart.com

**Occupational Safety & Health Administration**
www.osha.gov

**Pacific Gas and Electric Company**
www.pge.com

**PeopleSize 2000**
www.openerg.com/psz.htm

**Quebec Furniture Manufacturers' Association**
www.afmq.com/en

**Residential Lighting Magazine**
www.residentiallighting.com

**Retail Construction Magazine**
cc-mag.net

**Safework**
www.safework.com

**Underwriter's Laboratories Inc.**
www.ul.com

**U.S. Census Bureau**
www.census.gov/mcd

**Windows and Daylighting Group**
windows.lbl.gov

# GLOSSARY

## A

**accent lighting (focal lighting)** Illumination designed to highlight an object or area in a space.

**accommodation** A function of the eye that enables one to see objects at varying distances.

**adaptation** A function of the eye that adjusts to the amount of brightness entering the pupil.

**air-tight (AT) fixture** Luminaires that have been rated for being able to reduce the loss of heat or cold through a ceiling and attics.

**angle of incidence** The angle at which rays of light emitted from a light source strike an object or surface before reflection.

**anthropometric data** Detailed measurements of the human body that can be used to determine the location of luminaires, switches, and outlets.

**aperture** An opening in a wall or ceiling, such as a window or skylight.

## B

**backlighting** Illumination that is directly behind an object. Also referred to as silhouetting.

**baffle** A linear or round unit in a luminaire designed to shield light from view.

**ballast** A control device used with an electric-discharge lamp to start the lamp and control the electrical current during operation.

**bin** A method of sorting LEDs according to color properties.

**brightness** An effect from a light source at a high illuminance level that can be perceived as either positive or distracting.

## C

**candela (cd)** The SI unit of measurement of luminous intensity. One candela represents the luminous intensity from a source focused in a specific direction on a solid angle called the steradian.

**candlepower** The intensity of a light source, measured in candelas.

**candlepower distribution curve** A graph that illustrates the direction, pattern, and intensity of light emitted from a luminaire.

**central control system** An electronic system that uses a microprocessor to monitor, adjust, and regulate lighting in many areas or zones within a building, often in integration with other systems.

**charrette** A form of brainstorming that involves professionals and other people involved with a project. The compressed process is an interdisciplinary and collaborative activity that combines brainstorming with immediate feedback loops.

**chromaticity** The degree of warmness or coolness of a light source, measured in kelvins (K). Also referred to as color temperature.

**circadian rhythm** A biological function that coordinates sleeping and waking times through hormones and metabolic processes.

**coefficient of utilization (CU)** The ratio of initial lamp lumens to the lumens on a work surface.

**color-rendering index (CRI)** Measurement of how faithfully a light source reveals the colors of objects. The index range is from 0 to 100. The higher the CRI number, the better the color-rendering ability of the source.

**color temperature**  The degree of warmness or coolness of a light source, measured in kelvins (K). Also referred to as chromaticity.

**commissioning**  An extensive process that is conducted to ensure that energy building systems perform according to specifications.

**compact fluorescent lamp (CFL)**  A lamp made with one or more small, folded fluorescent tubes and equipped with a screw base. The ballast is a separate control gear or is built into the unit as an integral part of the system.

**construction drawing (working drawing)**  Graphic representations of a lighting system that supplements specifications.

**cornice lighting**  Illumination technique mounted on a wall or above a window, directing the light down.

**correlated color temperature (CCT)**  A color temperature in kelvins determined by the x and y location on a color diagram (developed by the International Commission on Illumination).

**cove lighting**  Illumination technique mounted on a wall or ceiling, directing the light up toward the ceiling.

**cross-lighting**  Light directed from the right and left of a task or object.

## D

**daylight (skylight)**  Desirable natural light in a space.

**daylight harvesting**  Capturing daylight for the purpose of illuminating an interior.

**daylighting**  Maximizing the benefits of sunlight into interior spaces while controlling for the ill effects of direct sunlight.

**decorative lighting**  Luminaires that provide illumination and are also artistic pieces.

**diffused luminaire**  Distribution of light in all directions.

**diffused reflectance**  The phenomenon that occurs when a material with a matte finish causes light to scatter in a variety of directions.

**diffuser**  Cover on a luminaire that scatters light in many directions, made from white plastic or etched glass.

**digital addressable lighting interface (DALI)**  A means of communicating through low-voltage wires, which allow information to be distributed to the lighting system and luminaires to report back.

**dimmer**  Electrical device designed to decrease light output by reducing power to a lamp.

**direct glare**  A distracting high-illuminance level, frequently caused by viewing a bare light source or by extreme contrast in illumination levels.

**direct luminaire**  Distribution of light when at least 90 percent of the illumination is downward.

**disability glare**  A distracting high-illuminance level that makes it impossible or difficult to see.

**discomfort glare**  A distracting high-illuminance level that is uncomfortable but still allows one to see.

**driver**  A type of transformer used to operate LEDs with a direct current.

## E

**efficacy**  A rating based upon the lumens per watt consumed, reflecting the energy efficiency of a lamp.

**electrical plan** Commonly used working drawing that designates electrical units and their location in a space.

**electric-discharge lamp** Electrical light source that produces illumination without filaments and operates on low or high pressure. An electric current passes through a vapor or gas.

**electrodeless (induction lamp)** A lamp that does not operate with electrodes, which extends the life of the lamp.

**electroluminescent lamp** Electrical light source that operates through an interaction between an electrical field and a phosphor.

**end-emitting fiber-optic lighting system** Light is visible at the end of the cylindrical optical fibers.

**evidence-based design (EBD)** Built environment solutions that are derived from research studies and/or professional practice.

**eye's field of vision** The central and peripheral areas that are visible to the eye.

## F

**fiber optic lighting** An electrical light source that utilizes a remote source for illumination. Light is transmitted from the source through a bundle of optical fibers.

**flame-shaped lamp** Small, decorative lamp in the shape of a flame. The bulb is clear or frosted glass.

**flood (FL)** A wide beam spread.

**fluorescent lamp** An electric-discharge light source that generally uses electrodes, phosphors, low-pressure mercury, and other gases for illumination.

**focal lighting (accent lighting)** Illumination designed to highlight an object or area in a space.

**foot-candle (fc)** Unit measuring the amount of light that falls on a surface within a one-foot radius of the source.

**furniture-integrated luminaire** Fixture mounted in a cabinet and generally hidden from view. The most common furniture pieces with integrated lighting are office systems, curio cabinets, breakfronts, and bookcases.

## G

**general lighting/ambient lighting** Overall illumination in a space, including lighting that allows people to walk safely through a room and that sets the mood or character of the interior.

**glare** A distracting high-illuminance level that can cause discomfort or be disabling.

**grazing** A lighting technique that places the light source close to a surface or object to highlight interesting textures and produce dramatic shadows.

## H

**halogen regenerative cycle** The operational process in which evaporated tungsten is redeposited on a halogen lamp's filament.

**heat sink** A unit that dissipates heat in some LEDs.

**HID high/low-bay** Cone-shaped surface-mount fixture designed to accommodate the shape of HID light sources.

**high hat** Recessed ceiling-mounted luminaire, also referred to as a downlight.

**high-intensity discharge (HID) lamp** Electric-discharge lamp with a light-producing arc stabilized by bulb temperature, including mercury, metal halide, and high-pressure sodium.

**high-pressure sodium (HPS) lamp** A high-intensity discharge lamp that uses sodium vapor for illumination.

**housing** The unit that contains various elements of a luminaire, including lamp(s).

# I

**illuminance (E)** The total amount of light falling on a surface, measured in lux (lx) or foot-candle (fc).

**illuminator** The box that contains the light source for a fiber optic lighting system. The fiber optics originate from the illuminator.

**incandescent carbon-filament lamp** A light source that uses an electrical current to heat the conductive material until incandescence is produced.

**indirect glare** A distracting high-illuminance level caused by reflection of a light source off a surface or object.

**indirect luminaire** Distribution of light when at least 90 percent of the illumination is directed toward the ceiling.

**indirect natural light** Illumination reflected from clouds, the moon, and stars.

**induction lamp (electrodeless)** A lamp that does not operate with electrodes, which extends the life of the lamp.

**initial lumens** The light output when the luminaire is first installed.

**insulation-contact (IC) fixture** A fixture that has been rated for contact with insulation.

**interreflection** Result of light bouncing back and forth within an enclosed space or structure.

# L

**lamp** Commonly referred to as a light bulb, a lamp is a source that produces optical radiation.

**lamp life** The operational time of a lamp expressed in hours.

**lamp lumen depreciation (LLD)** A measure of the loss of lumens resulting from the design of a lamp.

**layered lighting** An illumination plan that includes natural light and multiple electrical light sources.

**Leadership in Energy and Environmental Design (LEED)** An internationally recognized green building certification system that is sponsored by the United States Green Building Council (USGBC).

**light** A form of energy that is part of the electromagnetic spectrum.

**light-emitting diode (LED)** Semi-conductor device consisting of a chemical chip embedded in a plastic capsule. The light is focused or scattered by lenses or diffusers.

**light loss factor (LLF)** The amount of illuminance lost because of the type of lamp, ambient temperature of the space, time, input voltage, ballast, lamp position, interior conditions, or burnouts.

**light output** The amount of illumination produced by a lamp, measured in lumens.

**light pollution** Excessive illumination in the sky from electrical sources.

**light power density (LPD)** A unit that is used to calculate the watts per square foot for a space and/or type of building.

**light shelf** A horizontal unit that is placed high on an interior or exterior wall for the purpose of reflecting daylight into a space.

**light trespass** Occurs when a light source from one property directs unwanted light to adjacent properties.

**lighting plan** Commonly used working drawing that designates lighting units and their location in a space.

**lighting schedule** Commonly used on a working drawing for the purpose of listing and describing details of the lighting system.

**lighting/electrical plan** Commonly used working drawing that designates lighting and electrical units and their location in a space.

**localized lighting** A lighting technique that allows a user to position light sources where they are needed and at the appropriate illumination level.

**louver** A grid-shaped unit of a luminaire designed to shield light from view.

**lumen (lm)** A unit of measurement of the light output of a lamp.

**lumens per watt (lpW)** A rating that describes the amount of electricity consumed for a given amount of illumination.

**luminaire** An element of a lighting system that includes a light source, housing elements, ballasts, transformers, controls, a mounting mechanism, and a connection to electrical power.

**luminaire dirt depreciation (LDD)** A measure of the loss of light that results from dirt and dust accumulation.

**luminaire efficacy ratio (LER)** A ratio expressing the lumens per watts consumed for the entire luminaire system.

**luminance (L)** A measure of the objective brightness of a light source.

**luminous exitance** The total quantity of light reflected and emitted in all directions from a surface or material.

**luminous flux (F)** The total amount of illumination emitted by a light source; measured in lumens (lm).

**luminous intensity (I)** The intensity of light from a source pointing in a specific direction on a solid angle called the steradian.

**lux (lx)** The International System of Units (SI) unit of illuminance.

# M

**mean lumens** The average light output over the life of the lamp.

**mercury (MV) lamp** A high-intensity discharge lamp that uses radiation from mercury vapor for illumination.

**metal halide (MH) lamp** A high-intensity discharge lamp that utilizes chemical compounds of metal halides and possibly metallic vapors such as mercury.

**modeling** Emphasizing the three dimensions of a piece or surface through light, shade, and shadows.

# N

**nadir** Zero on a polar candlepower distribution curve.

**nanotechnology** A type of science that focuses on elements that are smaller than 100 nanometers (one billionth of a meter).

**natural light** Illumination from the sun and the stars.

# O

**occupancy sensor (vacancy sensor)** Device designed to turn lights on or off depending on whether people are present in a room.

**organic light emitting diodes (OLEDs)** A solid-state technology that is composed of extremely thin sheets of carbon-based compounds that illuminate when their electrodes are stimulated by an electrical charge.

# P

**PBT (persistent, bioaccumulative, toxic)** A classification indicating that a substance is toxic, remains in water or land indefinitely, and accrues in the world's ecosystems.

**photobiology**  The science that examines the interaction of light and living organisms.

**photometry**  A scientific discipline dealing with the measurement of light, including the effects of vision.

**photosensor**  Device that detects the amount of illumination in a space and then sends signals to control electrical light sources.

**polychlorinated biphenyls (PCBs)**  A toxic substance used in ballasts produced prior to 1978.

**portable luminaire**  Free-standing table and floor fixtures.

**postoccupancy evaluation (POE)**  A data collection process that occurs at various intervals after move-in to determine the effectiveness of a design.

**presbyopia**  A decrease in the eye's ability to change the shape of the lens, affecting an individual's ability to focus on near or distant objects.

# Q

**quality lighting**  A layered illumination plan that reduces energy costs, conserves natural resources, and allows users of the space to function comfortably, feel safe, and appreciate the aesthetic components of the environment.

# R

**radiometry**  A scientific discipline dealing with the measurement of radiant energy in the form of electromagnetic waves.

**recessed downlight**  Recessed ceiling-mounted luminaire, also referred to as a high hat or high-hat luminaire.

**recessed luminaire**  Fixture installed above a sheetrock or suspended-grid ceiling.

**recessed spot**  Luminaire mounted in a ceiling or furniture piece, with a lamp that distributes the light in a concentrated area.

**reflectance**  The ratio of incident light to the light reflected from a surface or material.

**reflected ceiling plan (RCP)**  A contract working drawing that illustrates the design of the ceiling, including the location of luminaires, architectural elements, and any HVAC equipment, as it would appear if seen in a mirror located on the floor.

**reflector contour**  A design feature of a luminaire serving to help maximize the reflection of light into a space.

**Restriction of the Use of Certain Hazardous Substances (RoHS)**  A European Union regulation that bans and restricts the use of hazardous substances.

**restrike**  Result of a lamp having to start again because of a power interruption or reduction in voltage.

**room-cavity ratio (RCR)**  A formula designed to take into account the proportions of a space and the potential distance from the luminaires to a work surface.

# S

**seasonal affective disorder (SAD)**  A condition associated with an individual's inadequate exposure to sunlight.

**semi-direct luminaire**  Distribution of light when most of the illumination is directed downward and some is directed upward.

**semi-indirect luminaire**  Distribution of light when most of the illumination is directed upward and some is directed downward.

**semi-recessed luminaire** Fixture whose housing is partly above and partly below the ceiling.

**semi-specular reflectance** The phenomenon that occurs when a partially shiny material causes light to be reflected primarily in one direction.

**shade** A device, either opaque or translucent, that shields a bare lamp from view.

**side-emitting fiber optic lighting system** Light is visible along the sides of the cylindrical optical fibers.

**sidelighting** The integration of daylight into interiors by gathering light through the walls of a building.

**smart textiles** Fabrics that can respond to a stimulus.

**soffit lighting** Illumination technique that is a built-in wall element close or next to the ceiling; directs the light down onto a task.

**solar geometry** The movement of the earth around the sun.

**solid-state lighting (SSL)** A type of illumination that operates with semiconductors and includes LEDs and OLEDs.

**specifications** Written descriptions of the parameters of the lighting system, which supplement the construction drawings.

**specular reflectance** The phenomenon that occurs when a shiny material causes light to be reflected in one direction.

**spot (SP)** A narrow beam spread.

**spotlight projector** Device that allows designers to select a very precise area to be illuminated.

**stepped switching** A means to conserve energy by turning lights on/off by controlling each lamp within a luminaire.

**steradian** A solid angle used to measure luminous intensity from a source in a specific direction.

**structural luminaire** Illumination technique that is an element of the architectural interior.

**sunlight** Light from the sun that enters a space directly.

**surface-mount luminaire** Fixture installed on a ceiling, wall, or floor, or under a shelf or cabinet.

**suspended luminaire** Fixture installed on a ceiling and extending into the room by a cord, chain, pole, or wire.

**sustainable design** Design focusing on products and processes that protect the environment and conserve energy for future generations.

**switch** A device that controls a luminaire by stopping and starting the flow of electricity. A circuit is closed when a light is on and is open when the light is off.

## T

**tandem wiring** One ballast that is wired to operate lamps in two or more fixtures.

**task lighting** Illumination that is specific to each task performed in a space.

**task tuning** A term for adjusting light levels to accommodate the needs for specific activities.

**timer** Device designed to control lighting systems by turning lights on and off at designated times.

**Title 24** California's energy efficiency standards, which includes requirements for lighting, for residential and nonresidential buildings.

**toplighting** The integration of daylight into interiors by gathering light through the roof of a building.

**toxicity characteristic leaching procedure (TCLP)** A procedure developed by the EPA to test the mercury content of lamps. To pass the TCLP test, the range of mercury content must be between 4 mg and 6 mg without additives.

**track luminaire** Fixture that has multiple heads mounted on an electrical raceway.

**transformer** An electrical device that increases or decreases voltages in a system.

**transmission** The passage of light through a material.

**tungsten** A conductive material used as a filament to heat because of its high melting and low evaporating points.

**tungsten-halogen lamp** Incandescent lamp that contains halogen.

## U

**universal design** An approach to the physical environment that focuses on accommodating the needs of all people, whenever possible, without modifications.

**uplight** Luminaire that directs the light up; generally a portable luminaire.

## V

**vacancy sensor (occupancy sensor)** Device designed to turn lights on/off depending on whether people are in a room.

**valance lighting** Illumination technique mounted above a window, directing the light up and down.

**veiling reflection** Reduction in light contrast on a task as a result of a reflected image on a surface.

**visual acuity** The ability of the eye to see details.

**visual display terminal (VDT)** A computer screen. The elimination of glare reflected from glossy work surfaces and proper lighting can enhance health and productivity.

## W

**wall bracket lighting** Illumination technique mounted on a wall and directing the light up and down.

**wallbox** A unit mounted on walls that contain a switch(s).

**wallslot** A structural lighting system integrated in the ceiling and distributing light down onto vertical surfaces.

**watt (W)** Unit measuring an electrical circuit's ability to do work, such as producing light and waste heat, in terms of the amount of electricity drawn.

**working drawing (construction drawing)** Graphic representations of a lighting system, which supplement specifications.

## Z

**zero-net-energy** A term that describes buildings that produce as much energy as they consume by using energy-efficient technologies and on-site renewable energy generation systems.

**zonal cavity calculation** A calculation to determine average illuminance. This method provides only the average illuminance in a space and does not factor in variation in light levels.

# INDEX

*Page numbers in italics refer to figures or tables.*